Veblen and Modern America

Veblen and Modern America
Revolutionary Iconoclast

Michael Spindler

Pluto Press
LONDON • STERLING, VIRGINIA

First published 2002 by Pluto Press
345 Archway Road, London N6 5AA
and 22883 Quicksilver Drive,
Sterling, VA 20166–2012, USA

www.plutobooks.com

British Library Cataloguing in Publication Data
A catalogue record for this book is available from the British Library

ISBN 0 7453 1960 7 hardback
ISBN 0 7453 0959 3 paperback

Library of Congress Cataloging in Publication Data
Spindle, Michael.
    Veblen and modern America : revolutionary iconoclast / Michael
Spindler.
      p. cm.
    ISBN 0–7453–0960–7
  1. Veblen, Thorstein, 1857–1929. 2. Veblen, Thorstein,
1857–1929—Influence. 3. Economics—United States—History. 4.
Sociology—United States—History. 5. Socialism—United
States—History. 6. United States—Economic conditions. 7. United
States—Social conditions. I. Title.
    HB119.V4 S67 2002
    330'.092—dc21
                                                        2002001204

Reprints: 10   9   8   7   6   5   4   3   2   1   0

Designed and produced for Pluto Press by
Chase Publishing Services, Fortescue, Sidmouth EX10 9QG
Typeset from disk by Stanford DTP Services, Towcester
Printed in the European Union by Antony Rowe, Chippenham, England

For my mother and my son, Rhodri

Contents

Preface   ix

Introduction   1

1   Veblen in His Time   4

2   The Early Work   26

3   The Later Work   61

4   Veblen's Reception   86

5   Veblen and Consumerism   110

6   Veblen and Modern American Fiction   126

Conclusion   142
References   151
Bibliography   166
Index   173

Preface

Thorstein Veblen was a major social theorist in the United States of the early twentieth century. Yet, there has been no book-length British discussion of his work and influence since 1936 (Hobson, 1936), and recent American contributions are very modest in number. So, in the wake of the centenary of *The Theory of the Leisure Class* and our entry into a new millennium it seemed timely to provide an introduction to this remarkable thinker and his long-running commentary on modern America. There follows then an outline of his books and ideas, a survey of his critical reception, an analysis of his contribution to understanding consumerism, a presentation of his presence in modern American fiction, and finally, a summing up and argument for his continued relevance in the twenty-first century. I hope this study will stimulate students in American Studies or in social theory to read him and follow up the debates concerning his concepts. The extensive bibliography is intended to facilitate that.

Inevitably, in discussing such a wide-ranging thinker some selection of material has had to take place and so I have paid less attention to his articles and books (*Imperial Germany and the Industrial Revolution, An Inquiry into the Nature of Peace*) that deal with the international dimension of World War One and its aftermath, percipient and prescient though these works were acknowledged to be.

Anyone who writes on Veblen is indebted to Joseph Dorfman's biography and collections of writings by and about Veblen (although it is plain from recent biographical work that some of Dorfman's portraiture should be treated with scepticism). I am also particularly indebted to the work of Rick Tilman and John P. Diggins. I should also like to record my gratitude to De Montfort University for study leave for a semester during the latter half of 2000 which allowed me to complete this project. Parts of this study have been aired at conferences of the British Association for American Studies and an earlier version of Chapter Six appeared in the *Australasian Journal of American Studies*.

Introduction

> I owe innumerable happy hours to the reading of [Bertrand] Russell's works, something which I cannot say of any other contemporary scientific writer, with the exception of Thorstein Veblen.
>
> Albert Einstein[1]

Thorstein Bunde Veblen was born in 1857 to Norwegian immigrants on a farm near Cato, Wisconsin and he died, poor, alone and neglected, in August 1929 in his ramshackle house in Stanford, California. In between, he had moved as a child of eight further west to rural Minnesota (while far to the east the Civil War was coming to a close), spent six years at Carleton College, gone on to study at Johns Hopkins and then at Yale where he gained a PhD in philosophy in 1884. He had returned to the farm for seven years, unable to gain an academic post, before securing a fellowship at Cornell to study economics. He had impressed his professor, J. Laurence Laughlin, who, becoming Head of Economics at the new University of Chicago, took Veblen with him on a fellowship. He had stayed at Chicago until 1906, then moved to Stanford University until 1909, then to the University of Missouri from 1911 to 1918. He was a contributing editor to *The Dial* and he had taught at the New School for Social Research in New York until 1926 when he retired and moved back to California.

In between, too, he had published a series of articles and books which established him as a key figure in early twentieth-century American intellectual life. Beginning with iconoclastic essays such as 'The Economic Theory of Women's Dress' (1894) and 'The Barbarian Status of Women'(1899) and then *The Theory of the Leisure Class* (1899) he had produced a set of works – *The Theory of Business Enterprise* (1904), *The Instinct of Workmanship and the Industrial Arts* (1914), *The Higher Learning in America* (1918), *The Vested Interests and the State of the Industrial Arts* (1919), *The Engineers and the Price System* (1921), and finally, *Absentee Ownership and Business Enterprise in Recent Times* (1922) which constituted an original, radical critique of American society. Public acknowledgement in his immediate academic field, economics, had come in 1925 when over two hundred

1

members of the American Economic Association petitioned him to become its President, but he declined on grounds of health.[2] Nevertheless, with his wide reading and his anthropological perspective he had transcended the boundaries of pure economics and showed how the economic was also social and how the cultural was also economic. One profound re-orientation he had achieved was to break from the production-centred economics of the the classical theorists, including Marx, and to focus on consumption, a focus which provided a basis for understanding the efflorescence of consumerism in the 1920s as well as its current vastly expanded dominance. Over a quarter of century, then, he had developed a theoretical analysis of American culture based on a number of categories – 'the leisure class', 'pecuniary emulation', 'the instinct of workmanship', and a series of dichotomies – 'peaceable traits' and 'predatory traits', 'production' and 'business', 'the vested interests' and 'the underlying population' – which became profoundly influential and provoked long-running debate.

He died just a couple of months before 'Black Tuesday', which brought on the Wall Street Crash and the ensuing Great Depression, and this collapse of American capitalism gave new impetus to interest in his ideas and revived his reputation. For, as 13 million people went without work and the most efficient factories in the world stood still, his barbed formulation of finance-dominated, profit-driven business as 'sabotage' struck home with especial force. In 1932 the Technocracy movement, which drew on his *Engineers and The Price System*, gave a further fillip to his public profile. In 1938 a survey of leading American intellectuals established that they regarded his impact on them as greater than that of Freud, Spengler, or Dewey.[3] Ten years after his death the editor of *The New Republic* could lament: 'Since Veblen died, we have not produced a social theorist of international standing.'[4] In response to the economic slump President Franklin D. Roosevelt set up the series of policies and institutions called the New Deal, and Veblen's posthumous influence was felt there, as will be discussed in Chapter Four.

He has been called 'the revolutionary iconoclast', 'the founder of technocracy', 'the American Gramsci', 'the most interesting social scientist the United States has produced', and the 'best critic of America that America has produced'. He has also been put in the company of Marx, Weber and Durkheim for achieving 'new and important insights into the nature of society'.[5] He has received continuous attention as a social thinker, though opinions have often been sharply divided, but there have been few reassessments of him for nearly two decades. He has usually been considered either as an economist or a sociologist, but in this study, multidisciplinary in its scope, I hope to establish him as a seminal analyst and critic of modern America.

So, in the following pages I have set out to place Veblen's thought in its historical and intellectual context, to delineate its main concepts and tensions, to re-establish the extent of his influence across the decades, to discuss his contribution to the understanding of consumption, and to outline his presence in the work of such novelists as Sinclair Lewis, Willa Cather, F. Scott Fitzgerald, Theodore Dreiser, and John Dos Passos. Finally, in the 'Conclusion' I first make an assessment of the usefulness and limitations of his views for understanding the early twentieth-century United States, and I then draw attention to his continued relevance for us in the twenty-first century, since much of the world that he dissected with clear-eyed, surgical realism – big corporations, conspicuous consumption, status rivalry, salesmanship and advertising, the domination of business for profit over production for use – is still very much with us, except in more extreme forms that would have brought only alarm to this aloof thinker who always wanted the best for humankind.

1 Veblen in His Time

The Historical Context

The years of Veblen's maturing, the last three decades of the nineteenth century, constituted a period of enormous economic change and attendant social tensions in the United States. This complex, multifaceted context is undoubtedly the major formative influence upon him and his emerging serious work in the 1890s was the beginning of his independent mind's struggle to understand and formulate what he saw happening around him.

Until the Civil War the United States had seen little industrial development except in some northeastern towns and its economy was predominantly a rural and handicraft one. However, the victory of the North in 1865 meant that the northern industrial and business interests, long held in check by a coalition of the agrarian South and Northwest, were free to develop the nation as they wished. With the compliance of a succession of federal governments sympathetic to the goal of economic expansion these interests began to exploit the resources of the American subcontinent and to take the economy through the process of rapid capital accumulation. Industrialisation took place on a massive scale.

All types of metal smelting expanded enormously in the post-bellum period and there was a correspondingly great increase in the output of the ore-producing mines. Pig-iron production doubled between 1860 and 1870 and doubled again by 1880. By 1900 the USA was producing more than a third of the world's output. There was also a huge rise in the production of steel following the commercial application of two technical developments – the Bessemer conversion process and the use of coal instead of wood. Steel rails quickly replaced iron rails in the construction of the railroads and late in the nineteenth century wide-flanged steel girders formed the framework for the multi-storey office-blocks being built in the rapidly expanding cities. Mineral sources of energy were increasingly exploited too, as the demand for power multiplied. Coal was used to supply heat for all the steam-driven machinery as well as being the basis of coke in the steel industry. In 1866 only 13 million tons of it were mined but in 1896 output had multiplied tenfold. Mineral oil used in the form of kerosene for lamps and burners replaced whale oil and became a main industry. In the 1880s electricity began to compete with these earlier means of power and by 1900 it was supplying about equal amounts of energy with steam. All machine manufacturing for both industrial and agricultural use developed enormously. Several new inventions, such as McCormick's reaper, were in great demand owing to the expansion of the West and the settlement of new land.[1]

As a result of this exploitation of natural resources the United States was transformed into a highly industrialised nation. In 1859 the ten leading industries were mainly those producing food, clothing, and other consumer goods, but by 1899 these had given way to capital goods industries such as iron and steel and forge manufacturing.[2] Manufacturing's share in the national income rose from under 14 per cent in the decade 1869–78 to more than 18 per cent in the decade 1899–1908, while agriculture's share fell from over 20 per cent to 16 per cent. The industrialisation of the economy is also reflected in the changing employment pattern. In 1860 the number of workers in agriculture and allied occupations was much larger than the number employed in non-agricultural trades, but by 1880 the number engaged in non-agricultural work had exceeded those in agriculture for the first time.[3]

Supplied by the American continent on the one hand with plentiful natural resources and by the European continent on the other with cheap, docile labour, American businessmen were able to accumulate capital at a prodigious rate. During the three decades to 1899 as much as 20 per cent of national output was devoted to capital formation, that is, investment in land, buildings and machinery. Virtually all this capital growth took place in the heavy industries, and virtually all of it was nationally generated, that is to say, it was not brought about by foreign investment.[4] Capital stock, that is, the number of factories, machines, miles of railroad, size of mines and steelworks, etc., increased much more rapidly than population during the period 1869 to 1899 – by 322 per cent while population grew only 87 per cent.[5] The overall effect of this heavy capital investment was a huge increase in national output; Gross National Product increased fourfold from 1869 to 1900 and per capita GNP more than doubled.[6]

Of course, the vast increase in national wealth represented by these figures was not shared equally by all those who helped to create it. As in Britain, so in America the members of the capitalist class appropriated the lion's share of it to themselves, and the names of some of the entrepreneurs of this period have remained bywords for unimaginable wealth well up to the present day. Andrew Carnegie, the Pennsylvania iron and steel magnate, left a personal fortune of 1,000 million dollars; J. D. Rockefeller made 1,500 million dollars out of his Standard Oil Company. Commodore Cornelius Vanderbilt made a fortune of 105 million dollars out of steamships and railroads; William Randolph Hearst made 400 million dollars, more out of mining operations than newspapers; and the Guggenheims obtained their fortune of hundreds of millions of dollars from silver, lead and copper mining, while the Du Pont family wealth was derived from gunpowder and dynamite.[7] Most of these tycoons gained their enormous profits from a monopolistic position which they had managed to achieve after ruthlessly ruining their rivals and then buying them out.

Another device they resorted to was the 'trust', by means of which key firms in a given industry maintained ostensible independence whilst in fact operating under the control of an overarching board of directors. In the 1880s trusts were established in cotton seed oil, linseed oil, whisky, lead, and sugar.[8] The Anaconda Mining Company was a trust established in this period between three or four erstwhile competitors to work the copper region of Montana. Standard Oil was built up by Rockefeller to be the biggest trust of these years, a leading position it did not relinquish until 1901 when Morgan formed the United Steel Company by merging the Federal Steel Company with several other firms including Carnegie's. In addition, when several business giants reached a stalemate in the struggle for domination of a market they would create a 'cartel' or price-ring which adminstered agreed, stable prices throughout that particular industry. In the railways in 1877 Vanderbilt, Jay Gould and Jim Fisk joined in a price-ring to raise rates and share revenues on operations in the area between New York and Chicago. In the 1880s the four big meat packers in Chicago, including the Armour company, also formed a cartel. The 1890s saw a further marked phase of combination between firms. Pure competition thus became a limited phenomenon in the closing years of the nineteenth century as major industries adopted these various devices to ameliorate, if not entirely abolish, price warfare.

Along with the decline of pure competition there went the decline of the family firm, of the situation in which the owners also managed. For with the rise of the stock market and huge corporations there developed a separation of ownership and control between the stockholders and the directors and managers. It was this period too that saw a huge increase in the urban population and the growth of the large industrial cities and towns. By 1900 New York, Chicago, and Philadelphia each had a population of over one million.

As a result of industrialisation then, the relatively homogenous ante-bellum society of independent producers gave way to one characterised by extremes of rich and poor. The opportunities for rapid capital accumulation afforded by industrial development created a class of millionaire entrepreneurs on the one hand and, on the other, a swelling tide of people, mainly European immigrants who owned no property and who lived by selling their labour. The formation of a massive proletariat on the one hand and a small, wealthy bourgeoisie on the other meant that the United States was no longer an egalitarian society. For those fortunate to be in regular work the average wage throughout the United States in 1886 was one dollar fifteen cents a day, a sum insufficient to keep a family. In the cities all the endemic diseases of poverty were rife and the problems of infant mortality, malnutrition, and premature death were aggravated by the intense overcrowding in slum tenements which often lacked sanitation or civilised amenities of any kind. In 1883 there were 25,000 tenement houses in New York with 1 million inhabitants. Often six or seven people shared a room and there were an estimated 19,000 tenements which accommodated 50 people each.[9] James Bryce observed in 1910 that, though equality of conditions was 'almost universal in the eighteenth century' and still general in the nineteenth, there was 'no equality now', a view supported by figures on the distribution of income. In 1910 the richest tenth of the population received almost 34 per cent of all personal income before taxes, a share greater than the share of the six lowest income tenths added together. One commentator estimated that in 1910, 17 per cent of American families lived on 'the pauper standard', 35 per cent on the 'minimum of subsistence standard', 44 per cent on the 'health and comfort standard' and 4 per cent on the luxury standard. Thus the relatively egalitarian, democratic society that de Tocqueville observed in the 1830s had been transformed into one characterised like European societies by stratification and great disparities of wealth.[10] Second- and third-generation descendants of successful entrepreneurs and financiers lost active contact with the commercial and manufacturing processes and lived entirely on their share income.

A new class thus emerged, an American leisured class, which indulged in the adoption of aristocratic codes of behaviour copied from Europe. They founded exclusive boarding schools, country clubs, and the *Social Register*. Polo ponies, huge mansions stuffed with Old World works of art, footmen, English butlers, and long sojourns in Europe, leading hopefully to a daughter's marriage to a bankrupt aristocrat, all became *de rigueur*. One of the examples of the excess the rich of the Gilded Age indulged in is provided by the descendants of Vanderbilt. In 1892 Cornelius Vanderbilt II built Newport, Rhode Island's Marble House, an $11 million mansion as a birthday present for his wife. In 1895 George Vanderbilt built a 250-room, Renaissance-style palace at Asheville, North Carolina, which remains the largest private house ever built in America. In addition, the Vanderbilt clan had by 1900 built eight lavish mansions between 51st and 59th Streets in Manhattan, one having 137 rooms.[11]

These economic changes brought new social tensions to which there were various political responses by the population at large. In the 1870s the agrarian population of the Midwestern states felt exploited by the railroads, banks, and millers, because of their charges. The railroad companies' pricing policy was simply expressed as 'charging what the market will bear' and, since these companies often held a monopolistic position, farmers had no alternative but to fall victims to rapacious rates for transporting their produce. A tide of opposition to the 'big interests' began to flow with Ignatius Donnelly emerging as its leading spokesman and, when in the next decade a decline in the price of wheat depressed farmers' incomes, this intensified. Answers were sought for the plight of the independent farmer in such ideas as Henry George's 'single tax'(to which we shall return) on which he campaigned in the 1886 New York mayoral election. Disillusionment with the two dominant political parties was widespread, and in 1890 voters deserted them in their thousands, to such an extent that in Minnesota they elected Donnelly and others in sufficient numbers to hold the balance of power. In May 1891 this disillusionment manifested itself in a huge conference of reform groups in Cincinnati, the outcome of which was the founding of the People's Party, which had its first national convention the following year. 'Populism', as the new political force was termed, raged throughout the Midwest in the 1890s and there was much in its proposed policies with which Veblen could agree. But neither he, nor any of his family, took any active role in the movement.[12]

The Intellectual Context

Thus, by the 1880s and 1890s, the United States had been transformed from a largely agrarian and handicraft society into a highly urban and industrialised one. Yet, the academic study of the economy was still profoundly dependent on assumptions fashioned during the earlier era. Neo-classical economics represented the orthodoxy, its precepts having been laid down by Adam Smith in *The Wealth of Nations* (1776), by Thomas Malthus, J. S. Mill, and David Ricardo. At the heart of this were the 'natural' right of property, the primacy of self-interest as the key motive for economic activity, a hedonistic psychology in which individuals behaved rationally to increase pleasure and reduce pain, the necessity of free competition unhampered by government regulation, and the 'invisible hand' which brought self-interested pursuit of gain into harmony with what was best for society. Adam Smith famously wrote: 'It is not from the benevolence of the butcher, the brewer, or the baker that we expect our dinner, but from their regard to their own interest. We address ourselves not to their humanity but to their self-love, and never talk to them of our own necessities but of their advantages.'[13] In the American context this doctrine was affirmed by Hector St John de Crèvecoeur who wrote in 1784: 'An American's labor is founded on the basis of nature, *self-interest*; can it want a stronger allurement.'[14] In a later passage in his *Wealth of Nations* Smith again emphasised the primacy of self-interest and brings it neatly (too neatly!) into line with society's interests:

> Every individual is continually exerting himself to find out the most advantageous employment for whatever capital he can command. It is his own advantage, indeed, and not that of the society, which he has in view. But the study of his own advantage, naturally, or rather necessarily, leads him to prefer that employment which is most advantageous to the society. ... By directing that industry in such a manner as its produce may be of the greatest value, he intends only his own gain; and he is in this, as in many other cases, led by an invisible hand to promote an end which was no part of his intention. Nor is it always the worse for society that it was no part of it. By pursuing his own interest he frequently promotes that of the society more effectually than when he really intends to promote it.[15]

The pursuit of private profit was thus validated as also contributing to the public good. It was also elevated to the dominant human motive. John Stuart Mill 's influential definition of Political Economy was that it was 'the science which treats of the production and distribution of wealth, so far as they depend on the laws of human nature', and he had written that: 'there is, perhaps, no action of a man's life in which he is neither under the immediate nor under the remote influence of any impulse but the mere desire for wealth.' In addition, a consequence of the harmonisation of the individual pursuit of wealth with the social good was that there ought not to be any regulation of economic activities by government since society gained most by the workings of an untrammelled, i.e. 'free', market. As Mill put it: 'Every restriction [of competition] is an evil, and every extension of it ... is always an ultimate good.'[16]

The major economists in America in the end-of-the-century period, such as William Graham Sumner, Laughlin, and the writers in the influential *Nation*, acknowledged that there were unresolved issues, but, according to Dorfman, believed that 'the present competitive or laissez-faire system was as satisfactory as possible under the circumstances', and that 'the tasks remaining were largely those of extension, interpretation and refinement'.[17] Depressions were conceived as 'natural tides' in business, and deemed as beneficial through ridding the community of weak and inefficient companies. There was thus a well-entrenched paradigm in economics, largely uncritical of current business practices, that came under threat from two directions.

The first of these was the rise of a socialistic literature which was highly critical of industrial capitalism and its ideology of individualistic competition, calling for its modification or overthrow. Chief among the intellectual broadsides was, of course, first, Marx and Engels' *Communist Manifesto* of 1848 which pointed to the schism between the two great classes of bourgeoisie and proletariat and called on the workers of the world to unite, followed by Marx's *Capital*, the first volume of which came out in 1867 and the second in 1885. Marx offered a radical analysis of industrial capitalism and proposed a 'labour theory of value'. According to this, the real source of prosperity was the workers' labour power, and capital was accumulated by the capitalist only by expropriating the 'surplus value' created by the labourer. Entrepreneurs, then, far from being the engines of increased industrial development and benefactors of society were in fact parasitic both upon that development and the working community, the profits they seized enlarging their wealth while the poor sank into greater immiseration. However, according to Marx, factory conditions and urban crowding were creating a revolutionary consciousness among the working class that would lead to their overthrowing the capitalist order and establishing a socialist state.

Veblen read Marx and appreciated his originality and brilliance. He certainly absorbed Marx's social determinism and his critical animus towards capitalist society, but he was later to write a penetrating analysis and critique of Marxism, and some commentators have overstated the 'intellectual kinship' between the two great thinkers and have underestimated the degree to which Veblen moves beyond Marxist analysis.[18]

Much more popular attacks in America were Henry George's *Progress and Poverty* (1879), Laurence Gronlund's *The Cooperative Commonwealth* (1884), and Edward Bellamy's utopian socialist novel, *Looking Backward: 2000–1887* (1888). George attempted to counter the Malthusian basis of the struggle for existence as well as the emphasis on the virtues of competition. He argued that the main conditions of social progress were association and equality, and that America was threatened by the inequality and poverty the present untrammelled system had bred. He focused on the issue of land and argued that the rental value did not derive from the effort of an individual, but was a product of society. To eliminate poverty and depressions, therefore, he argued the state should levy a 100 per cent tax on this 'unearned increment' as he termed it. Gronlund also set out to rebut competitive individualism and to argue the benefits of cooperation and combination.[19]

Written in response to the irrationality and waste Bellamy saw everywhere in the capitalist system, *Looking Backward* is set in Boston and relates how its narrator, Julian West, is transported during a trance forward 113 years to the year 2000. There he discovers a socialist utopia in operation in which money has been abolished (individuals are issued with credit cards!), private wealth has given way to collective wealth, economic egalitarianism reigns, and production and distribution are planned rationally. This was accomplished not by abandoning industrialism and returning to a quasi-medieval handicraft system in the manner later proposed by the noted English socialist, William Morris, in his utopian novel *News from Nowhere* (1891), but by following through the logic of the increasing centralisation of capital and establishment of monopolies to the point where, by nationalisation, the state becomes the sole owner of capital: 'The nation, that is to say,' Dr Leete, West's tutor in the new order, explains, 'organized as the one great business corporation in which all the other corporations were absorbed.' Thus, by eliminating the 'prodigious waste' of 'private enterprise' and harnessing the productive capacity of the factory system it is possible to share its gains so that everyone can live amongst abundance at the cost of only a short working life (retirement at 45) and hours of work per day set in inverse ratio to the severity of the labour. Bellamy points out, through Dr Leete, that in the nineteenth century there was a dichotomy of interests between the business class and the community, and that it was business which restricted production: 'This, Mr West, is what was called in the nineteenth century a system of production. I will leave it to you if it does not seem, in some of its aspects, a great deal more like a system for preventing production.'[20] Economic depressions had been eliminated, since they were caused by the needs of private capital, and were not inherent in the factory system.

Bellamy also attacked the hedonistic pyschology of neo-classical economics, by pointing out that under different social conditions different motivations would come to the fore:

> 'Does it really seem to you,' answered my companion, 'that human nature is insensible to any motives save fear of want and love of luxury, that you should expect security and equality of livelihood to leave them without possible incentives to effort?'

He also pointed out that the huge increases in productivity brought about by industrialism were not due to the expertise of the entrepreneurs but to the communal 'heritage of past knowledge and achievements' which the business class exploited for their own gain at the cost of the community.[21] The book was hugely popular, selling a million copies in a short time, spawning Bellamy Clubs organised by such men of letters as William Dean Howells, a magazine, and even a Nationalist Movement whose title was derived from Bellamy's proposal to nationalise industry and whose function was to propagate his vision.[22]

Veblen first encountered neo-classical economics at Carleton College where he was taught by John Bates Clark, then at Yale where he took a minor in economics with Sumner, and then at Cornell where he was a fellow under Laughlin. He read Marx during his years in rural retreat, wrote a penetrating analysis and critique of Marxism in 1891, and provided a note on the third volume of *Capital* when it was published by the Chicago firm of Charles H. Kerr in 1894. He read Henry George whilst at Carleton, and he and his wife, Ellen Rolfe, read Bellamy together in 1888. It was this encounter with *Looking Backward* which, according to his wife, led Veblen to decide on economics as the focus of further study.[23] According to Tilman, Bellamy influenced Veblen more than any other socialist writer, including Marx, for they shared many views, particularly on the obsolescence of neo-classical economics and its individualist premises.[24]

However, Daniel Bell has also emphasised the influence of the French utopian socialists, Fourier and Saint-Simon, claiming that the 'parallels with Fourier in Veblen's writings are astonishing'. In particular, he points to Fourier's description of the earlier stages of society as savagery and barbarism, and to the focus of Fourier's critique of capitalism as being on the rapacity of the stock-market, the squandering of resources, and the recurring miseries of economic crises.[25] Veblen was also sympathetic to anarcho-syndicalism as manifested in the United States in the International Workers of the World (IWW), which was successful in organising workers in the western lumber and mining regions.

The second of the factors that threatened the paradigm of economic thinking was a general intellectual ferment which led to the demise of so many cherished inherited assumptions. This was not centred on economics, but via such wide-ranging iconoclastic thinkers as Veblen, it did lead to a shift in 'the dismal science'.

The general intellectual context of the 1870s and 1880s was dominated by Darwinism. *The Origin of Species* was published in November 1859, and copies had begun reaching the East Coast during the last days of the year. Substantively, it had grown out of Lyell's geology, Malthus's law of population, Darwin's own round-the-world trip on the *Beagle*, especially his encounter with the Galapagos Islands, and subsequent material that he had managed to accumulate through many years of correspondence. It was a highly structured and strongly rhetorical work.[26] Its revolutionary contribution was not the idea of evolution, which had already been proposed by others such as Lamarck, but the proposition of a materialist explanation for it, namely natural selection. The work dealt solely with plants and animals, with only one sentence in the 'Conclusion' alluding to its application to humankind: 'Light will be thrown on man and his origins.' Despite this it provoked fierce controversy in England because of its implications for the Biblical account of creation in the *Book of Genesis*, a controversy dramatised by the heated exchange between Bishop Wilberforce and Thomas Henry Huxley at the 1860 meeting of the British Association.

It provoked similar heated debate in the United States with strong resistance not only from theologians but from scientists imbued with the assumptions of design and harmony in nature perpetuated by early nineteenth-century natural theology. The pro-Darwin camp was led by the botanist Asa Gray, who took on the role of America's chief proponent of natural selection. Gray had received an abstract of the book from Darwin in 1857, and on publication he energetically arranged an American edition, wrote favourable reviews and defended the book against its critics. He began with an article in the *American Journal of Science and Arts* in March 1860, followed by a discussion in the *Proceedings of the American Academy*, and went on to publish three articles in the *Atlantic Monthly*, which were reprinted as a pamphlet and later included in his book *Darwiniana* (1876).[27] He also defended Darwin against the Harvard zoologist Louis Agassiz's attack on him in the 1860 meeting of the American Academy of Arts and Sciences. Despite his efforts, however, Darwinism did not gain widespread acceptance in the United States until the late 1870s. This was cemented by O. C. Marsh's discoveries of American fossil horses and his publication in 1874 of a paper laying out the evolution of the horse, and by Darwin's vociferous champion, T. H. Huxley, giving an American lecture tour in 1876.[28]

Darwin's *The Descent of Man* (1871) also made an impact with its focus on sexual selection as a refinement of natural selection, including sexual selection in humans, and its proposal that humankind had evolved from lower life forms:

> The main conclusion arrived at in this work ... is that man is descended from some less highly organised form. The grounds upon which this conclusion rests will never be shaken, for the close similarlity between man and the lower animals in embryonic development, as well as in innumerable points of structure and constitution, both of high and the most trifling importance, – the rudiments which he retains, and the abnormal reversions to which he is occasionally liable, – are facts which cannot be disputed.

In the latter part of the volume he pointed to the biological basis for some aspects of human social behaviour, particularly in relation to sexual selection. Dress, fashion, cosmetics, and ornamentation could all be viewed as enhancing or exaggerating secondary sexual characteristics. In addition, marriage in the civilised world operated under certain canons of selection:

Civilised men are largely attracted by the mental charms of women, by their wealth, and especially by their social position; for men rarely marry into a much lower rank of life. ... in civilised nations women have free or almost free choice [and] their choice is largely influenced by the social position and wealth of the men.

Wives, too, in earlier times had been obtained either through capture, or by physical competition between two suitors:

That the habit of capture [of wives] was most extensively practised during former times, even by the ancestors of civilised nations, is clearly shown by the preservation of many curious customs.

The Descent provoked even more hostility in clerical circles, but a review of it in *The Nation* praised it as 'the most lucid and impartial exposition of the present state of scientific opinion respecting the origin of man and his relations to the lower animals'.[29]

Particularly influential was Social Darwinism as espoused by its English proponent Herbert Spencer whose popularity in the United States reached its peak in 1882 when he visited the country and met prominent business and intellectual leaders. Veblen had read Spencer and Spencer gave a lecture at Yale, while Veblen was there, since one of his prominent disciples was William Graham Sumner under whom Veblen was studying. Spencer tried to demonstrate that the methods of investigation used in the physical sciences could be applied to social life. He also employed anthropological material to explain the evolution of social and economic institutions. He posited a two-stage development from military/status types of society to industrial/contract types. In the former, status – that is, the esteem gained by subordinating others – is the dominant social motive. He also viewed social evolution as a process of advance leading to a state of equlibrium and harmony: 'Evolution can end only in the establishment of the greatest perfection and the most complete happiness.' Yet this goal would be bought at the price of inescapable suffering since the 'survival of the fittest' meant that many of the weakest would fall by the wayside. The poor were unfit and not only would be, but should be, eliminated. In the 1872 American edition of *Social Statics* he asserted that: 'The whole effort of nature is to get rid of such, to clear the world of them, and make room for better.'[30] Sumner would later declare:

Let it be understood that we cannot go outside of this alternative: liberty, inequality, survival of the fittest; not liberty, equality, survival of the unfittest. The former carries society forward and favors all its best members; the latter carries society downwards and favors all its worst members.'[31]

Such views were eagerly seized upon as validating *laissez-faire* economics, the ruthless competition of late-nineteenth-century American business, and the existence of millions of the poor. James J. Hill, the railroad magnate, in an essay defending consolidation argued that the fortunes of the railroad companies are determined by the law of survival of the fittest, and John D. Rockefeller would apply the Spencerian analogy: 'The growth of a large business is merely a survival of the fittest.'[32] Steel king Andrew Carnegie would write:

While the law [of competition] may be sometimes hard for the individual, it is best for the race, because it ensures the survival of the fittest in every department. We accept and welcome, therefore, as conditions to which we must accommodate ourselves, great inequality of environment; the concentration of business, industrial and commercial, in the hands of a few; and the law of competition between these, as being not only beneficial, but essential to the future progress of the race.[33]

When, however, through trusts, amalgamations, and cartels competition was significantly diluted by the early twentieth century, as we have already noted, Spencer's philosophy lost its force and by the end of World War One Social Darwinism was a dead letter.[34]

The impact of Darwin on Veblen was immense, though he never accepted the relevance for social science of such notions as 'natural selection', 'the struggle for existence', or 'the survival of the fittest' in the way that Social Darwinists did. In fact, he was negative towards Social Darwinism, partly because it justified the present economic order and social inequities as being the result of natural laws. He absorbed some elements of Spencer's approach but could not accept it fully because he found it teleological in that it posited a libertarian political order and the market economy as the final outcome of the evolutionary process, and because it sanctioned pecuniary values.[35]

In *The Origin* Darwin had devoted a chapter to 'Instincts' and had proposed that with natural selection psychology could be put on a new basis:

Psychology will be securely based on the foundation, already well laid by Mr. Herbert Spencer, that of the necessary acquirement of each mental power and capacity by gradation.[36]

And as a result of his influence there developed the evolutionary school of psychology associated with William James, William McDougall, C. Lloyd Morgan and Jacques Loeb, in which instincts became a significant category for the explanation of much human behaviour. James published *The Principles of Psychology* in 1890, Morgan *Habits and Instincts* (1896), Loeb *Comparative Physiology of the Brain and Comparative Psychology* (1900), and McDougall *Introduction to Social Pyschology* (1908). Veblen cites these sources in *The Instinct of Workmanship* (1914) and his use of such terms as 'reflex,' 'habit,' 'instinct,' and 'tropism' arise from these pioneering works. James believed that instinct is usually defined as the faculty of acting in such a way as to produce certain ends, without foresight of the ends, and without previous education in the performance. Yet, James was inconsistent in his use of the term and these different, hazy meanings spill over into Veblen's own use in his published writings.[37] Morgan lectured at Chicago in the 1890s when Veblen may have heard him and he describes 'habit' as behaviour 'stereotyped through repetition,' a meaning Veblen takes over for his explanation of the way certain behaviour generated in the past persists into a radically different historical era. Loeb was both a colleague and friend of Veblen's at Chicago and a committed materialist who was dedicated to establishing the chemical basis of all living processes, including human psychology. Veblen read Loeb's books and papers and, unfortunately, transferred Loeb's vagueness about the distinctions between 'tropisms' and 'instincts' to his own discussions. McDougall laid out what he saw as the major instincts and Veblen used several of these, as well as defining new ones such as his 'instinct of workmanship.'

Any discussion of the influences upon Veblen would be incomplete without an acknowledgement of the earliest of all, namely his home and his family. The impact of being of Norwegian background upon his idiosyncratic perspective has received some discussion, the main point being that it may have contributed to his own sense of marginality. However, the isolation from the Anglo-American community seems to have been exaggerated, and it is to more general bases that we have to look for any origins of his later attitudes and ideas.[38] Raised largely on the farm in Minnesota he was imbued with a countryman's self-reliance and a distrust of the town. He identified with the Midwestern farmers and their victimisation at the hands of an exploitative business class as represented by both the small traders in the country towns and the big corporations such as the railroads. From his father, who had to be carpenter as well as agriculturist, he derived a sense of craftsmanship, of the inherent value of a well-made thing. (The house Thomas Veblen built is still standing.) His father, too, was keen that his sons and daughters should be well educated and so it was with his sister and brother that Thorstein went in 1874 to Carleton College, the three of them inhabiting a house built by their father on land nearby. From there he went to Johns Hopkins where one of his courses was under the logician, Charles S. Peirce, and he eventually ended up in Yale studying economics, and philosophy with the Kantian, Noah Porter. His training in philosophy, it has been argued, underpinned his development of evolutionary economics.[39] It taught him how to look at concepts critically, how to understand the historically determined nature of concepts, and how our ontological categories shape our sense of the world, so that there is no such phenomenon as 'naive vision'. When he returned from Yale he remarked to Ellen Rolfe, his wife-to-be, that he had never met his father's intellectual equal, and his biographer tells us that if he had an intellectual problem he would walk by his father in the fields and discuss it with him, and in the Minnesotan evening they would chew over abstruse topics together.[40]

Chicago

The story of Thorstein Veblen's productive life really begins in 1892 with his arrival at Chicago. The years of disappointment and indirection were behind him and at last he seemed to have found both a mentor to support him in Laughlin (he was ever to be dependent on the good offices of generous friends) and a *métier* – political economy. Yet, when he stepped out early in the Fall from the looming massiveness of the railroad station to marvel, perhaps, at the electric lighting and the 20-storey buildings, awesome instances of technological innovation that would shape a very different new century, he was no more than a novice academic. Multilingual and widely read he may be, but at 35 he was considerably older than others in such a junior position as his, and over the 14 years there he had to suffer the sight of others, more conventional, less original, more favoured, climbing the academic ladder, while he barely hung on to its lowest rungs.

At that time he was a tall, brown-bearded, quiet man who spoke slowly, and who had an air of wry detachment. A thick moustache drooped over his mouth; keenly intelligent eyes gazed out from above the cheekbones; and his hair, parted in the middle, fell in limp locks each side of his forehead. Habitually, he wore a sombre suit and a black necktie. He seemed languorous and disinclined to any physical effort. In the day he taught a course on socialism, adding in 1898 a new course, 'Economic Factors in Civilization,' and in the evenings, alone in the room he rented in the house of a friend, he wrote. Then, like a late harvest, his most important ideas and and his most famous book came. Out of his immense reading, his philosopher's under-standing of how our constructed concepts and ontological categories shape our sense of the world, his long conversations with his father, his outsider's fresh view, and his encounter with 'eighties and 'nineties America, particularly Chicago, there precipitated a stream of articles and two volumes which asked awkward questions and provided original answers.

For Chicago in the 1890s was a good place to test out economic theories and to observe rapid social change. It was in the throes of breakneck expansion and brutal economic competition, a vast, living experiment in the gains to be had and the ravages to be suffered under *laissez-faire* industrial capitalism. After the disastrous fire of 1871 the 'windy city' had grown tremendously in size and importance to overtake Philadelphia and be second only to New York. Situated on Lake Michigan with access to the Great Lakes water routes and as the hub of Midwestern railroads it enjoyed enormous advantages as a trading and manufacturing centre, and was regarded as the 'Great Gateway to the West'. Its major areas of activity were grain (the Board of Trade was the largest corn exchange in the world), lumber, iron and steel, agricultural machinery, livestock and meat-packing. Thousands of immigrants poured in during the late nineteenth century to take up jobs in the mills, factories, stockyards and packing plants, swelling the population to 1.2 million by 1893. They faced harsh conditions, fierce competition for work, and exploitative bosses and landlords. It is little wonder that the emancipatory perspectives of anarchism and socialism were popular, that strikes were widespread, and that class antagonism was intense. The situation reached a flashpoint on 4 May 1886 when, after a weekend of clashes between workers and police, the Haymarket Riot occurred. A bomb was thrown; shots were fired; and one policeman was killed and many injured. The trial of the people detained became a trial of anarchism, and on questionable evidence four defendants were found guilty and executed. Radicalism went into retreat until the publication of Bellamy's novel in 1888 and the founding in 1891 of the People's Party.

Class antagonism in Chicago was fuelled by the huge gulf between rich and poor. At one end of the social scale there were the destitute, cared for, if at all, by the likes of Jane Addams and her Hull House settlement in the Nineteenth Ward, while at the other the dynamic expansion of business and the rapid rise in land values had created a wealthy entrepreneurial class, whose members were not averse to bribing city politicians in order to establish lucrative monopolies. According to the *Tribune* there were over two hundred millionaires in the city in the 1890s with Marshall Field (retail stores) topping the list at an estimated 75 million, and Philip D. Armour (meat-packing) following behind with 40 million.[41] They consolidated themselves into a plutocracy with an *Elite Directory and Club List*, with exclusive societies such as the Entre Nous Club and the Assembly Association, built lavish mansions on Lake Shore Drive, and furnished them with rare paintings and antiques from Europe. Charles Yerkes, the streetcar magnate, possessed works by the Dutch masters, and McCormick (agricultural machinery) owned four of Napoleon's royal chairs, while his wife's jewel collection included an emerald necklace by Cartier valued at over one million dollars. In their halls and parlours were Buddhas from Chinese temples and tapestries from Brussels, and at large dinners guests were served on a golden service consisting of one thousand pieces that had been given by Napoleon to his sister, Pauline.[42] Max Weber in *The Protestant Ethic and the Spirit of Capitalism* had described the ideal type of entrepreneur as 'one who avoids ostentation and unnecessary expenditure as well as conscious enjoyment of his power', and whose 'manner of life is distinguished by a certain ascetic tendency', and Andrew Carnegie would urge that the duty of the man of wealth was 'to set an example of modest, unostentatious living, shunning display or extravagance'.[43] These features of sobriety and restraint may have been characteristic of early nineteenth-century businessmen, but in contrast the millionaires of late-nineteenth-century Chicago, like those of New York, loved to display the symbols of wealth, and major events in the social calendar such as the Assembly Ball or the Grand Charity Ball provided opportunities for ostentation.

The booming economy had a strong cultural impact. Architecture flourished with Louis Sullivan the leading practitioner, and Chicago pioneered two distinctively modern types of building: the steel-framed skyscraper with the Home Insurance Building of 1884, and the large department store, as instanced by the construction in 1892 on State and Van Buren of Siegel, Cooper and Company's new store housing 73 departments. The Grand Opera House was erected (it provided the opening scene for Norris's novel *The Pit* of 1903), and in 1890 a city orchestra established. Numerous famous speakers – Charles Dickens, Oscar Wilde, Mark Twain, Matthew Arnold, Henry M. Stanley – came to Chicago and addressed large audiences.[44]

A literary culture began to flourish as it became a centre for writers. The major intellectual journal of the city, *The Dial*, had been founded in 1880, and in 1892 it went bi-monthly, carrying reviews and literary criticism as well as articles on such issues of the day as the Columbian Exposition or the popularity of Ibsen. Harriet Monroe was a Chicago poet who published her 'Columbian Ode' in 1893 and who later founded *Poetry* in the same year that Margaret Anderson founded *The Little Review*. The poet, Edgar Lee Masters, settled there in 1891, and Theodore Dreiser was in the city as a reporter for the *Chicago Globe*. He drew on his newspaper experience in his first novel set in Chicago and New York, *Sister Carrie* (1900). Henry Blake Fuller published *The Cliff-Dwellers*, a vivid portrait of workers in a skyscraper in 1893, and later, *With the Procession* (1895). These novels were anti-business, and anti-materialistic just like those of Robert Herrick, also at the University, who published novels such as *The Web of Life* (1900), *The Common Lot* (1904) and *Memoirs of an American Citizen* (1905), a sceptical look at politics. Fuller was one of a group of writers and artists who met and went by the name of 'the Little Room'. This included Hamlin Garland and Floyd Dell. To this little colony centred on Dell and his wife Margaret Curry came Veblen, the poet Eunice Tietjens with her oriental dances, Robert Morss Lovett, also from the University, and later Sherwood Anderson, Ben Hecht, and Carl Sandburg.

Through the 1890s there was a flowering of museums, art galleries, and educational institutions. The most significant was the University of Chicago, brought into being by a grant from John D. Rockefeller and a parcel of land from Marshall Field. Yerkes donated an astronomical observatory. When it opened in October 1892 it had nearly

600 students and 120 faculty members.[45] It was headed by William Rainey Harper, a former professor of Hebrew, and despite its newness there was still a heavily traditional weighting towards religion with ten out of the original 31 professors specialising in theology.[46]

As one of these members, Veblen came under new influences that would shape his thought and outlook for years to come. The first experiential influence upon the man from a Minnesota farm was, of course, the city itself with its brash energy, variety, and crowdedness, celebrated in Sandburg's free-verse ode in the following terms:

> Laughing the stormy, husky, brawling laughter
> of Youth,
> half-naked, sweating, proud to be Hog
> Butcher, Tool Maker, Stacker of Wheat, Player with
> Railroad and Freight Handler to the Nation.

'Chicago' (1914)

All too evident was its *laissez-faire* economics, its class polarisation, ethnic diversity, and close contiguity of industrial production with aristocratic extravagance and display. An associated influence was the event that crowned Chicago's coming of age – the World's Columbian Exposition of 1893 (Veblen makes a passing reference to it in *The Theory of the Leisure Class*). This was held to mark the 400th anniversary of Columbus's discovery of America, and it was sited on land next to the university. Dvorak conducted his Eighth symphony there, and in six months it was visited by over 21 million people including Hamlin Garland and Henry Adams, who was prompted to profound reflections. He spent a fortnight there and wrote of its impression upon him: 'Chicago asked in 1893 for the first time the question whether the American people knew where they were driving ... . Chicago was the first expression of American thought as a unity; one must start there.'[47]

It was a vast fair designed to demonstrate the progress of civilisation, and around the classically styled Fine Arts Building were arranged the pavilions of 39 states and 18 foreign countries. There were stark juxtapositions of the contemporary and technological with the ancient and primitive. An Electricity Building showed the latest and largest dynamos, while the Japanese pavilion was modelled on an eleventh-century temple. In a part of the Jackson Park site called the Midway was the newly invented Ferris wheel, a massive mechanism which could carry over two thousand people at a time. In its shadow were clustered native exhibits such as a Samoan village, the 'streets of Cairo', and a Javanese village. Placed there partly to illustrate by contrast the superiority of Anglo-Saxon civilisation, they were also part of a purposeful effort to encourage the study of ethnology and so offered an introduction to anthropology.[48]

It was in the last two decades of the nineteenth century that this study of cultures was attaining the status of a distinct discipline. Veblen had been deeply interested in it since his days at Carleton and the two pioneers in the field were Lewis H. Morgan and Franz Boas. Morgan in his *Ancient Society* (1877) made the point that the institution of private property (the cornerstone of classical economics) was a relatively late invention in humankind's cultural development, not appearing until the organisation of civilised societies. He went on to point out that recently ownership had given rise to a 'greed philosophy' which seemed to be getting out of control and becoming a threat to society. This developing area also impinged on Veblen's mind at the university with the anthropological perspectives of W. I. Thomas and Carlos Closson, and, particularly, with the fascinating work of the curator of the Field Museum, Franz Boas. He had studied the Kwakiutl Indians of British Columbia and in reports he presented in 1895 and 1899 he drew attention to the custom of the 'potlach', by which individuals gained prestige, and trumped rivals, by the amount of property they distributed at gift-giving ceremonies. He noted that in an earlier period 'feats of bravery counted as well as distribution of property, but nowadays as the Indians say "rivals fight with property only"'. He noted too that there was an equivalent to the potlach in modern society in the ostentatious spending carried out to demonstate superiority over a rival, and that the potlach was 'founded on psychical causes as active in our civilised society as among the barbarous natives of British Columbia'.[49]

Only days after the close of the Exposition the stock market collapsed, to be followed by a long depression. Unemployment soared and the winter of 1893/4 saw a large increase in poverty in Chicago with huge demonstrations on the lakefront by the unemployed. In response, Jacob Coxey set up a movement, the Army of the Commonweal, centred on Chicago, and organised a march of the jobless to Washington. Later in 1894 Chicago experienced bitter class conflict with the Pullman strike, or the 'Debs Rebellion' as it was called. The railroad-car manufacturer had cut wages by 25 per cent but would not cut the rents of the company tenements where its workers lived. A strike was called; the main union officials were arrested; large demonstrations were held; President Cleveland declared a state of insurrection and sent troops into the city to control the situation.[50] Two years later the American Socialist Party was organised with Eugene Debs as its leader and Chicago as its base. It was to make great gains in the city until it really seemed poised to take over the municipal government and Debs could raise nearly a million votes in the presidential election of 1912.

On the other side of the social and political divide, the ability of a few rich individuals to manipulate the so-called 'free' market was spectacularly demonstrated in 1897 by Joseph Leiter's attempt to corner the world's supply of wheat through aggressive buying on the Wheat Pit at the Chicago Board of Trade. However, when he seemed to have secured his monopoly, his main rival, Armour, learned that 7 million bushels were lying in Duluth. Leiter had left them out of his calculations because, owing to the frozen Lake Michigan, they could not be shipped until the spring. Armour hired ice-breakers and tugs and brought it all to Chicago where he dumped it on the market. The price plummeted and Leiter sustained a loss of 2½ million dollars.[51]

Thus, the newly arrived economics instructor had within his immediate purview rich material to observe. He enjoyed the unconditioned responses of the outsider and the newcomer both to the city and to his academic discipline and he saw with clear-eyed realism that neo-classical economics, the orthodoxy in his field, could not explain the behaviour he saw around him. As inherited from Adam Smith, this based itself, as we have seen, on Enlightenment assumptions that economic behaviour was rational and that self-interest and competition were natural phenomena and intrinsic to human societies. Veblen began to question these premises, and recognised both that in the behaviour of the entrepreneurial class a spirit of barbarism flourished (they were later memorably termed 'the robber barons') and that irrational considerations underpinned many facets of social life.

Novelists such as Frank Norris in *The Pit* (1903), his fictional account of a doomed attempt to manipulate the grain market based on Leiter's 'corner', Upton Sinclair in *The Jungle* (1908), his study of immigrants working in the stockyards, and Theodore Dreiser in his novels based on Yerkes's life, *The Financier* (1912) and *The Titan* (1914), drew on Social Darwinism to conceptualise the phenomenon of Chicago and employed the Darwinian tropes of 'the struggle for existence' and 'the survival of the fittest'. But Veblen drew from

Darwin a more profound perspective. He knew how present-day features may have a long genealogy stretching into the distant past and how residues of the past can survive into, and adapt to, a very different environment. He also adopted Darwin's emphasis on process and change and demanded in an early article, 'Why Is Economics Not An Evolutionary Science?'(1898) that economics cease being merely taxonomic and adopt an evolutionary approach to phenomena. It should be, he proposes, 'the theory of a process of cultural growth as determined by the economic interest, a theory of a cumulative sequence of economic institutions stated in terms of the process itself'.[52] Thus, drawing on his immense reading, his adoption of an anthropological orientation, and his iconoclastic view of prevailing institutions and theories, he embarked on a project to theoretise and reformulate the significant elements of turn-of-the-century economic behaviour and social relations.

2   The Early Work

One with a genius for taking the cosmic point of view.

Wesley C. Mitchell[1]

While he was at Chicago Veblen was extremely busy. Besides his teaching, he took on the time-consuming role of managing editor of *The Journal of Political Economy*, and was a prolific reviewer, writing 25 reviews for his own journal, and 15 for other academic publications. In addition, he wrote 21 articles and three books, as well as translating two books from German. Four of his early articles illustrate his iconoclasm, his anthropological perspective, his drawing on eclectic sources, and his innovations in bringing within economics phenomena that had traditionally been ignored. The four – 'The Economic Theory of Women's Dress' (1894), 'The Barbarian Status of Women' (1899), 'The Instinct of Workmanship and the Irksomeness of Labor' (1898), and 'The Beginnings of Ownership' (1898) – can be profitably read together and treated as a unit, as 'variations on a theme'.[2] For though they deal ostensibly with widely different topics, they share an underlying conceptual schema or interpretive framework which was evidently coalescing in Veblen's mind at the time and which was to receive fullest expression in two of his early books.

These articles introduce what were to become his key terms – 'conspicuous consumption', 'leisure class' and 'instinct of workmanship' – as well as a dualistic model of early human cultural evolution. For Marx the decisive break in history leading to changed economic and social relations had been that between the feudal and capitalist eras, but for Veblen the primary shift had occurred in prehistory. Initially, he proposed, primitive society had enjoyed a long period of being peaceable and productive, but with advances in technical efficiency and mastery of the environment leading to greater productivity a surplus was produced. At the same time crowding in 'the struggle for subsistence' caused hostilities to break out between neighbouring groups. A new predatory phase given over to exploit, seizure and martial prowess supplanted the peaceable one and ushered in the barbarian era. A consequence of this was a division of status between

26

those activities relevant to exploit, which were regarded as superior, and those relevant to peaceable productivity, which were regarded as inferior. Veblen then employs this historical hypothesis (and we have to recognise that it can never be more than a hypothesis) as the basis for explaining a wide range of phenomena, including contemporary ones, since in his view these betray the heritage of that long-ago change in patterns of behaviour and habits of thought.

Veblen, therefore, in addition to drawing on Darwin for a perspective, is working in a very Darwinian manner. For, just as Darwin could not 'prove' that natural selection generated new species in the way required by the hypothetico-deductive method of the experimental sciences, so Veblen cannot 'prove' his prehistorical bifurcation. Nonetheless, just as Darwin, using the accumulation of his vast range of examples, could argue for the validity of his theory because of its unsurpassed explanatory power, so Veblen can claim validity for his hypothesis through its explanatory power in dealing with a range of diverse phenomena. Implicitly, in these articles he is saying that, given these two contrasting modes of social life with the later dominating the former, we can account for economic institutions and other social features by tracing their genealogies to this decisive bifurcation. We can, therefore, explain what has not been adequately explained before.

Of course, to render his novel perspective acceptable he first has to consider conventional approaches and either implicitly subvert, or explicity demolish them. The former manoeuvre is evident in 'The Economic Theory of Women's Dress', where three views of dress as, firstly, a functional expression of the need for warmth and protection, secondly, an expression of aesthetic pleasure in colour and fabric and design, and, thirdly, as an element in sexual display and attraction, are all implicitly repudiated. It is even more evident in the associated essay, 'The Barbarian Status of Women', which focuses on the institution of marriage, one of the cornerstones of the bourgeois social structure and bourgeois morality. Without actually saying so, it ruthlessly undercuts not only the romantic and sentimental perspectives on marriage but also the religious one in which, within a consecrated space and conducted by a sacerdotal official, it becomes 'holy matrimony', given supernatural force by means of its recognition by the Deity.

The latter manoeuvre is manifest in the other two essays, 'The Instinct of Workmanship and the Irksomeness of Labor' and 'The Beginnings of Ownership', in which he focuses on two axioms of classical economics, demonstrates their invalidity, and then substitutes his own interpretation. 'The Instinct of Workmanship' opens with a consideration of the axiom that underpins the hedonistic psychology of classical economics, namely that work is repugnant and humankind seeks to escape it by securing wealth. Yet, Veblen points out, humankind seems to differ from other species in that productive effort is necessary for survival, and since *Homo sapiens* has survived it must possess this capacity for productive effort in great measure. How, then, are we to account for the negative view of work? As it stands it seems that 'the alien propensity in question must have been intruded into his make-up by some malcontent *deus ex machina*'.

The strong Darwinian perspective is clear in such comments as: 'Like other animals, man is an agent that acts in response to stimuli afforded by the environment in which he lives.' Natural selection presses on humankind, eliminating the unfit, just as it presses on other species, and so out of selective necessity 'man is endowed with a proclivity for purposeful action', which Veblen, drawing perhaps on C. Lloyd Morgan's *Habits and Instinct* (1896), labels 'the instinct of workmanship'. This instinct, as the biological term suggests, is 'a more generic, more abiding trait of human nature' than the aversion to work that is currently affirmed. During the peaceable, industrious phase of development the instinct of workmanship was conserved and developed. Further, this phase was marked by collective existence and group solidarity was necessary for survival. Thus, Veblen points out, we can identify the historical origins of another of classical economics' axioms, namely, self-interest as the motive for economic action. This motive could not have existed in the peaceable phase and only came into being during the next stage: 'Self-interest, as an accepted guide of action, is possible only as the concomitant of a predatory life.'

However, Veblen is inconsistent, even contradictory, in his treatment of the instinct of workmanship. At one point he proposes a kind of determinism in which social and work practices determine habits of thought and commonsense values: 'a habitual line of action constitutes a habitual line of thought'. Thus it was the habits of industry in the peaceable phase which developed the instinct of workmanship. But later he uses the 'instinct of workmanship' in the sense of an innate quality, like a drive: 'Under the canon of conduct imposed by the instinct of workmanship efficiency, serviceability commends itself and inefficiency or futility is odious.' He has thus taken over the ambiguities of the term from such psychologists as

James, and it is never clear whether Veblen means a heritable trait in the strict biological sense, or a complex of values transmitted through learning from generation to generation, but pushed into the background during the predatory phase. In this phase exploit, raiding, becomes the chief activity and emulation, together with the desire for social honour, also appears. With the difference in status between exploit and productive activities, the latter fall under 'a polite odium' and are regarded as being 'substantially ignoble'. 'Labor', Veblen concludes in a paragraph that introduces the phrase 'the leisure class', 'carries a taint and all contamination from vulgar employments must be shunned by self-respecting men.' This is the explanation for work having the low esteem it has and possessing that 'irksomeness' economists have conceived as a quality intrinsic to it.

Veblen's first step in 'The Beginnings of Ownership' is to demolish the orthodox view of the natural-rights basis of private property through calling into question the individualist focus of classical economics. According to received theory, the notion of property rights originated in individual productive work; that is to say, when a workman made a thing it was 'natural' that he owned it. Yet this axiomatic basis of the theory of property ignores the fact that human beings are social animals living in collective units: 'All production is, in fact, a production in and by the help of the community, and all wealth is such only in society.' In addition, Veblen says, echoing Bellamy in *Looking Backward*, all production is dependent on the inheritance of knowledge and techniques that are the common store of the industrial community. He sums up his case thus: 'Since there is no individual production and no individual productivity, the natural rights preconception that ownership rests on the individually productive labor of the owner reduces itself to absurdity.'

If then this is not the basis of ownership and property rights, then what is? Lewis H. Morgan was already the acknowledged dean of American anthropology when he brought out his highly regarded and influential *Ancient Society* in 1877. He argued that cultural evolution had proceeded through three stages – 'savagery', 'barbarism', and 'civilisation', each divided into 'early', 'middle', and 'late' phases, and that private property did not become a central institution until the late phase of barbarism, that is to say, it was not intrinsic to human society but was a relatively late cultural institution. The book impressed Marx and it spurred Friedrich Engels to expand on a historical–materialist interpretation of its main points in *The Origin of the Family, Private Property, and the State* in 1884. Veblen always read widely in anthropology and ethnology, and he, too, seems to have been influenced by Morgan and others in the field. In 'The Beginnings of Ownership' he draws on ethnological material to consider the possibility that the concept of ownership arose from the possession of weapons and ornaments, but drawing on Frazer's *The Golden Bough*, the early volumes of which had begun appearing since 1890, he suggests these constituted part of a 'quasi-personal fringe,' and so cannot explain the origin of ownership. He also dismisses the idea of ownership as having an instinctual basis. For ownership, he insists, is not a natural fact but a cultural one which grew into an institution 'through a long course of habituation'. Finally, he traces the notion of private property to 'tenure by prowess' in barbarian culture. During the earlier peaceable stage, 'there is no leisure class resting its prerogative on coercion, prowess and immemorial status; and there is also no ownership'. In the barbarian, predatory phase ownership arises not so much with the seizure of goods as with the seizure of persons and their enslavement. Veblen is in harmony with Morgan up to this point since he had also noted how systematic slavery had originated in this phase and 'stands directly connected with the production of property'.[3]

However, Veblen deviates from him in focusing on the seizure of women and its consequences. (He possibly has in mind Viking raids on Anglo-Saxon coastal villages.) Female captives thus became trophies, evidence of an individual warrior's prowess. Since they were separate from him but controlled by him and their services enjoyed not communally but exclusively by him, they could be said to be 'owned' by him and this is the origin of ownership. Furthermore, Veblen, implicitly taking up remarks by John Ferguson McLennan in *Primitive Marriage* (1865) and Darwin in *The Descent of Man* (1871) that marriage had its origin in capture, then proposes that out of this relationship arose a form of ownership-marriage in which the man is the master and the wife a chattel. This institution soon encompassed women who were not captured but were from the same group and so constituted 'the original both of private property and of the patriarchal household'. (Morgan by the way does not associate the capture of women with either the origin of property or of marriage.)

This linkage between the origins of ownership and of marriage is also at the heart of the argument in 'The Barbarian Status of Women'. There he proposes that a woman captured from another group is 'a trophy of a raid', and therefore 'evidence of exploit'. Being of relevance to the man as an individual rather than as a member of a group this leads to 'a form of marriage based on coercion and ... to a concept of ownership'. Eventually, the institution of ownership-marriage 'makes its way into definitive acceptance as the only beautiful and virtuous form of the relation'. When it comes to marrying women from within the group, this is effected by a 'mimic or ceremonial capture', and so marriage for the woman becomes 'an initiation into servitude' for it is 'the woman's place to love, honor and obey'. Thus, the patriarchal household derives from the predatory and barbarian phase of culture and 'the ownership of women is a gratifying evidence of prowess and high standing'.

It is, therefore, a wife's status within the patriarchal household, the domestic unit of modern American society, which endows her dress with an economic dimension. For 'what constitutes dress as an economic fact,' he states in 'The Economic Theory of Women's Dress,' 'properly falling within the scope of economic theory, is its function as an index of the wealth of its wearer – or, to be more precise, of its owner, for the wearer and owner are not necessarily the same person'. A wife's or daughter's costume indicates the wealth of her patriarchal household and, since social respect or status is gained by the display of wasteful expenditure, 'the first principle of dress, therefore, is conspicuous expensiveness', and another central principle is 'conspicuous waste'. To highlight the wastefulness there must be a constant succession of items of apparel, to the extent that some items such as ballgowns and wedding dresses can be worn only once. Fashion aids the display of wastefulness by requiring the repeated re-equipping of female wardrobes in deference to the latest designs. Dress is also evidence of leisure, another key element in social honour, given the low esteem in which work is held. For, typically, women's dress (and we are thinking of the late nineteenth century here, the era of the Gibson girl) demonstrates with its voluminous skirts, delicately perched hats, and high heels that the wearer is incapable of doing any useful work. Wives and daughters then serve to advertise the wealth of their patriarchal household, gaining social honour for the paterfamilias. Even young children have a role to play, for 'the child in the hands of civilised woman is an accessory organ of conspicuous consumption'.

'Marriage', 'the patriarchal household', 'property rights', 'self-interest', 'status', 'fashion' – it would be difficult to identify foundations that were more central than these for the world-view of respectable people in turn-of-the-century America. Yet, here was Veblen in these articles systematically undermining them, and in so doing undercutting any complacent sense they might enjoy of being part of an advanced civilisation, for what was the origin of property and marriage but the brute capture of female slaves by barbarian marauders! If these were outcomes of the predatory phase of history, the only hope of overcoming them lay in a resurgence of the habits of thought characteristic of the earlier, peaceable period. Two of these essays accordingly close with hints of a need for radical social change and of where hope for such change may be best placed. 'The Instinct of Workmanship' concludes: 'There is no remedy for this kind of irksomeness, short of a subversion of that cultural structure on which our canons of decency rest.' 'The Barbarian Status of Women' ends on a note of revolutionary hope, based on what he saw as a weakening of marriage among the industrial working class:

> There may seem some ground for holding that the reassertion of ancient habits of thought which is now apparently at work to disintegrate the institution of ownership-marriage may be expected also to work a disintegration of the correlative institution of private property.

To sum up, we can see that, though Veblen's immediate focus is on contemporary phenomena as befits a sociologist, he looks beyond them to their roots and, as befits a cultural analyst, is able to establish their derivation from the heritage bequeathed the present by the past. This brings about a new understanding, enables new linkages to be made between phenomena previously thought unconnected, and offers some hope of revolutionary change. His project in these articles is also a demythologising one. In *Mythologies* (1973) Roland Barthes points to the dependency of bourgeois ideology on 'myths', in which by a characteristic manoeuvre the historical and political is reduced to the 'natural'. He writes: 'We reach here the very principle of myth: it transforms history into nature', and later, 'myth is constituted by the loss of the historical quality of things; in it, things lose the memory that they once were made.'[4] Myths, therefore, place practices and beliefs outside culture, so rendering them eternal and immutable. So, Veblen here takes such givens in conventional social and economic thought as dress, marriage, ownership, and work's low esteem, and by tracing their historical evolution exposes them as cultural artefacts. This opens up the possibility that, given a change of culture, new artefacts, new institutions, could be brought into being.

The Theory of the Leisure Class

Veblen began writing *The Theory of the Leisure Class : An Economic Study of Institutions* in 1895, and, since these essays represent an initial articulation of ideas central to that work, it is logical to turn to his first book, the one that brought him to a much wider audience and by which he is still most commonly remembered. It was published in 1899, but the general idea he said had been formed in his boyhood in a large part by remarks made by his father.[5] Its purpose, he announced, in the 'Preface' was 'to discuss the place and value of the leisure class as an economic factor in modern life'. The book was divided into two parts of seven chapters each, the first part elaborating on the major features of the leisure class, and the second detailing the widespread influence this stratum has upon modern economic and social life. The first part, then, tends to be empirical as he draws on an eclectic range of sources to illustrate key aspects of this élite. He moves from ethnological material concerning the Andaman Islanders, say, to historical material, to observations on present-day practices in order to demonstrate both the ubiquity and persistence of this phenomenon from the barbarian past.

Underlying his presentation is the same historical-dualistic model that underlay the four essays, but it is refined here by the addition of two subsequent stages: the quasi-peaceable stage (with slavery and status), followed by the peaceable stage of modern industry (with wage labour and cash payment), also referred to as 'the pecuniary culture'. In the first peaceable, productive phase people, he suggests, had 'a sense of the merit of serviceability or efficiency and the demerit of futility, waste or incapacity', and that this 'aptitude or propensity may be called the instinct of workmanship'.[6] For Veblen the prime motivation in social life is the attainment of honour or esteem and in this first phase esteem is gained through efficiency or productivity, by the degree to which one exemplifies the instinct of workmanship. In groups that are peaceable and sedentary and where there is no individual ownership there is also no leisure class. The conclusion Veblen draws is that this institution emerged during the transition from a peaceable to a predatory or warlike phase. He then reprises material from the articles to link the origins of ownership and marriage with the capture of female slaves. With the transition the basis of social honour changes, for now it is evidence of prowess or exploit that gains most esteem, and productive labour falls into low esteem. Evidence of prowess becomes manifest, through the institution of ownership, in personal wealth. Veblen takes issue with the doctrine of classical economists that the motive for acquisition of wealth is consumption. Rather, he says, the key motive for ownership is emulation, for 'the possession of wealth confers honor,' and 'the end sought by accumulation is to rank high in comparison with the rest of the community in point of pecuniary strength' (p. 39). Thus, there is instituted the regime of pecuniary emulation, at the head of which is the leisured class, whose members are exempt from industrial employments and indulge only in occupations such as war or sports that confer social honour.

The possession of wealth, however, is not sufficient in itself; it must be shown off, advertised, for 'esteem is awarded only on evidence'. There are two main strategies for this. The first is to abstain from useful, productive work, since a life of leisure must be based on substantial riches: 'Conspicuous abstention from labor therefore becomes the conventional mark of superior pecuniary achievement and the conventional index of reputability' (p. 43). Leisure, however, does not necessarily mean idleness, but the 'non-productive consumption of time' and this may be instanced through the knowledge of dead languages, or of dog and horse breeding, facility at music and sports, and good manners. These last are evidence of time and effort spent wastefully and must be cultivated by anyone wanting to succeed in 'the regime of status'. Servants, by their abstention from useful work, are engaged in 'vicarious leisure' and so provide additional proof of their master's wealth.

The second strategy is the conspicuous consumption of goods, and Veblen, echoing Boas, draws a comparison between the Kwakiutl potlatch and the aristocrat's or millionaire's ball as examples of ostentatious consumption. Now centring his discussion much more on contemporary conditions, Veblen identifies two factors that have led to the relative dominance of conspicuous consumption over conspicuous leisure as a means of demonstrating superior wealth. Firstly, the greater mobility and anonymity of modern industrial society means that the display of goods prevails over the display of leisure as the basis for esteem (p. 71). Secondly, the instinct of workmanship, which 'is the ultimate value by which activities can be measured ... for it is an instinct more fundamental, of more ancient prescription, than the propensity to predatory emulation' (p. 179), affects even the leisure class, particularly in the modern industrial period, so that they feel impelled to engage in quasi-purposeful activities, such as 'social duties,' charity work, or artistic and scholarly pursuits.

The whole system of pecuniary emulation or status is governed by imitation of the habits of the leisure class, which 'stands at the head of the social structure in point of reputability' and whose 'manner of life and standards of worth therefore afford the norm of reputability for the community' (p. 70), so that the canon of conspicuous consumption becomes widespread. People become accustomed to a certain amount of wasteful expenditure as necessary to their standard of living. This has a profound implication for social development in a time of increasing industrial efficiency and output. Since conspicuous consumption, being relative to the consumption of the leisure class, is indefinitely expansible, increased factory productivity will not lead to less working time and more leisure for workers (as envisaged by Bellamy for instance) but to the use of the surplus in further consumption in the service of pecuniary emulation:

> As increased industrial efficiency makes it possible to procure the means of livelihood with less labor, the energies of the industrious members of the community are bent to the compassing of a higher result in conspicuous expenditure, rather than slackened to a more comfortable pace. (p. 85)

This was remarkably prescient, for, as Gary Cross has shown in *Time and Money: The Making of Consumer Culture* (1993), in the 1920s American workers chose to forego campaigning for a shorter working week in favour of higher incomes. Veblen instances the decline in the birth-rate and the increased habit of domestic privacy as demonstrating the pervasive influence of the canon of conspicuous consumption.

He then expands his field of enquiry to demonstrate how this 'canon of conspicuous waste' has an impact not only on economic activity *per se* but also on facets of social life traditionally thought to be autonomous and far from the sway of economics or class. These include the sense of duty, of beauty, of utility, and of devotional or ritualistic fitness. It even modifies the moral judgement, he suggests, since (in a veiled reference to the swindles and frauds perpetrated by some nineteenth-century entrepreneurs), if great wealth is gained by crime the thief or swindler is less likely to be prosecuted than if only a small amount of money is involved, and if he spends his gains in conspicuous consumption this will 'dissipate any opprobrium he may suffer' (p. 89).

In the case of the Christian churches, which he iconoclastically terms 'the maturer cults', the canon of conspicuous waste is plainly at work in 'devout consumption'. This refers not only to the elaborate sacred buildings or churches, but also to the highly wrought articles and works of art that fill them, as well as the costly vestments worn by the priests. Then, using the example of a hand-made silver spoon compared with a factory-made aluminium one, he points out the strong linkage between our sense of beauty and awareness of cost. Though they both do the same job and the latter may well be lighter and easier to use and maintain, it is the former that is considered beautiful, for 'a beautiful article which is not expensive is accounted not beautiful'. Thus, hand-wrought items have higher status than mass-produced goods, and because of their absorption into the system of pecuniary emulation Veblen rejects the exaltation of handicraft goods and the call for a return to handicraft production associated with Ruskin and Morris.

If our aesthetic sense is infected by the rule of waste, so too, Veblen proposes, is our evaluation of female beauty. This can be seen in the shift from the classical ideal of beauty as a well-built, strong physique to the delicate features and narrow waist of the feudal ideal and its modern imitators such as the Pre-Raphaelites. For such physical slightness connotes an abstention from productive work and therefore membership of the leisure class. However, Veblen believes that there is a shift back to the ideal of the well-built woman in the West.

Dress is one of the best examples of conspicuous consumption, and the first part of *The Theory of the Leisure Class* concludes with a chapter on 'Dress as an Expression of Pecuniary Culture'. Here Veblen reprises many of the points he first made in 'The Economic Theory of Women's Dress', such as the role of fashion, but enlarges the discussion to embrace men's dress. Under the canon of conspicuous waste, dress should not only be expensive but should make plain the wearer's exemption from useful work. Women's dress in particular, most clearly advertises a freedom from productive labour, and is part of the woman's role as a vicarious consumer bringing honour to her household and its patriarchal head.

It is not until the beginning of Part Two with Chapter Eight that we are offered an explication of the theoretical foundation that underlies this assemblage of social data concerning this particular stratum. This foundation is unequivocally Darwinian:

The life of man in society, just like the life of other species, is a struggle for existence, and therefore it is a process of selective adaptation. The evolution of social structure has been a process of natural selection of institutions. (p. 131)

Veblen has taken Darwin's view of the natural selection of varieties and the evolution of species according to definite laws and here is applying it to society, thus developing 'an evolutionary economics'. He dispenses with the teleological dimension of Spencerian social evolution, namely that there is a process of meliorism towards a perfectly stable society, and points out the various factors and pressures which lead to the survival of some features and the extinction, or near-extinction, of others. Among the most powerful of these factors, he suggests, drawing (through the slight shift in his terminology) on an analogy with the law of natural selection, is 'the law of conspicuous waste'. It is thus a wholly materialistic theory that he is proposing, in that he posits the operation of material forces shaping society's development in accordance with the Marxian base/superstructure model of economic determinism, for 'the forces which make for a readjustment of institutions, especially in the case of the modern industrial community are, in the last analysis, almost entirely of an economic nature' (p. 134).

He proposes that ideas or attitudes are themselves subject to selection and only 'the fittest habits of thought survive'. What is necessary for survival is the adaptation of such habits of thought to prevailing conditions. The implication of this is that the reigning ideology is not necessarily the most truthful, most useful, rational or ethical; it is simply the congeries of habits of thought that have survived. Institutions change and develop in response to changing circumstances, but there is often a cultural lag, for they 'are products of a past process, are adapted to past circumstances, and are therefore never in full accord with the requirements of the present' (p. 133). These inherited habits of thought, residues from an earlier historical period, may well impede successful adaptation to contemporary needs. The leisure class, as a barbarian residue, is a key example of this and, because it is sheltered from the economic forces that make for change and adjustment, it has not had to adapt to the modern age.

These broader considerations prepare the way for Veblen's central charge against the leisure class: it is hampering cultural advancement by impeding the full adjustment of society to a contemporary industrial economy. It does this, he suggests, in three main ways: through the conservatism of the class itself, for it has a 'material interest in leaving things as they are'; through setting an example of conspicuous waste and conservatism, which become honorific and are imitated by the lower classes; and through the unequal distribution of wealth on which it rests, for 'the accumulation of wealth at the upper end of the scale implies privation at the lower end of the scale,' so depriving the working class of the energy required for 'the learning and adoption of new habits of thought' (pp. 140–1). We can thus see that, like Antonio Gramsci, Veblen is concerned with the question of hegemony: how a ruling class manages to maintain its dominance in the face of the numerical and technical superiority of the subordinate classes, and how it manages (to borrow a phrase from Noam Chomsky) to 'manufacture consent'.[7] The answer is that it maintains political supremacy through command of the ideological field, and the latter half of the book sets out to demonstrate how leisure-class canons of conspicuous consumption, status, and invidious distinction ramify through such diverse surface phenomena as manners, sports, religion, and university education. This pecuniary culture, promulgated throughout society and participated in by the middle class, is thus demystified by Veblen and exposed as masking class interests and ensuring the continuation of the ruling class's dominance.

Modern America, for Veblen, is not an example of a unified, harmonious system but, because of its leisure class, is riven by two sources of tension, by what may be labelled 'the cultural contradictions of capitalism'.[8] The first of these concerns a distinction he expands upon in his later work, namely that between business, the pecuniary process of making profit, and industry, the technical process of making goods. Industry as factory production selects for habits of thought which constitute a *matter-of-fact* attitude (that is, an empiricism which stresses the need for demonstrable, physical evidence) towards objects and processes informed by an understanding of scientific causality. By contrast, business has as its basis financial or pecuniary activities and it is with these that members of the leisure class are occupied. Their relation to the economic process is 'a relation of acquisition, not of production; of exploitation, not of serviceability', and their 'office is of a parasitic character, and their interest is to divert what substance they may to their own use' (p. 143). They are, therefore, not affected by the progressive demands of industry and harbour archaic traits, such as spiritualism, that are out of kilter with the secular modern order. Veblen then expands on how the leisure class's archaic values influence industrial society and infect many different fields.

The second source of tension, connected to the first, arises out of the dual nature of the individual as both a sole agent and a member of a group. The collective interests of any modern community, Veblen points out, centre on industrial efficiency, and this is best served by 'honesty, diligence, peacefulness, good-will, an absence of self-seeking, and an habitual recognition and apprehension of causal sequence'. These traits, however, come into conflict with those required of the individual under the regime of pecuniary emulation, for 'the immediate interest of the individual under the competitive regime is best served by shrewd trading and unscrupulous management' (p. 154), and so the traits that serve the collective interest are 'disserviceable to the individual.' Business carries over and cultivates predatory aptitudes from the barbarian past as exemplified by the captain of industry, but the industrial process impinging on the majority of the population 'acts to adapt their habits of thought to the non-invidious purposes of collective life.' There is thus a bifurcation of habits of thought with 1) business and its pecuniary activities based on exploit-conserving predatory traits and 2) modern industry eliminating them.

Thus, while the factory system fosters certain aptitudes, these are countered by the general aptitudes fostered in the pecuniary culture by the leisure class. The result, Veblen concludes, is that the leisure class 'lowers the industrial efficiency of the community,' and retards 'the adaptation of human nature to the exigencies of modern industrial life' (p. 164). It does this by conserving archaic traits, such as traditional acts of prowess, for example, in war, duels, and sports, an irrational belief in luck that underpins gambling, and devout or religious observances. Veblen devotes much of the last quarter of the book to elaborating on these points. He asserts that the 'body of habits of thought which make up the character of an individual is in some sense an organic whole,' and so 'the habit of thought formed under one stimulus will affect other habits of thought'. A belief in luck, say, has, in his view, a deleterious effect on a worker's fitness for work in an industrial society which demands that 'matter-of-fact temper which recognises the value of material facts simply as opaque items in a mechanical sequence' (p. 199). This is a little too simplistic in that he fails to acknowledge the extent to which individuals are able to compartmentalise their attitudes in accordance with their immediate activities. Ordinary people, just like Whitman, can embrace contradictions, being rational and scientific in the factory during the week but still placing a bet at the race-course on Saturday and going to church on Sunday. He sees some hope in the decline of religious attendance among the working and middle classes, in a falling away from what he dismissively terms 'the anthropomorphic creeds' (p. 210).

He sums up 'the substantial canons of the leisure-class scheme of life' as 'a conspicuous waste of time and substance and a withdrawal from the industrial process' (p. 218), and expands in his last chapter on how such canons have shaped even university education. This, like fashion, like ostentatious architecture, is an expression of the pecuniary culture, and arose out of a priestly class and their development of doctrine and ritual (p. 237). He was no doubt thinking here of the preponderance of theology professors at the University of Chicago. As evidence he points to the large number of American colleges and universities affiliated to some religious denomination, as well as to the rituals and vestments, the initiation and graduation ceremonies, the caps and gowns, that are prevalent in universities. Leisure-class canons of waste are evident too in the high honour given to knowledge of Greek and Latin – a mark of conspicuous leisure – though he remarks that college athletics now rivals the classics 'for the primacy in leisure-class education' (p. 256).

Thus he brings to a close his radical analysis of modern America and its pecuniary culture. In doing so he has punctured many illusions, and debunked many bastions of respectability. He has demonstrated that, far from being the acme of the progressive spirit, this culture, because of, not in spite of its universities, its architecture, its opera houses, its fashions, its religion, its institutions of marriage and property, but most of all because of its leisure class, is bedevilled with survivals from a vicious barbarian past. Its governing principle, persistent through history, is 'conspicuous waste' in the service of a competitive regime of pecuniary emulation, in which individuals strive to outdo one another in gaining social status. In this way Veblen countered Marx's belief in the triumph of bourgeois over feudal modes of thought and of the inevitability of human progress, and Max Weber's view of the inexorable spread of rationalisation in modern societies. Rather, he proposed, modern American culture was marked by the atavistic survival of primitive forms which fostered irrational social needs.

Using as his key example Benjamin Franklin, Max Weber had presented America as the home of the Protestant Ethic, an ideology centred on work as worldly vocation and on abstinence from luxury as befitting the period of early capital accumulation.[9] That era was now past, overtaken by industrialism and the growth of huge personal fortunes, and the American rich shifted from a code of frugality and restraint (despite the calls, already noted, of such millionaires as Andrew Carnegie for its retention) to one of monumental expenditure and luxury. One consequence was that work was no longer regarded as a 'vocation', but was now degraded, 'irksome,' of low esteem, so that the commonest dream of all was to escape from it, by means of an unexpected inheritance, say, or 'a lucky break,' such as striking a vein of gold ore in the Klondike.

The implications of the hegemony of the leisure class are disturbing and affect everyone. The life-ideal or rather pseudo-ideal that prevails is saturated with the image of the leisure class, that is to say, a composite of idleness, high status, and hedonistic gratification through consumption. Thus, the key notions of happiness and freedom are reconfigured and perpetuated as happiness *away from* productive labour, rather than happiness *in* productive labour, as freedom *from* work, rather than freedom *in* work. Yet, if we accept with Veblen that the human individual is a purposeful agent, and if there is a human propensity 'more fundamental, of more ancient prescription than the propensity to predatory emulation', so primal in fact as to deserve the label 'instinct', an instinct of workmanship, one directed toward production *in itself*, such a notion of happiness is both false and injurious, for it involves a repression of a fundamental constituent of human nature. (This may account for the noted *ennui* of the leisured classes.)

However, happiness in production is impossible under capitalism for at least four reasons. Firstly, as the young Marx pointed out, there is the condition of alienation the workers feel, since they do not own their product, nor express themselves through it.[10] Secondly, industrial manufacture is fragmented into many small steps so that the worker is condemned to endless repetition of the same task and denied the satisfaction of creating the whole product. Thirdly, the large-scale organisation of factory production requiring the integration of many different stages in the manufacturing process removes all autonomy from the individual. And fourthly, the imperative of maximising profitability demands a pace of working, a productivity, which is exhausting and life-destroying. Ford's workers, their lives dominated by the speed of the assembly line, were soon to find this out.

William Morris's solution proposed in *News from Nowhere* was to abandon both capitalism and industrialism. To his mind happiness *in* production could only be secured through a return to handicraft manufacture, thus restoring both ownership of the product and autonomy over his labour to the worker. However, as we have seen, Veblen is dismissive of this option, not only because this would abandon the huge productivity gains attained by the factory system (soon to be augmented through Ford's methods) which provide for the elimination of want, but also because he sees in factory discipline itself, as his later work makes clear, a progressive force shaping humanity for the future. Yet, Veblen's 'instinct of workmanship' does offer a revolutionary potential. For if this is really a primary constituent of human nature, humankind can be reconceived as *Homo faber*, the creating, shaping mammal, and the reign of pecuniary emulation can simply be viewed as an historical distortion. If there once was a social organisation (in the peaceable, industrious phase) which allowed this instinct full expression, then a future organisation which does the same could be envisaged and a full humanity recovered.

Four Essays on Economics

At the turn of the century Veblen also produced another group of closely related articles – four methodological essays about economics, beginning with 'Why Is Economics Not An Evolutionary Science?'(1898), and ending with the three-part discussion 'The Preconceptions of Economic Science,'(1899–1900).[11] They present a discussion of the obsolete procedures of academic economics, that is to say, neo-classical economics, in contrast to the evolutionary method of modern science in physics, chemistry, biology, psychology, anthropology and ethnology.

The first article begins Veblen's attack on classical economics as represented by Adam Smith and John Stuart Mill and also the Austrian Historical School represented by Gustav Schmoller. Late in the piece he points out that for people engaged in modern industry, and imbued with a matter-of-fact habit of mind and understanding of causal sequence, there is an 'unreality' about the axioms and laws of traditional economics, for 'it is helplessly behind the times', incapable of dealing with economic life in ways that could be called 'modern'. Drawing on an analogy with the development of sciences such as biology, psychology, and anthropology which, post-Darwin, have become evolutionary, Veblen attributes economics' outdatedness to its being stuck in an earlier phase and not having yet become an 'evolutionary science'. The 'premises and point of view' for this to happen have been absent, since economics is still dominated by notions of the 'natural', and the 'normal', of 'verities', and of 'controlling principles'. These 'normal' or 'natural' laws developed by economists represent principles which they thought should, rather than those which actually did, govern economic behaviour; they were 'a projection of the accepted ideal of conduct'.

A second charge he makes is that, just as biology before Darwin was concerned with classification, so economics is still engaged in elaborating 'a system of economic taxonomy'. This, he concedes, may be useful up to a point, but it presupposes the static nature of the system and fails to deal with change; it is unable to explain the causes of development. In order to do this, it must focus on the human material, as it is here that 'the motor forces of the process of development' are to be found; this 'economic action' must become the subject of economics if it is to become evolutionary in character.

At the root of economics' failure to deal adequately with modern life is a mistaken conception of human nature, for within the classical schema humanity is 'conceived in hedonistic terms, that is to say, in terms of a passive and substantially inert and immutably given human nature'. (The notion of 'immutability' in the natural world was terminally discredited by Darwin's theory of natural selection.) Within this concept the individual is 'a lightning calculator of pleasures and pains', largely swayed by the environment. However, Veblen points out, recent psychology and anthropology have rendered the notion of 'the hedonistic man' obsolete, for they have provided a conception of human nature which stresses not passivity but the human capacity for action, for being an agent devoted to purposeful activity: 'it is characteristic of man to do something, not simply to suffer pleasures and pains through the impact of suitable forces.' The individual then is 'a coherent structure of propensities and habits which seeks realisation and expression in an unfolding activity'. There is thus a dynamic, never-to-be-concluded relationship between the individual, as well as the group, and the environment, in which each effects changes in the other, producing a new situation which in turn leads to further changes. Humankind's interest in the 'material means of life', or 'the economic interest' has played a large part in 'shaping the cultural growth of all communities', and since its impact is felt everywhere, all institutions can be considered 'economic institutions'. This, we can see, greatly enlarges the scope of economics and is the theoretical position underpinning Veblen's treatment of dress, marriage, aesthetic standards, religious devotion, and the leisure class in the contemporaneous publications we have just considered.

What then would an evolutionary economics be like? It must, Veblen proposes, be 'the theory of a process of cultural growth as determined by the economic interest, a theory of a cumulative sequence of economic institutions stated in terms of the process itself'. There is thus the assumption of an economic determinism at play in the evolution of cultural institutions, and an emphasis on change and adaptation. But, Veblen points out, this is an open-ended process; it does not have a purpose, nor, *vis-à-vis* Spencer or Marx, a predetermined goal or state.

Veblen followed this with his long, three-part essay, 'The Preconceptions of Economic Science', in which he surveys the historical development of economic theory from the French Physiocrats, through the classical, utilitarian, and neo-classical phases up to recent work by Keynes and Marshall. In addition, he reiterates in a much more detailed and refined treatment his exposure and critique of the metaphysical assumptions underlying traditional economics. He points to the preconceptions of a 'natural order' and teleological process in economic life which underlie Adam Smith's influential works. He also points to the hedonistic psychology introduced by Bentham, and to the way in which for post-Bentham economists exchange value rather than the contribution of industry to the material welfare of the community becomes the central focus. This leads to an emphasis on 'the pecuniary side of life', involving acquisition, ownership, and monetary gain, with a consequent shifting of production to a subsidiary role in practice and to the background in theoretical consideration. In classical economics pecuniary gain is thus viewed as the only motive for economic activity, and industrial production is merely a means to that end. One consequence of this is 'the classical failure to discriminate between capital as investment and capital as industrial appliances' with the result that two distinct aspects of capitalistic industry, the financial and the productive, have been conflated into a false unity. In his last few pages Veblen qualifies his comments in the earlier article and allows that 'economists of the present day are commonly evolutionists, in a general way', but he goes on to make the point that neo-classical political economy manifests only a 'quasi-evolutionary tone' and still has a long way to go to explain economic behaviour and development in terms of a scientific causal sequence.

At the turn of the century American capitalism was changing in structure and character. The individualistic entrepreneur, the owner-boss, who directed his firm as well as owning it, was becoming a thing of the past. The growth of the stock market led to the dispersal of ownership among the stockholders, and the direction of the company was left in the hands of a trained, professional élite of managers and technicians. In addition, as noted in the previous chapter, the phase of pure competition between firms had given way by the 1880s and 1890s to a phase marked by amalgamation, the formation of cartels, and the creation of 'trusts' and holding companies. J. D. Rockefeller built up Standard Oil to be the biggest trust of these years, a position it did not relinquish until 1901, when J. P. Morgan formed the United States Steel Company by merging the Federal Steel Company with several other large steel firms, including Carnegie's Pennsylvania Steel Company. This was achieved through the device of the 'holding company' and it inaugurated the era of finance capitalism as well as the displacement of the entrepreneur by the investment banker as the dominant force in American business.

The investment banker usually organised a holding company for two reasons: first, to obtain a commission for promoting and selling the securities issued by the new concern; and second, to realise a further gain through the appreciation of the common stock issued, part of which he retained. J. P. Morgan and Company organised a syndicate of bankers to finance the setting-up of United States Steel. The Morgan firm received $12.5 million in Steel corporation securities for organising and managing the group and an additional amount for participating as a member of the syndicate. The syndicate as a whole obtained securities that netted $62.5 million when sold. Such massive gains could be made through the way in which the corporation was capitalised since, though it was essentially a coming together of ten major iron and steel producers, it was valued by the bankers at much more than the sum of its parts. The initial capitalisation was over $1.4 billion, but the physical assets of the controlled, participating companies, i.e. their plant and equipment, inventories of raw materials and finished products, were worth only $676 million. The difference equalled the value of the 'watered' or 'inflated' securities issued on Wall Street. The value of these stocks and bonds represented the estimated value of an intangible asset called 'goodwill,' which derived its worth from the trust's competitive advantage and its capacity to achieve economies of scale. (The people who actually made the steel were denied any share in the fortunes created by amalgamation, since US Steel maintained the 12-hour working day until August 1923 when it finally yielded to pressure from the Harding Administration).[12]

In the early 1900s up until the collapse of the stock market in 1929 such trust-making and upward recapitalisation by means of holding companies proceeded apace so that the large investment banks were able to gain a widespread grip on the American economy. By 1912 J. P. Morgan and Company and associated concerns held numerous directorships in 112 corporations across a wide range of business activities with combined assets of over $22 billion.[13] By 1928 holding companies accounted for 395 of the 593 corporations listed on the New York Stock Exchange.[14] It is in response to this rise of finance capital that Veblen wrote his next book, as well as the much later *Absentee Ownership and Business Enterprise in Recent Times: The Case of America* (1923).

The Theory of Business Enterprise

In an article, 'Industrial and Pecuniary Employments', Veblen had made the distinction between industrial capital and pecuniary capital.[15] The former refers to the factories and the machines, while the latter describes the paper wealth involved in the firm's capitalisation on the stock market. The industrial employments, then, are to do with the factories and machines, while the pecuniary employments are concerned with the financial activities associated with pecuniary capital. This fundamental dichotomy informs *The Theory of Business Enterprise* (1904), which up to a point is a further development of the ideas in the article.

This is a bifocal work that offers an analysis of what Veblen sees as two contradictory aspects of modern manufacturing. The first of these is the reliance of business on industrial production or the machine process, which requires fine adjustments between its different stages leading to the standardisation of tools, units of measurement, goods and services, and even patterns of living and thinking. However, in modern America 'industry is carried on for the sake of business', whose motive is 'pecuniary gain'. So the second aspect is the pecuniary dimension of business devoted to making profits.

In his discussion Veblen draws on both Werner Sombart's *ModernismusKapitalismus* (1900) and Marx's *Capital* (1865), and points out an aspect of the businessman which militated against the idolisation and idealisation of business leaders by serious intellectuals and the popular press alike. William Graham Sumner could write in 1902 in 'The Concentration of Wealth: Its Economic Justification' that millionaires were a product of natural selection and as such were 'the naturally-selected agents of society for certain works'. Their role was to organise production 'so that the cost of it will be reduced to the lowest terms'. Carnegie, the same year, wrote: 'I can confidently recommend to you the business career as one in which there is abundant room for the exercise of man's highest power, and of every good quality in human nature.'[16] However, Veblen points out, businessmen can in certain circumstances gain from disrupting the industrial system and their relationship to the productive capacity of modern industry may well be an obstructive one: 'the captain of industry works against, as well as for, a new and more efficient organisation.'[17] One of the ways in which he may act as a brake is by resisting the inevitable trend towards consolidation and combination. For the best way to secure profitability is 'to establish as much of a monopoly as may be' (p. 54). This process of amalgamation has led to a rise in the importance of loan credit through the issuance of bonds, preference shares and debentures. So advanced are such devices that the market for capital has superseded the market for goods, since those firms interested in combining need large amounts of capital for buying out competitors. The source of this capital is the investment banker, who also acts as the promoter to sell the securities in the newly amalgamated concern to the institutional as well as private investors who ultimately finance the amalgamation.

Often the banker was the instigator in forming a trust or a holding company to effect the merger of competing firms as this was also a means for him to acquire a portion of the issued stock. As Veblen points out, as reward for his organisation of the trust he would receive 'a bonus which commonly falls immediately into the shape of a share in the capitalization of the newly organized concern' (p. 124). His opportunity for maximising his 'bonus' depended on inflating the trust's capitalisation by exaggerating the value of its chief intangible asset – goodwill. As well as economies of scale and the trust's competitive advantage, this 'goodwill' included the value of the banker's involvement in the reorganisation, for this brought with it the cooperation of other financiers and the promise of further credit if need be. 'It is safe to affirm,' Veblen comments in a reference to J. P. Morgan and Company, 'that this good-will of the great re-organizer has in some measure entered in capitalized form into the common stock of the United States Steel Corporation, as also into that of some of the other great combinations that have latterly been effected' (p. 172).

The process of stock market capitalisation which set up the trust was entirely a paper affair and added nothing to the total quantity of an industry's concrete assets. It also led to a bifurcation of ownership. Veblen estimated that in a usual reorganisation the amount of bonds and preference shares issued represented the capitalised value of the material assets, while the common shares equalled the capitalised value of the intangible assets. So purchasers of the former were effectively the real owners of the physical assets, while purchasers of the latter were owners of the inflated goodwill. He concluded: 'This method of capitalization, therefore, effects a somewhat thoroughgoing separation between the management and ownership of the industrial equipment' (p. 146).

One of the consequences of this separation was a greater distancing of the businessmen and their pecuniary occupations from the industrial process, a distancing that had cultural implications he would expand on later in the book. Another consequence was that, by manipulating the flow of information about the company or even its actual performance, stockholders on the board of directors could 'buy or sell securities of the concern with advantage to themselves', and so would 'manage the affairs of the concern with a view to an advantageous purchase and sale of its capital rather than with a view to the future prosperity of the concern' (p. 156). Since, therefore, the businessmen's interests lay in the artful manipulation of the share price more than in the efficient production of industrial goods, a dichotomy of interests arises 'between the industrial needs of the community and the business needs of the corporation' (p. 158). Veblen is here undermining the myth of a harmony of interests between the community and business, as well as the conventional status of the businessman as a benefactor to society. Berle and Means were later to voice a similar concern about the ways in which certain stockholders may manipulate the business for their own advantage rather than for the general benefit of the corporation's investors.[18]

Despite exposing how great fortunes were being made spuriously from the formation of such trusts, Veblen was in favour of further combination and amalgamation, unlike some radicals who regarded the trend towards monopolies as a threat. In his view business since 1870 had been suffering 'chronic depression' and the only refuge from this lay in 'thoroughgoing coalition in those lines of business in which coalition is practicable' (p. 263). This would eliminate the waste of competition and would lead, or rather ought to lead, to the integration of whole industrial sectors:

> As the exigencies which enforce the resort to coalition uninter-ruptedly gain in scope and urgency, the 'trust' must take the same course of growth to meet these exigencies; until with some slight further advance along the accustomed lines, the trust which shall serve the modern business situation must comprehend in one close business coalition virtually the whole field of industry within which the machine process is the dominant factor. (p. 265)

The aim of the book, Veblen explained early on, was 'to show in what manner business methods and business principles in conjunc-tion with mechanical industry influence the modern cultural situation' (p. 21), and he now proceeds first to delineate the influence of business on American culture. This, he emphasises, is widespread and dominant. In the political sphere, Veblen echoes Marx and Engels' comment in *The Communist Manifesto* that 'the executive of the modern state is but a committee for managing the common affairs of the whole bourgeoisie', for 'the management of the affairs of the community at large falls by common consent into the hands of businessmen and is guided by business considerations. Hence, modern politics is business politics' (p. 268), and, 'Representative government means, chiefly, representation of business interests' (p. 283). All the chief agencies and activities of the state – police sur-veillance, the justice system, diplomatic relations, military expeditions, are at the service of business. A policy of war and armaments, he points out, benefits business, as does colonial expansion (the United States had fought Spain over Cuba in 1898 and had annexed the Philippines) which provides access to raw materials and new markets. It also brings about competition between states which in turn leads to increased military spending which benefits business.

In Chapter Nine he turns to the second aspect of his enquiry, the influence of 'mechanical industry' upon cultural life, and in a long, wide-ranging, and ambitious essay he expounds a technological deter-minism to counter the economic determinism arising from business. In general, Veblen's view of factory manufacture as a social force is a positive one, similar to Marx's, but in contrast to the negative views of such commentators on industrialism as Carlyle, Ruskin, and Morris. In 'Signs of the Times' (1829) Carlyle had bemoaned the pervasive cultural and psychological effects of machine industry: 'Not the external and physical alone is now managed by machinery, but the internal and spiritual also.' What he noted and feared was the displacement of the human capacity for imagination and intuition by a process of mechanisation of the human spirit: 'For the same habit regulates not our modes of action alone, but our modes of thought and feeling. Men are grown mechanical in head and in heart, as well as in hand.'[19] Morris also, as we have seen, could only conceive Utopia as an economy based on handicraft. Veblen agrees with Carlyle on the pervasiveness of 'mechanical' thinking, but he views it as ultimately a progressive intellectual and social influence, the one hope for the evolution of a better society and the supersession of the pecuniary regime of the leisure class.

Machine production impacts most forcibly, of course, on the factory workers, engineers, and technicians who experience it for most of their waking hours and it shapes their habits of thought in definite ways. Frederick Winslow Taylor had published his first essay on factory management the year before, and with the spread of the application of Taylorism, the analytical breakdown of activities that could be measured and the integration of human and machine into an efficient unity, with the increased discipline it demanded, that impact was becoming ever greater. In addition, the advent of 'scientific management' in the factory, a rational, quantified organisation of production enhanced the view of the shop floor as the locus of 'progress' and increased rationality.[20] So, in Veblen's view, machine production is corrosive of traditional or conventional forms of thought and values and inculcates thinking governed by 'regularity of sequence', 'mechanical precision' and 'measurable cause and effect' (p. 309).

One consequence of this is a contrast in the mentalities of businessmen and technicians: the former base their thinking on the natural-rights doctrine of property, 'a conventional anthropomorphic face having an institutional validity, rather than a matter-of-fact validity', while the latter are 'occupied with matters of causal sequence, which do not lend themselves to statement in anthropomorphic terms of natural rights' (p. 318). Thus, Veblen argues, those engaged in industrial manufacture become sceptical of the natural-rights basis of property and incline to a socialistic view that seeks the abolition of private ownership. He then refines Marx's notion that only the working classes can be truly socialist, by claiming that it is only those engaged in industrial occupations who will adopt the revolutionary standpoint. As evidence he cites the pervasiveness of socialism among industrial centres and its absence from the peasantry and rural working class. In addition, he sees the matter-of-fact mentality inculcated by the machine process as underlying a decline in religious faith, as well as a growth of scientific enquiry. Veblen sums up the general impact of industrial production thus: 'the cultural growth dominated by the machine process is of a sceptical, matter of fact complexion, materialistic, unmoral, unpatriotic, undevout' (p. 372).

However, he fails to consider the experience of Britain where industrialism was a least half a century older than in the United States (Carlyle was complaining about it in 1829) and where there was little evidence of more reduced deference to the leisure class or more scepticism in general than among American workers. Rather optimistically he believes that as industrialism spreads so the habits of thought shaped by it will become pervasive, and the traditional habits of thought associated with the pecuniary culture will greatly weaken. At the heart of industrial capitalism lies a cultural contradiction: 'the growth of business enterprise rests on machine technology as its material foundation', but 'the discipline of the machine process cuts away the spiritual, institutional foundation of business' (p. 375). Thus, Veblen, echoing Marx on the inevitability of the collapse of capitalism, argues in his final chapter, 'The Natural Decay of Business Enterprise', that the property-rights basis of business is bound to decline and the sceptical, socialistic temper bound to prevail. He concludes the book with prescient remarks on how this process may well be stopped, however, by war, for ten years later the Great War with its eruption of patriotic fervour was to bring about a huge setback for socialism in the United States.

The Higher Learning in America

At this time Veblen also completed a third book, *The Higher Learning in America,* but was unable to find a publisher for it until 1918.[21] Since it expands on the final chapter of *The Theory of the Leisure Class* and belongs to his early work, it seems appropriate to discuss it here. His focus is the American university system and the trends he discerns within it. The work's originality lies, firstly, in attempting a sociology of the modern university, that is to say, in identifying how it is embedded in the dominant economic and social value system and, secondly, in establishing how increasing bureaucratisation and quantification are destroying the university's traditional Enlightenment qualities. He begins with proposing that all esoteric knowledge arises from two traits of human nature: 'Idle Curiosity' and the 'Instinct of Workmanship'. Curiosity is thus added to Veblen's list of human instinctual proclivities and it is 'idle' in the sense 'that a knowledge of things is sought, apart from any ulterior use of the knowledge so gained'. The university is the one social institution whose role is the quest for knowledge and the teaching of it to the upcoming generation. University staff are therefore dedicated to the pursuit of knowledge for its own sake through scholarship and scientific inquiry. This is Veblen's ideal formulation of the nature of the modern university.

However, America is a business-dominated society, and Veblen laments the way in which this ideal has been corrupted by the infection of university practice with business principles. This has occurred, and is increasingly occurring, in a number of ways. The first is the universities' annexation of colleges and training schools with the result that practical or vocational courses have become 'a conspicuous feature' of the university curriculum and technical and professional trainers become part of the faculty. This can have only a deleterious effect on the central purpose of a university for 'the technologist and professional man are, like other men of affairs, necessarily and habitually impatient of any scientific or scholarly work that does not obviously lend itself to some practical use' and are likely to divert resources away from disinterested science and scholarship towards utilitarian ends. The most evident invasion of business concerns is in the development of schools of commerce, which divert resources away from legitimate university interests and which create a hostile bias against scholarly and scientific work.

The second important factor is the predominance on universities' boards of governors of businessmen, who thereby control overall policy, while in Veblen's view being utterly unsuited to the task: 'the final discretion in the affairs of the seats of learning is entrusted to men who have proved their capacity for work that has nothing in common with the higher learning'. The businessmen on the board control the budget and thereby what can be taught and how much money should go to teaching and how much into the development of the real estate. Yet, there is a real contradiction between the perspective of the businessmen governors and that of the university staff devoted to pure research.

Thirdly, universities have been pervaded by a paradigm of business efficiency and performance, so much so that they operate as if they were businesses. They have a hierarchical structure with a President and an executive and the scholars and scientists become no more than hired hands to do the work required. The President becomes something like the Captain of Industry concerned not with the advancement of scholarship, but with the success of his corporation in the competition with other universities. Also, because of the businessmen on the board, any work that is likely to be critical of existing business practices is frowned upon and its practitioner regarded with disapproval:

> It is further of the essence of this scheme of academic control that the captain of erudition should freely exercise the power of academic life or death over the members of his staff, to reward the good and faithful servant and to abase the recalcitrant.

This is a veiled reference to his own experience at Chicago where, despite his books, articles and reviews, and his fame, he never rose above the rank of Assistant Professor, while the sports coach Amos Alonso Stagg was quickly made a full professor.[22]

In addition, college presidents conceive of themselves as 'dealing in merchantable knowledge' and set out to produce 'the largest feasible output'. A university 'is a corporation with large funds, and for men biased in their workday training in business affairs it comes as a matter of course to rate the university in terms of investment and turnover'. The result is a standardisation and quantification of the university's programme and the use of statistics to measure performance. As quasi-businesses, universities come into competition with each other for two vital resources – endowments and enrolments. This leads to a large diversion of funds to salesmanship, as carried out through publicity, through ostentatious parades and rituals, and through the construction of impressive buildings which conform to the architectural norms of a traditional seat of learning, what Veblen terms with acid wit 'bastard antique'. Also the upper classes are courted as they are the more likely sources of gifts and of students.

Staff, too, are expected to engage in 'an endless chain of conspicuously expensive social amenities, where their social proficiency and their ostensible ability to pay may effectively be placed on view'. Thus a preference is shown for members of the faculty who have sources of private money to fund such consumption and inevitably in appointments the well-to-do scholars are favoured. Thus, Veblen emphasises, 'the intrusion of business concepts into the universities goes to weaken and retard the pursuit of learning, and therefore to defeat the ends for which a university is maintained.' However, there are obstructions to the full sway of business principles. These include the dedication of the major proportion of the staff to learning, as well as the university's avowed aim to advance scholarship. Also, there are advantages in terms of prestige and hence marketability in hiring prominent scholars and scientists.

Finally, Veblen implicitly refers to the examples of Chicago and Stanford, both established with sizeable endowments and therefore not in urgent need of finance, and complains of how even these places, despite their favoured position, have failed to maintain the scholastic ideal in the face of the contamination of business principles. As a provocative parting shot more than a serious proposal, our iconoclast suggests as remedial action the abolition of the governing board and the university executive for, 'as seen from the point of view of the higher learning, the academic executive and all his works are anathema, and should be discontinued by the single expedient of wiping him off the slate'.

The book, then, to sum up, is a jeremiad on the state of American higher education under the injurious influence of businessmen and business principles. And what was happening in American universities justified his concern and invective. So many major universities had been founded on the basis of personal or corporate wealth: Johns Hopkins, a banker, bequeathed $3.5 million to establish a university in Baltimore; Leland Stanford, a railroad tycoon, provided $24 million to a university to be named after his son and based on the family farm in California; and, as we have already seen, John D. Rockefeller funded the establishment of the University of Chicago. Also, there had been serious threats to academic freedom with the 'heresy' trial of the University of Wisconsin's Richard T. Ely in 1894, and the sacking in 1894 of Edward Bemis from the University of Chicago for making comments on trusts, unions, and the Pullman Strike which the university hierarchy regarded as anti-business. Yet, as John Kenneth Galbraith points out, there were limits to business influence in the universities for a 'large amount of legislation or policy regarded as inimical by the entrepreneurial enterprise received its initial impetus from the academic community'. He goes on to list anti-monopoly laws, regulations concerning access to capital markets, welfare measures, and progressive taxation, as instances of successful anti-business measures which originated in academia.[23]

In March 1906 Veblen published 'The Place of Science in Modern Civilisation', in which he reiterated his technological determinism, namely that industrial processes were the chief factor in 'shaping men's habits of thought', and linked the matter-of-fact mentality inculcated by the machine process to the rise of modern science.[24] Industry changes the conception of the world and makes it less anthropomorphic, leading to the idea that 'the run of causation unfolds itself in an unbroken sequence of cumulative change'. At the root of science too is a human characteristic, 'idle curiosity,' which has no functional or pragmatic aim, but which generates disinterested enquiry. This propensity mutates into 'the scientific spirit' and is the driving force behind an ever-expanding system of knowledge. In April he gave a series of lectures to the Department of Economics at Harvard, which were later published as a two-part essay, 'The Socialist Economics of Karl Marx and His Followers'.[25] These marked a considerable development in Veblen's thinking on Marxism since his earlier 'Some Neglected Points in the Theory of Socialism' (1892), but still meant that, although Veblen paid homage to the brilliance and originality of Marx, he found fundamental flaws in aspects of the theory. As a result of his training in philosophy, Veblen was expert at unearthing the premises underlying a particular position, and he traced Marxist economics' roots to classical economics and Hegelian metaphysics, both of which he now regarded as having been superseded. He contrasted Marxism's teleological position, that social development tended towards a final outcome in the attainment of a socialist society, with Darwinism's dismissal of teleology and proposal that evolution of species or human societies has no final predetermined goal. He also saw the labour theory of value as being at the heart of Marx's system, but Marx had offered no proof of that theory. Finally, he concluded that Marxism had largely become a dead letter through the obsolescence of its metaphysical preconceptions, the growth of trade unions and amelioration of the workers' lot, and the growth of nationalist and imperialist attitudes.

The same year Veblen, feeling that, due to the animus of President Harper, he would never advance his career at the University of Chicago, moved to Stanford, where he bought a property. However, he was able to stay there only three years before being made to resign, when he was embroiled in a scandal caused by his lover moving in with him.[26] He was unable to find a suitable post until his friend

William Davenport at the University of Missouri managed to secure a position for him in 1911. Veblen, then, remained a marginal figure in the academy, rather like his Berlin contemporary Georg Simmel who, despite his brilliance, also spent most of his working life without a regular faculty appointment.

The Instinct of Workmanship

In 1914 Veblen completed *The Instinct of Workmanship and the State of the Industrial Arts*, which draws heavily on anthropological material in an attempt to identify the factors that shape the development of culture. It was according to his biographer essentially a summary of his course on 'Economic Factors in Civilisation' and it merges together all the basic ideas he had used previously. John P. Diggins rates it 'perhaps his greatest book', because it operates at a philosophical level setting out propositions concerning Veblen's views of human nature.[27] If any comparison can be fruitfully made, it seems that *The Instinct of Workmanship* is more akin to Freud's *Civilisation and Its Discontents* (1934), a fairly rarefied discourse full of provocative ideas but with little attention paid to empirical fact, rather than to a conventional work of economics or sociology. Since it makes little direct commentary on modern America it must play only a minor role in this study.

The post-Darwinian perspective, placing humankind firmly within the natural realm as having drives just like any other species, is made plain from the start: 'For mankind, as for other animals, the life of the species is conditioned by the complement of instinctive proclivities and tropismatic aptitudes with which the species is typically endowed.'[28] Veblen also draws on William James in his view of instinct as being purposive, as being a factor in making the human animal an agent engaged in operating on his or her world to secure certain goals. He identifies two instinctive predispositions as being concerned with the welfare of the race, 'the sense of workmanship', and 'the parental bent' (p. 25). The latter is not concerned solely with the bringing up of children, but with the welfare of the community and reaches out as a 'solicitude for the welfare of the race at large'. Thus it provides, as we can see, an explanation for those charitable and altruistic aspects of human behaviour which classical economics' proposition of the primacy of self-interest as a motive for action could not account for. The instinct of workmanship is in Veblen's schema the most powerful drive, since it 'is effective in such consistent, ubiquitous, and resilient fashion that students of human culture will have to count it as one of the integral hereditary traits of mankind' (p. 27). This instinct for effective work and 'efficient use of the means at hand' is crucial in the development of tools and later technology, what Veblen terms 'the industrial arts'. This technological advance, as Morgan had pointed out in *Ancient Society*, is fundamental to the growth of culture, as the dynamo of social change.

Technology is not only a means of manipulating the material world more effectively; the practice of it leads to new habits of thought, to a change in world view. It is conducive to a matter-of-fact mentality and an awareness of causal sequence, as well as an emphasis on tangible performance, yet there is an obstruction to the full dominance of this mentality in another human proclivity, namely animism. This, in Veblen's usage, is the tendency to anthropomorphise things, that is to say, to endow them with human attributes and the capacity for action. Ultimately, animism gives rise to myth and theology.

In 'The Place of Science in Modern Civilisation' Veblen had formulated another hereditary proclivity 'the instinct of idle curiosity', and he returns to this notion in this volume. It comes into play, he suggests, only after the more immediate needs of subsistence have been met, and it is this which leads to the race's 'systematical knowledge and quasi-knowledge of things' (p. 87). Its essential quality is that it has no utilitarian aim or sentiment; it is not directed to the achievement of any end. That is why it is 'idle', but paradoxically because it is freed from the necessity of engaging with practical problems and practical solutions, it may well generate insights or make connections or initiate theories which will 'serve the ends of workmanship'.

Next, Veblen lays out his usual view of prehistory. Initially, there was a long period of savage culture which was peaceable and sedentary, since it is unlikely that such advances as the domestication of plants and animals (emphasised by Morgan) would have been achieved otherwise. This was a matriarchal scheme of things with a prevalence of fertility goddesses and it was a highly collectivised existence. As an example he cites the Pueblo Indians of the American southwest, for example, Colorado. Veblen stresses the point that technological knowledge is of 'the nature of a common stock, held and carried forward collectively by the community' (p. 103). He thus emphasises that technical know-how is a group resource, and plays down an individualistic interpretation of technical advance as being due to the inventiveness of extraordinary individuals.

Next comes the second stage of cultural evolution, the 'barbarian' or 'predatory' phase. By now agrarian communities, because of increased productivity, have risen above the level of subsistence to generate a surplus. A predatory mode of life now comes into being for some groups, since they can make a living through warlike exploit raiding other groups and seizing their goods and their women. As Veblen pointed out in 'The Beginnings of Ownership', the acquisition of female captives leads to a break with the collective nature of property and initiates the concept of individual ownership. This leads to a far-reaching change in human society:

> since predation and warlike exploit are intimately associated with the facts of ownership through its early history (perhaps throughout its history) there results a marked accentuation of the self-regarding sentiments; with the economically important consequence that self-interest displaces the common good in men's ideals and aspirations. (p. 160)

As he noted in 'The Instinct of Workmanship and the Irksomeness of Labour', prowess in exploit now becomes the source of personal wealth and exemption from work, and consequently productive work becomes denigrated. Also, with individual ownership invidious comparisons can be made between different individuals as to their possessions. So, to reiterate the point he makes in *The Theory of the Leisure Class*, Veblen points out that 'the conspicuous consumption of goods becomes a mark of pecuniary excellence, and so it becomes an element of respectability in any pecuniary culture' (p. 174). This pecuniary culture with its origin in the predatory phase can be described as 'invidious, personal, emulative, looking to differential values in respect of personal force or competitive success, looking to gradations in respect of comparative potency' (p. 177). The next stage is the commercial phase of the predatory culture which sees the emergence of the middle class, an advancement in the industrial arts, and an acceleration in the accumulation of wealth.

In Chapter Five, 'Ownership and the Competitive System', he turns to the modern period and picks up the point made in *The Theory of Business Enterprise* about there being a dichotomy of functions – production and business. In business the prime motive is 'invidious self-aggrandisement', and the goal is 'the conspicuous waste of goods and services' (p. 194). Yet, despite the dominance of business, the instinct of workmanship which is at play in the sphere of production still asserts itself and brings about technological progress. This technological progress has several cultural consequences. Veblen then proceeds with a narrative of the vicissitudes of the instinct of workmanship from prehistory to the handicraft era, when it came into a dominant position, to the industrial period. In Veblen's view it influenced religious concepts (with God conceived as the master craftsman) and the development of science, since the notion of causality, crucial in that development, is 'a particular manifestation of the sense of workmanship' (p. 263). Veblen, then, is presenting the thesis that the instinct of workmanship through its various manifestations has shaped the culture at large, including the eighteenth-century doctrine of natural rights.

Veblen completes his historical overview by considering the era of machine industry, i.e. from the Industrial Revolution, and elaborates on what he sees as the cultural effects of the factory system. Repeating some of the points he had made in *The Theory of Business Enterprise*, he points out that the machine process involves a training in 'impersonal, quantitative apprehension and appreciation of things' and its outcome is 'an unqualified materialistic and mechanical animus in all orders of society, most pronounced in the working class' (p. 318). However, there is a separation of ownership and control as businessmen employ engineers to run the factories for them and so lose contact with the machine process and advances in technology. A conflict is thus set up between the demands of business and the emphasis on efficiency and productive work derived from the instinct of workmanship:

> Habituation to bargaining and to the competitive principles of business necessarily brings it about that pecuniary standards of efficiency invade (contaminate) the sense of workmanship, [and the] prevalence of salesmanship, that is to say, of business enterprise ... is perhaps the most serious obstacle which the pecuniary culture opposes to the advance in workmanship. (p. 350)

This instinct, which is so fundamental to humankind and has been so instrumental in its advance, is now contaminated or even obstructed by the demands of capitalism, which seeks to turn the community's collective productivity into private gain. The book then, after all its excursions into prehistory and the handicraft era, finally homes in on Veblen's favourite target, the American businessman 'who gets something for nothing' and who, far from being a benefactor to the community is in fact predatory upon it.

As Diggins points out, Veblen's theory of instincts makes many modern scholars uncomfortable, since it is full of terminological vagueness, and it has led some sociologists to dismiss this kind of theory as crude.[29] Yet, we can see that Veblen is attempting to provide a theory of cultural change, and, implicitly as a post-Darwinian, he believes any such theory must take account of humankind's biological make-up, which includes heritable traits such as instincts. Although in many ways he is a cultural determinist, his stance here is essentialist. His proposition of an active principle of human nature which leads men and women to seek knowledge and to work for other than financial reasons is profoundly radical in stressing the non-profit-seeking, constructive impulses in the human psyche. In redrawing the lineaments of humankind as *Homo faber*, Veblen is implicitly subverting the underpinning assumption of *laissez-faire* economics theory and current capitalistic practice – that acquisitive self-interest is the prime human motive and is what powers production and economic development. The notion of an 'instinct of workmanship', though hazy, provides some explanation for the development of human society, as well as allowing Veblen to portray the modern phase of business-dominated production as being a repression or distortion of a drive to provide for the welfare of the community. A consequence of this is that it is possible to imagine a society in which this instinct would be given free rein, and so revolutionary hope is born.

Conclusion

This volume brings his early work to a close. The cycle began with his papers 'The Economic Theory of Women's Dress' and 'The Beginnings of Ownership', and moved through *The Theory of the Leisure Class*, *The Theory of Business Enterprise*, and *The Higher Learning in America*. It is marked by intellectual and social iconoclasm and the employment of anthropological perspectives to try and explain modern America. The iconocalsm would remain, but his writings would take a different direction from now on.

3   The Later Work

Civilization and profits go hand in hand.

Calvin Coolidge (1920)

The work Veblen produced up until World War One is marked by a certain wry distance from the social issues he is considering. His stance is that of a disinterested observer, a scientist, simply discoursing on the social phenomena he has come across and seeking to employ anthropological material to illuminate it. The tone is ironical, satirical, the writing full of tongue-in-cheek remarks that he is only being neutral and does not mean anything derogatory by terms such as 'conspicuous waste'. However, the war that erupted in August 1914 – ostensibly because of the assassination in Sarajevo of the Crown Prince Ferdinand, but really because of imperial rivalry between Britain and Germany – radically changed the social climate.

After promising to keep the United States out of the conflict, Woodrow Wilson plunged America into it, in April of 1917. American soldiers died in their thousands in the French mud, and American front-line witnesses wrote of modern war's horrors with unforgettable power – Dos Passos' *Three Soldiers* (1922), Cummings's, *The Enormous Room* (1923), and, most notably, Hemingway's *In Our Time* (1925) and *A Farewell to Arms* (1927). In the face of casualty figures for the battles of the Somme (1.3 million all told) and Passchendaele Spencer's proposition that society was evolving to an ever higher and more perfect state now seemed a cruel mockery. All the old, comforting, nineteenth-century certainties regarding the progress of civilisation were gone, and the Great War opened up the prospect of a future in which everything was more bleak and more uncertain than any American (even Henry Adams) had ever conceived.

Then, also in 1917, came another blow to the established order: the Russian Revolution with the popular revolt based on the slogan 'Land, Peace, Bread,' leading to the storming of the Tsar's Winter Palace in St Petersburg, the establishment of a Provisional Government under Kerensky, and then in October, under Lenin's leadership, the Bolshevik seizure of power. For the first time an explicitly anti-capitalist government was in power in a major country. Huge landed estates were confiscated; privately owned businesses were abolished; and the economy was organised on state socialist lines.

Inevitably, many American intellectuals began to be more international in their perspectives and, though the War provoked grim anxieties about a possible Apocalypse, for those on the Left the Revolution provoked dreams of Utopia. The improbable had happened; out of the Steppes an exemplar of Marx's prophecy had materialised: capital could be overthrown; the people could gain power and organise from the bottom up, soviet-style. So, given Veblen's concerns for the shape and direction of society, his critique of the dominance of the pecuniary culture in American life, and his disdain for business, these momentous events produced a shift in tone to one which was much more *engagé*, much less aloof and ironic. He now demonstrates far greater concern with social reorganisation, his scope is international, and his postwar writings become 'oriented towards revolutionary change'.[1]

Veblen was actually in Europe when the war broke out and when he returned to the United States he worked on his first book in connection with the War, *Imperial Germany and the Industrial Revolution* (1916). However, despite its seemingly topical focus Veblen says in his 'Preface' that he had begun it before the War started, and there are in fact few references to the contemporary conflict. The primary focus is 'a comparison and correlation between the German case on the one hand and the English-speaking peoples on the other hand, considered as two distinct and somewhat divergent lines of cultural development in modern times'. He wrote the book hastily,[2] and at the end are appended five lengthy notes, one of which dealt with the American country town as an illustration of the predatory workings of American business.

The main thrust of Veblen's argument is that Germany has taken over the industrial technology of England but not its democratic political institutions and, consequently, the progressiveness of industrial culture comes into conflict with the dynastic state which is feudal in nature. Yet, this is only an extreme variant on the contradiction in English-speaking societies between the matter-of-factness of machine production and the legacies of a predatory past embedded in business principles. The operations of the small American town are instanced by Veblen as reflecting the backwardness of business values and methods. Veblen is optimistic, however, that the discipline of technology would bring the technician to the fore and would eventually lead to the decay of the dynastic state.

By December 1916, in contrast to many others on the Left, he was keen that America should enter the War on the side of Britain and France, and he began writing *An Inquiry into The Nature of Peace and the Terms of its Perpetuation* which was published in 1917.[3] Here, he analyses the origins of the War in relation to the role of the state and its fostering of patriotic fervour and nationalistic ambitions as part of a system of invidious emulation between nations. Veblen also links the pursuit of a military build-up which preceded the War to the interests of the business class who stand to gain most from war, while it is the working class who pay the cost of it. It is these class interests which stand in the way of securing a lasting peace. This can be achieved, Veblen suggests (after reiterating his radical critique of capitalism now broadened to include European business), only by the abolition of privilege and royalty, and the establishment of a pacific league of neutral peoples. Undemocratic institutions must be eradicated and estates over a certain modest size are to be confiscated. Thus, in future war can avoided by abolishing those institutions which bring it about and by setting up a number of socialist states, in which the ruling business and political class has been overthrown.

In October 1917 such an overthrow did take place with the Bolshevik seizure of power in Russia and the establishment of a Soviet Socialist Republic in which capitalism was abolished. That month Veblen took leave of absence from the University of Missouri to go to Washington where he did some work for the Food Administration, contributing papers on the prices of foodstuffs and on the farm labour supply, the latter advising the government to liaise with the anarcho-syndicalist International Workers of the World to improve the availability of labour.[4] Early in 1918 he delivered an address to the Institute of Social Sciences which was printed in the April 13 edition of *The New Republic* as 'A Policy of Reconstruction'. Then, in June 1918 Veblen moved to Manhattan to become one of the contributing editors of *The Dial*, a well-established literary journal, which had been reoriented under one of its owners, Helen Marot, to have a wider scope including 'internationalism and a program of reconstruction in industry and education'.[5]

Though now 61 years of age, he was to enjoy another spurt of productivity that would result in three books. Also, freed from the constraints of surviving in academe, he was able to inject more venom and a sharper bite into his writing. The anthropological perspective drops by the way as does the early vocabulary – 'the leisure class', 'the instinct of workmanship', 'conspicuous consumption' – and the discussion picks up from *The Theory of Business Enterprise* to centre much more on contemporary developments and American finance capitalism with its dynamics and its opposition of interests to the general population. This leads to a focus on the capital-owning class, what Veblen referred to as 'the vested interests' and 'the absentee owners'. For *The Dial* he contributed editorials and articles, and, writing for a general audience, was able to comment on the implications of the Russian Revolution as well as to excoriate 'the vested interests' for their mismanagement of industry. From reading them it is clear that Veblen is intent on several objectives. He is seeking to combat right-wing propaganda from the press and the conservative Administration in relation to both the Russian Revolution and American business. He is setting out to demystify the economic processes and class relations underlying American capitalism, as well as to expose the waste of the business system. He is also attempting to heighten class consciousness and hostility by characterising the absentee owners as parasitic 'kept classes' and bringing home to the mass of the population just how badly the business system is letting them down, given the immense productive capacity of industry.

The Vested Interests

The first series of his essays under the general heading 'The Modern Point of View and the New Order' were published from 19 October 1918 to 25 January 1919 and were collected in a volume as *The Vested Interests and the Common Man* in 1919. The immediate context is supplied by the Great War, its coming to a close, and the issues of peace and reconstruction that arose in its aftermath. In between the last of the essays and the appearance of the book he also published 'Bolshevism is a Menace – To Whom?' in *The Dial*.

Veblen begins *The Vested Interests* by invoking one of his favourite themes, namely the longevity of the framework of law and order in the United States. It was set forth in such documents as the Declaration of Independence and the Constitution in the late eighteenth century and was based on notions of natural rights derived from Adam Smith, John Locke and Montesquieu. As he states in his early essays, Adam Smith's views of property rights applied in his own time, but the huge changes in the industrial economy since then have rendered the American natural-rights doctrine of ownership obsolete. The era of handicraft has passed away, as indeed has the era of the captain of industry, to be replaced on the one hand by complex factory production and on the other by corporations, capitalised in securities on the stock exchange. The 'New Order' that has come into being has changed everything. Nowadays, 'the workman has become subsidiary to the mechanical equipment, and productive industry has become subservient to business'.[6] He reiterates the materialist position he first introduced in *The Theory of Business Enterprise* that factory work will inculcate a particular mentality, 'a mechanistic conception of things, ways, means, ends, and values' (p. 40), as well as a preference for tangible performance and results, and this industrial mindset should eventually work its way through into a revision of the outdated notions of ownership and the law.

This is needed because, in respect of industry, the character of ownership has greatly altered. The owner-employer of the mid-nineteenth century has been replaced by the corporation and ownership 'has taken the form of an absentee ownership of anonymous private capital', and 'the ownership of capital foots up to a claim on the earnings of the corporation' (pp. 44–5) in the form of interest and dividend payments. These returns look to the common man like unearned or 'free' income, for, though it is the factory workers who make the goods, they do not reap all the rewards. 'Productive industry yields a margin of net product over cost', and this has become 'an overhead charge payable to anonymous outsiders who own the corporation securities' (p. 48). These outsiders thus own a 'vested interest', which is the 'marketable right to get something for nothing' (p. 100), and vested interests can be identified with stocks and securities, that is, 'immaterial wealth' or 'intangible assets'.

One outcome of the rise of the corporation as the dominant institution is a distinction between tangible assets, i.e. the factory plant, equipment, and inventories, and intangible assets, such as 'goodwill', the possession of a patent or a franchise, or a monopoly, which may provide a profitable advantage and so have market value. Curiously, these intangible assets as capitalised in securities have vastly outgrown the physical assets which produce the material goods; so a discrepancy exists:

> Capital ... is capitalized prospective gain. From this arises one of the singularities of the current situation in business and its control of industry; viz., that the total face value, or even the total market value of the equipment and resources ... always and greatly exceeds the total market value of the equipment and resources to which the securities give title of ownership. (p. 104)

What gives these intangible assets their value is the income they generate for their holders:

> The free income which is capitalised in the intangible assets of the vested interests goes to support well-to-do investors, who are for this reason called the kept classes and whose keep consists in an indefinitely expansible consumption of superfluities. (p. 113)

We have a passing allusion here to the leisure class and its practice of conspicuous consumption.

This income is obtained at the expense of the underlying population. For, while the productivity of industry has greatly increased with more efficiency and finer integration, industry is not allowed to run at full capacity because this would lower prices. What interests business is the largest net gain it can make from the price minus cost, this gain being the source of the vested interests' free income. 'The rate of production in the essential industries has habitually and by deliberate contrivance fallen greatly short of productive capacity', and Veblen charges the owners not with a marginal but with a substantial curtailment of output, as he estimates that under normal circumstances the rate of production is 'something like one-fourth of the industrial community's capacity' (p. 81). To understand this restriction one has to remember the dichotomy between production, 'a mechanical process incidental to the making of money', and business, 'the making of money, a pecuniary operation carried on by bargain and sale'. Veblen could have pointed out that in Bolshevik Russia or in fictional utopias such as that presented in Bellamy's *Looking Backward* one can see production carried on free of the need of business to provide a return on intangible capital. What he does point out is that this dichotomy is the source of a clash of interests, for 'the common good, so far as it is a question of material welfare, is evidently best served by an unhampered working of the industrial system at its full capacity'. However, for the businessmen it is necessary to curtail output to meet the overhead charges that constitute the free income. 'Sabotage of this kind is indispensable to any large success in industrial business' (p. 93). Businessmen and stockholders, far from being benefactors to the community as politicians' speeches and newspaper editorials (and conservative responses to Veblen by such as Cummings and Teggart) would have it, are actually injurious to it, keeping prices higher than they need be and expropriating unearned income.[7]

In the sixth of his essays Veblen turns his attention to the role of the nation state, for (as in *An Inquiry into the Nature of Peace*) he sees a strong linkage between the vested interests and the activities of governments. Since he had recommended such a move in a memorandum to the House committee in 1917,[8] it is not surprising that he comments favourably on Woodrow Wilson's proposal to set up a League of Nations which would limit the right of nations to self-aggrandisement as well as their use of force to further national ambitions. He is scathing in his portrayal of national governments as being tools of vested interests, carrying out imperialist expansion for the sake of big business while making the common man bear the cost. Nationalism is, he believes, out of date, since the new order enforces a spirit of internationalism, for 'the industrial order overlaps the national frontiers as business increasingly reaches round the globe'. He is highly critical of the United States' Administration's use of protective tariffs, which he characterises as being 'like any other method of businesslike sabotage' (p. 132), as they are designed to keep supply limited and prices up by hindering competition.

With the ending of the war there was the optimistic assumption that lessons had been learned, that society would be fairer, that things would get better for ordinary people, but Veblen paints a blistering picture of America returning complacently to the *status quo ante*:

> Already the vested interests are again tightening their hold and busily arranging for a return to business as usual, which means working at cross-purposes as usual, waste of work and materials as usual, restriction of output as usual, labor quarrels as usual, competitive selling as usual, mendacious advertising as usual, waste of superfluities as usual for the kept classes, and privation as usual for the common man. (p. 140)

In postwar America, the culmination of the eighteenth-century egalitarian republic, he sees an increasing polarisation into two classes: 'those who own wealth invested in large holdings and who thereby control the conditions of life for the rest; and those who do not own wealth in sufficiently large holdings, and whose conditions of life are thereby controlled by these others' (p. 160). This seems to echo *The Communist Manifesto*, but he emphasises that this is a revision of the class conflict as proposed by socialism: 'It is a division, not between those who have something and those who have nothing – as many socialists would be inclined to describe it – but between those who own wealth enough to make it count, and those who do not' (p. 140).

Thus, Veblen is implicitly including the the white-collar middle class in the category of the exploited strata of society, just as some pages later he explicitly brings in the farmers, who have fallen under the rule of the vested interests but who still delude themselves they are independent producers. Unfortunately, the polarisation of society and its attendant opposition of interests is not widely recognised, for there is a lack of awareness, a lack of class consciousness among most of the population: 'The common man does not know himself as such, at least not yet, and the section of the population which goes to make up the common lot as contrasted with the vested interests have not yet learned to make common cause' (p. 174). The reason for this is that the residual ideology inherited from the eighteenth century still deludes them (inculcates in Marxian terms a false consciousness) into thinking they are free, independent agents, in a society of equal opportunity. However, he concludes, there is some hope that 'the mechanistic logic of the new order of industry' may engender a frame of mind that insists on tangible performance, on real work done, thus ushering in an era when 'all income from property, simply on the basis of ownership, will be disallowed, whether the property is tangible or intangible' (p. 170). Already he sees evidence in the International Workers of the World and the NonPartisan League of increasing dissent from the conventional view and scepticism about the right of vested interests to their free income.

The Engineers

In April 1919 Veblen began a new series of essays for *The Dial* on 'Contemporary Problems in Reconstruction' which, according to an announcement in the magazine, were intended to be 'a concrete application of [Veblen's] theory' as outlined in *The Vested Interests*. The immediate background for these articles, later collected together in *The Engineers and the Price System* (1921), was provided by the so-called 'Red Scare', the campaign of repression initiated by Attorney General A. Mitchell Palmer against radical groups through 1919 and 1920. Because of the success of the Bolshevik Revolution and the attempts at revolution elsewhere such as in Berlin and Turin, there was an official fear of insurrection in the United States. John Reed had published *Ten Days That Shook The World*, his eye-witness account of the Russian Revolution and had set about founding the

Communist Party of America. Labour conflict was intense with a wave of strikes, including the national steel strike. As a result of these heightened tensions and political paranoia, wartime political conformity in the United States was perpetuated in the form of hostility towards left-wing groups, which were seen as unpatriotic. Because of the strikes, similar attitudes were directed towards the labour unions. These factors contributed to the violent repression in which many radicals were attacked (like members of the anarcho-syndicalist International Workers of the World) or jailed (like Eugene Debs, the leader of the Socialist Party) or deported (like the prominent anarchist, Emma Goldman).

Another shaping element in their context were developments in the engineering profession. Frederick W. Taylor with the publication in 1911 of *The Principles of Scientific Management* had established a new field and put the pursuit of efficiency at the head of the goals of industry. One of his disciples, Henry L. Gantt, came under the influence of Veblen's ideas and in 1916 founded a group called the 'New Machine'. Critical of the incompetence of the financiers, he argued that the community should not have to bear the costs of their inefficiency. He assumed that the business system was close to breakdown and that the group to take over in the aftermath were the engineers. In one of the essays he declared:

> We can no longer follow the lead of those who have axes to grind, disregarding economic laws; but must accord leadership to him who knows what to do and how to do it for the benefit of the community. This man is the engineer.[9]

The 'New Machine' held a few meetings drawing about three dozen interested engineers and its only offical act was to write to President Wilson in February 1917 informing him that the industrial system would grow 'only through a progressive elimination of plutocracy and all other forms of arbitrary power'. Gantt was friendly with one of Veblen's disciples, Leon Ardzrooni, and was one of the chief sources for Veblen's notions about the engineers.

A second source was another disciple of Taylor, Morris L. Cooke, whom Veblen met. In 1915 Cooke was elected a vice-president of the American Society for Mechanical Engineers and became the leader of a faction intent on reforming the association. He criticised the Society's links with the big companies, alleging that the professional status of the engineers was being undermined by their subservience to big business. As a result of his campaign, the Society had by 1919 broken its ties with business and trade associations, and an ethical code was adopted according to which the first professional obligation of the engineer was to the standards of his profession, not to his employer. This reform movement, then, and some of Cooke's papers provided another stimulus for Veblen's hopes on the radical potential of the new class of technicians. By the time the articles appeared in book form, however, the American Society for Mechanical Engineers had reverted to a conservative agenda.[10]

The Engineers is Veblen's shortest (114 pages) and most clearly written book with a novel central thesis. It is more rhetorical than any of his books, and its rhetorical structure is classically simple: statement of a problem; followed by a suggested solution to the problem. The heart of the matter lies in the price system and business's over-riding imperative to secure the largest net profit from its products. In the earlier era of industrialism free competition often led to full production in order to lower unit costs and, thus, the final price, but as a result of mergers, trusts, holding companies, and interlocking directorates and the establishment of semi-monopolistic control of the market price, competition has virtually disappeared in the major industries. Also, with technical advances industry has become more productive than ever, and so in order to maintain optimum net return businessmen restrict output by resorting to (in Veblen's appropriation of a term conventionally associated with strikers) 'sabotage,' that is to say the deliberate under-use of plant and labour. Business, he says, cannot tolerate full production, for output 'must be adjusted to the needs of the market, not the working capacity of available resources, equipment or manpower, nor to the community's needs of consumable goods'.[11] The implication here, then, is that there is an inescapable opposition of interests between the needs of business and the needs of the community, rather than that harmony of interests which American politicians and business-funded newspapers were always claiming. A second implication is that unemployment (which in the welfare-less society of early modern America meant extreme hardship) is not due to some malfunctioning of the business system which may one day be remedied, but rather is intrinsic to it, since the attainment of full production and so full employment is contrary to the pecuniary needs of the corporations.

The United States Government, he points out, also plays a role in sabotage through various means, particularly the protective tariff which obstructs price competition from outside the country. It acts to keep the supply of goods low and the prices high. This secures satisfactory dividends for the vested interests who own the corporations 'at the cost of the underlying community' (p. 49).

In the next chapter Veblen traces the rise of the captain of industry from the early pioneers in the Industrial Revolution in England, people who were just as knowledgeable about the technical processes of manufacture as about the financial processes of running the business. With the growing complexity of the factory system, however, the entrepreneur withdrew from engagement in the technical aspects to concentrate on the financial aspects. The captain of industry thus mutated into the captain of finance, who has been superseded by the impersonal corporation. With the corporation has come the completion of the separation of ownership (absentee ownership through stocks and securities) and management (by a cadre of trained professionals) begun with the captain of finance. This separation had widened over the past twenty years with the coming to the fore in the American economy of the investment banker, as instanced by J. P. Morgan and Company and his formation of the United States Steel Corporation. His model has been followed to the extent that various investment banks now rule over much of the country's industry (p. 66).

As part and parcel of this evolution of American business, manufacturing is now under the control of industrial experts or production engineers, who constitute 'the general staff of industry whose work is to control the strategy of production at large and to keep an oversight of the tactics of production in detail' (p. 72). Veblen argues that these experts and engineers should be allowed to manage industry as efficiciently as possible; however, the absentee owners, represented by the investment bankers, limit their discretion 'arbitrarily for their own commercial gain, regardless of the needs of the community' (p. 83). The expertise of the technicians, their knowledge of the 'industrial arts', is derived from the community and is part of the community's common heritage, but at the moment it is confined to meeting the needs of business, not the needs of the community. The implication is clear that full production and all the fruits it would bring in the form of full employment and the satisfaction of the population's material needs is being held back, not by the limitations of industry itself, but by the vested interests for the sake of their free income in the form of dividend and interest payments. Drawing implicly on the efforts and writings of Gantt and Cooke, Veblen remarks that the engineers have begun to realise they are 'the indispensable General Staff of the industrial system,' and have begun to develop a 'class consciousness' manifest in 'a growing sense of waste and confusion in the management of industry by the financial agents of the absentee owners' (p. 83). They are also coming to understand, he asserts, that 'the whole fabric of credit and corporation finance is a tissue of make-believe', an encumbrance which could be sloughed off 'provided only that men made up their mind to that effect' (p. 86). Here, then, Veblen introduces an original and provocative idea he expands upon later, namely that this professional class of engineers and technicians possesses revolutionary potential, for it is a small, homogenous grouping, able and trained, which could easily organise itself for a common purpose: the overthrow of the capitalistic price system which fetters industry at the expense of the community. His adoption of military terminology – 'general staff', 'strategy', 'tactics' – is a rhetorical device to exaggerate the degree of the engineers' coordination and to suggest that as a disciplined body they could marshall themselves for a battle.

Referring to the 'Red Scare,' Veblen points out that much of it is hysteria on the part of both government and the business class, because Bolshevism's success in Russia does not guarantee any similar success in the United States. It 'is not a present menace to the Vested Interests in America' (p. 96), primarily because there is no working-class organisation with revolutionary potential. He dismisses the American Federation of Labor as just another of the vested interests, concerned only with raising the price of labour, and he dismisses the International Workers of the World as lacking the expertise necessary to take over and run a complex, highly integrated industrial system. Next, he redraws the lineaments of a revolutionary overthrow, substituting for the traditional seizure of political power – the organs of the State, a seizure of the industrial system: 'The main lines of revolutionary strategy are ... essentially lines of industrial engineering; such as will fit the organization to take care of the highly technical industrial system' (p. 103).

In his penultimate chapter Veblen sees the wastefulness and inefficiency in industry increasing to the point where a change may occur. In particular, he attacks the wastefulness of 'salesmanship,' or marketing which is integrally bound up with the need to maintain net profits, and which leads to much higher prices than are necessary, thus causing a rise in the cost of living for the general population. He estimates that by eliminating salesmanship and sales cost (which are increasing in proportion to production costs) the 'burden of workday production for the underlying population' would be reduced by half (p. 115).

The problem he has focused on then is a wasteful, underproducing industrial system run for the profit of the vested interests rather than for the needs of the community, and the only solution lies in the hands of those who run the system, the technicians. So 'the chances of anything like a Soviet in America ... are the chances of a Soviet of technicians' (p. 125), if only they will acknowledge their responsibility to the community, realise their power in respect of industry, and act in concert. One can see Veblen here trying to convince the technocrats of their potential. Though the realist in him acknowledges that such an eventuality is extremely remote, the utopian in him cannot forego the pleasure, as well as the rhetorical effect, of sketching the revolutionary scenario, as if by presenting it in words he could convince the engineers of, first, its possibility, then its desirability, and finally, its viability.

So in his final piece, 'A Memorandum on a Practicable Soviet of Technicians,' he sets out the main lines by which such a revolutionary organisation could come about, what preparations for it would need to be made, and how the new order would be run. By way of laying the ground, solidarity would have to be established with the workers in industry and transport and a campaign of education carried out to inform them of the current state of affairs. Other prerequisites include a study of existing conditions and available ways and means, a survey of available personnel, and the setting up of practicable organisation tables. As for the revolutionary overturn itself, there need be no violence nor mass demonstrations; all that would be needed would be a general strike of the country's technicians, bringing industry to a standstill. The absentee owners would then either abdicate or be dispossessed by a legal order cancelling all corporation securities. The Soviet of technicians would constitute itself as an industrial directorate, when it would be in a position to 'avoid virtually all unemployment of serviceable equipment and man-power on the one hand and all local or seasonal scarcity on the other'. It would also ensure 'an equitable and sufficient supply of goods and services to consumers' (pp. 134–5). This utopian scenario carries strong echoes of Bellamy's future industrial wonderland in *Looking Backward*, which Veblen read all those years before. While he gives rein to his yearning for radical change here, he is also sufficiently clear-eyed to know that the possibility of it ever happening is very remote. He concludes the book on a note of sober realism, while hinting at a ray of hope for the future: 'There is nothing in the situation that could reasonably flutter the sensibilities ... of the absentee owners, just yet.'

Veblen then was percipient in recognising that this new class of white-collar expert and technician who ran industry could, but would not necessarily, form a third force for change alongside the traditional groupings of labour and capital. In the aftermath of the War and the Russian Revolution there was a widespread hope for radical change, and the severity of the offical repression of left-wing groups and individuals only served to foster the impression that this was a serious possibility. However, it is evident that Veblen grossly overestimated the radical bent of the engineers, who through their salaries and status had much to thank the business system for. As Theodor Adorno was to point out later, they are deeply assimilated into the status hierarchy and tend to identify with the owners of the corporations rather than with the blue-collar shop-floor workers.[12] Veblen failed to address the problem of social relations within the factories, in the way, for instance, that workers identify the 'boss' as the manager of their section and focus their hostility on him rather than on the absentee owners hidden behind the anonymity of their shareholdings.

A further inadequacy lay in his neglect of the problem of planning and distribution. Who is to decide how many items of such a kind are to be produced and to whom they are to be distributed? If the market is abolished, what other mechanism will take its place to ensure a match of supply and demand? His solution, too, as Daniel Bell points out, suffers from being apolitical, from neglecting to engage with the civil government, either in terms of its power, or in terms of its economic role via its budgets.[13]

Later Articles

In the autumn of 1919 Veblen left *The Dial*, which had become a literary journal once more, and joined the newly established New School for Social Research in New York, where he stayed until it was reorganised in 1922. In May 1921 he published an article in *The Freeman* entitled 'Between Bolshevism and War', followed in June 1922 by another there, 'Dementia Praecox'.[14] These pieces contain some of Veblen's most extreme statements and show him at his most disaffected with modern America. In the first he begins by proposing that since the Armistice of November 1918 the western countries including the United States have faced a stark choice between Bolshevism or preparing for war. By Bolshevism, a term taken from Lenin's victorious Party in Soviet Russia, Veblen means a revolutionary overturning of the economic and social *status quo*, and though such an event seems remote in America, it 'too, seems to be headed that way'. In particular, it would disallow absentee ownership, and displace democracy and representative government, because they 'have proved to be incompetent and irrelevant for any other purpose than the security and profitable regulation of absentee ownership'. In their place would be organisation by means of the soviet, a kind of council, 'very closely analogous to the town meeting as known in New England history'. Since Bolshevism is a 'menace' to absentee ownership and is growing in appeal, the guardians of capital, that is to say the politicians, have no choice but to try and deflect this revolutionary drift through stoking up nationalistic rivalries and patriotic fervour. Bellicose attitudes turned outwards thus distract people's attention from their economic deprivation and the internal mismanagement of industry and the country's resources. Veblen concludes with some of the most explicitly anti-capitalist statements he ever made. Beginning with the claim that 'the established businesslike system of ownership and control will no longer work,' he goes on to condemn it as 'no longer fit to manage the country's industry in such a way as to yield a decent livelihood for the country's population'. Finally, absentee ownership is at 'cross purposes with the country's industrial needs'. The implication is clear that what is needed is a soviet-style reorganisation of industry, with a strong likelihood of this taking place but for the manipulation of public attitudes (for example, patriotism) by the national government.

'Dementia Praecox' is a savagely satirical article which drives home the point that America's entry into the European War in April 1917 was 'a highly deplorable mistake,' which has had deleterious effects both abroad and at home. Firstly, America's intervention brought about a premature cessation of the conflict, so saving the German ruling class, the Junkers, from conclusive defeat, so pre-empting social reformation in Germany, the ending of rule by privilege and property and the establishment of an industrial democracy. It also prevented the collapse of the financial system in Europe, thus keeping the world safe not for democracy as Woodrow Wilson claimed, but for the vested interests.

Secondly, in America, intervention has turned the United States into 'a psychiatrical clinic' and has brought on the psychopathology of dementia praecox, that is to say 'an illusion of persecution and a derangement of the logical faculty'. As evidence of the illusion of persecution Veblen points to the 'Red Scare' of 1919–20 when pacifists, Wobblies, and radicals were regarded as threats to the established order, and as evidence of weakened rationality he cites the popularity of Reverend Billy Sunday, the evangelist, and the growth of Christian Fundamentalism with its opposition to Darwinism. 'These evidences of a dilapidated mentality', he wrote, 'are growing more and more obvious.' (Three years later John T. Scopes, a high school science teacher in Tennessee, was to be pubicly tried for teaching Darwinism.) Veblen lists other disastrous consequences of America's involvement in the War as: the incorporation of military ritual into public schools; interference with the right of popular assembly; the reinvigoration of the Ku Klux Klan (in the years immediately after the War it enlisted hundreds of thousands of men in a crusade to intimidate racial, religious, and political minorities[15]); the profiteers at business as usual; and the Federal administration's bringing in protective tariffs to enhance business profits.[16]

Absentee Ownership

In 1923 Veblen published *Absentee Ownership and Business Enterprise in Recent Times: the Case of America* , a large work of some 445 pages, offering a comprehensive overview and analysis of the current American economic situation. The medium-term context and stimulus for the book was provided by the decline since the 1890s of the individualistic entrepreneur-manager of industry, his supersession by the impersonal corporation with stocks listed on the stock-market, and then the rise of a new business institution, the holding company, the prime example of which was the United States Steel Corporation, as we noted in the previous chapter. The holding company effected amalgamation among firms in specific industries, thus reducing competition, and brought to the fore the investment banker as a leading shaper of American business, the prime example here being John Pierpont Morgan and Company. The whole development Veblen summed up in the phrase 'absentee ownership,' in contradistinction to the earlier 'hands-on' ownership of the traditional employer-manager who took an active part in running the industrial plant. He, therefore, sets out to answer two implicit major questions: What is the new structure of American capitalism that has come into being in the first two decades of the twentieth century? And, what are its ramifications and consequences?

The immediate context for his discussion is provided by the post-Armistice period which in America was characterised by economic uncertainty and considerable conflict. Immediately after the war there was a brief period of prosperity during which the cost of living rose dramatically but which came to an end in the summer of 1920 with the onset of a depression. At that time the cost of living stood at 104.5 per cent above the 1914 level, but by March 1921 it had fallen to 68.7 per cent above the 1914 level and there were 4 million unemployed.[17] Also, as already noted, various factors contributed to the 'Red Scare' of 1919–20.

In 1920 there followed the Presidential election which was won by the Republican candidate, Warren Harding, with his running mate, Calvin Coolidge. Early in 1921 they instituted a strongly pro-business Administration, and in the spring and summer of 1922 faced their first labour crisis. There was a national coal strike, brought on by employers trying to reduce wages, followed by a national railways strike as the railroad companies, forced to cut freight-rates, also tried to cut wages. Harding tried to bring an end to these highly damaging disputes through negotiation but was unsuccessful and the partisan quality of his Administation soon became apparent when the Attorney-General Harry Daugherty procured a court order enjoining workers from interfering with the free functioning of the railroads and from doing anything to continue the strike. As a result, the railway workers were forced to accept the reduced pay-rates set by the Railroad Labor Board.[18] Along the way Veblen also deals with such ancillary questions as: Why is there unemployment? Why is there industrial strife? Why do the state agencies of this democratic republic side with business interests against working people? Why is there price-inflation when industry is becoming more and more efficient and productive?

Absentee Ownership adopts Veblen's typical structure of two parts of roughly equal length, in which themes introduced in the first half are taken up and expanded upon in the second. As usual this leads to some repetition and this must count as the most repetitive and prolix of Veblen's books. Though he can be sharp and to-the-point when he wishes to be, e.g. 'the present businesslike management of the industrial system is incompetent, irrelevant, and not germane to the livelihood of the underlying population', these defects of style tend to blunt the radical thrust of his analysis.[19] Yet, radical it truly is, going to the root causes of the economic malaise and social unrest, and, despite the sometimes tiresome verbiage, providing a penetrating critique of modern corporate America.

He begins by emphasising the importance and international scope of the issue of absentee ownership, citing the First World War as evidence of its dominance in world affairs: 'The Great War arose out of a conflict of absentee interests and the Peace was negotiated with a view to stabilise them' (p. 3). The continuing industrial conflict and public anxieties about the role of trusts and holding companies have focused popular attention on the topic. Thus, he implies, a discussion and analysis of absentee ownership is called for in order better to understand the contemporary situation. Following on from his proposition that absentee ownership is 'the prime institutional factor that underlies and governs the established order of society' (p. 4), he points out how national politics and the law serve the absentee owners at the cost of the mass of the population. This is evident abroad in the use of national rivalries and imperialist acquisition of territory to promote the interests of the big corporations. America in 1920 had a sizeable empire including the Philippines, the Hawaiian Islands, the Virgin Islands, Alaska, Puerto Rico, the Panama Canal Zone, and Guantanamo Bay in Cuba. It was also evident at home, Veblen pointed out, in an implicit allusion to the 'Red Scare' and the use of the law to break the railway strike, in the repression of radicals and labour activists.

Why was this so? The historical reason lay in that the American Revolution and War of Independence brought into being simultaneously a new nation-state and a new form of (albeit limited) democratic government. The late eighteenth century, when the laws of this novel entity were being codified in the Constitution of 1787, also saw the ascendancy of the natural-rights doctrine of ownership derived from handicraft industry and articulated by Adam Smith and John Locke. Thus, the inviolability of property rights was enshrined in United States law, and the American legal and political system became closely identified with defending ownership. By a process of extension, this now applies in the twentieth century to absentee ownership, though Veblen, in his reprise of his by now familiar criticism of the natural-rights argument, points out this has nothing in common with the original basis of a workman and his product. Yet, the doctrine lives on unquestioned and so absentee ownership is 'legally and morally secure' (p. 11).

Veblen has a particularly cynical view of contemporary American politics and the way it operates in an amoral fashion. 'The personnel of official life [i.e. holders of office] come to be made up, in the main, of such persons as will be at home in the resulting spiritual twilight of official life by native gift or sedulous training,' he says, adding in a scathing footnote: 'This will ordinarily imply a degree of arrested development, particularly of the moral faculty, such as goes to create what is called a "moron"' (p. 28). He goes on to accuse the Harding and Coolidge Administration of being nothing more than a tool of the big financial interests, acting against the interests of the ordinary person:

Any Business Administration will be a Big Business Administration. So the constituted authorities of this democratic commonwealth come, in effect, to constitute a Soviet of Business Men's Delegates whose dutiful privilege it is to safeguard and enlarge the special advantages of the country's absentee owners.

Thus, the early promise of the revolutionary republic has been betrayed, for

democratic institutions which were once designed to serve the ends of liberty, equality, and the brotherhood of man, have under these latterday conditions come to converge upon the security and free income of the absentee owners, at the cost of the underlying population (p. 38).

There is thus a tension between the legal and political system which still rests on eighteenth-century foundations derived from a handicraft economy and the twentieth-century industrial system which is in perpetual evolution. The economy has changed so much since the late 1700s, and in a wide-ranging historical survey Veblen shows how the handicraft era, the era of free competition, and the captain of industry have all been superseded by the impersonal corporation capitalised on the stock exchange. Since such new arrangements as absentee ownership have come to the fore, nineteenth-century formulations of economic issues are out-of-date and new formulations are required. (Some nine years later Berle and Means were to make exactly the same point.[20]) So, implicity revising Marx, he writes, 'the issue now is turning not on a question of ownership, as such, but on absentee ownership,' and 'the standard formalities of "Socialism" and "Anti-socialism" are obsolete in the face of the new alignment of economic forces' (p. 9). As a result, the significant issue is not, as egalitarian social reformers would have it, the distribution of income and wealth, but 'the effectual use of the country's industrial resources, man-power, and equipment' (p. 10). For America, Veblen suggests, once offered the possibility of an almost utopian general prosperity. Given the country's rich natural resources – the coal, oil, ores, timber, land, waterways, together with the people's workmanship, it would have been possible for the American population to have gained 'an unexampled material abundance on unexampled easy terms' (p. 124). Two factors, however, prevented and continue to prevent this outcome. The first is that the United States's natural resources were not retained in public hands for public benefit, but were handed over to private owners for private profit, eventuating in the absentee ownership of these resources. The motive for all business he points out is to to get 'something for nothing at the cost whom it may' (p. 71), and by means of a comprehensive survey of agriculture, timber, precious metals, and oil he shows that 'the American Plan' of seizure of public resources and conversion to private gains (p. 186) has led to huge waste and inefficiency and the commanding position of the absentee owners.

The second factor is that industry, or the underlying population's workmanship, is not allowed to operate at full capacity and thereby enjoy all the productivity gains that modern technology has brought, despite the fact that this would benefit the population the most: 'The material interest of the underlying population is best served by maximum output at a low cost, while the business interest of the industry's owners may best be served by a moderate output at an enhanced price' (p. 10). This early statement introduces the central theme of the book which he expands upon in the latter half, namely that under absentee ownership output is deliberately restricted in order to maintain or enhance profitability. Technological advance increases output and brings unit prices down, but lower prices (though a necessary competitive tool in the era of free competition) would in the era of the corporation be deleterious to business by harming net gains. So, 'the remedy by which the inordinate productivity of the industrial arts is to be defeated or minimised is always a business-like sabotage, a prudent measure of unemployment and curtailment of output' (p. 97). The startling corollary of this, unacknowledged by liberal reformers, is that underproduction and unemployment are not aberrations of the system that can be remedied, but are central to it, are an essential feature of its *modus operandi* under corporate ownership and control.

In the second part of *Absentee Ownership* Veblen amplifies this point through an analysis of what he calls 'the new order,' in which Big Business is paramount. The onset of the reorganisation of the key industries into larger and larger conglomerates he traces to 'the era of trust-making' begun around 1897 and so 'the point at which the New Order may be said to have set in was reached and passed so soon as a working majority of the country's industrial resources had been brought under absentee ownership on a sufficiently large scale for collusive management' (p. 213). In 1899 some 66.7 per cent of all manufacturing was carried on by corporations, but this had grown to 87 per cent by 1919.[21] Competition on price between industries, at least the key industries, has largely been eradicated with the establishment of situations of either monopoly or duopoly, and this reorganisation has several significant features and several serious consequences.

The first feature is the dependency of the corporation as a business institution on credit. Picking up from his discussion of this topic in *The Theory of Business Enterprise*, Veblen points to the vastly expanded use of business credit, i.e. bonds, debentures, preference shares, ordinary shares or common stock, to fund business and maintain its profitability in the twentieth century. As he explains, it forms the basis of the corporation thus:

> The corporation arises out of a collective credit transaction whereby funds supplied by the stockholders (shareholders) are entrusted to the corporation as going concern to be administered for their benefit ... The company ... is therefore an impersonal incorporation of liabilities to the stockholders and by employing these liabilities as collateral ... it will then procure further capital by an issue of securities (debentures, bonds) bearing a stated rate of income and constituting a lien on the assets of the corporation. The securities outstanding make up the capitalisation, and the stated income rates ... are fixed charges on the corporate earnings. (p. 90)

It is imperative, therefore, for the corporation to meet these fixed charges, payable as interest, and so its profit must always be sufficient to meet them. According to Veblen, it consequently cannot expand production to the full because to do so would lower its prices and reduce the net business gain to 'below the danger point – the point below which the fixed charges on outstanding obligations would not be covered by the net returns' (p. 96). Corporations have to raise earnings to match their capitalisations and there two ways of doing this: keeping costs down by reducing wages, or increasing sales through salesmanship. The former has led to conflict with the labour unions, as Veblen points out, and the resort to salesmanship has led to a huge increase in expenditure on promotion and advertising which in turn is a cost that has to be met in the price of the item sold. In a rare recourse to numerical data, Veblen quotes estimates of over $60 million on outdoor advertising for 1921, over $800 million for national newsprint advertising in 1922, and over $1 billion for newsprint advertising in 1923 (p. 315fn).

The conditions, *vis-à-vis* capitalisation and associated fixed charges, have been exacerbated, Veblen points out, by the rise of the holding company, as developed by John Pierpont Morgan. For in the reorganisation which constitutes bringing a number of firms together into a holding company, such as happened in the case of United States Steel, there is a recapitalisation of the whole business, thus drawing on more credit through the usual instruments. Within this recapitalisation room has to be made for the investment banker's bonus for achieving the restructuring, usually in the form of a tranche of stock. Morgan, Veblen notes, came in for a block of United States Steel's securities of $50 million (p. 342). The result is an expanded quantity of liabilities without any increase in the material or tangible assets, namely the land, factories, equipment and inventories (p. 344). With the increase in securities the fixed charges have increased and can only be met by higher earnings – to be more precise, a higher net gain brought about by lower wages and/or higher prices. Due to the semi-monopolistic position of the holding companies in their fields, they are able to raise prices, which in turn are eventually passed on to the ultimate consumer, bringing about price inflation.

As we have seen, the cost of living more than doubled between 1914 and 1920, and as Veblen observes, 'it will be evident that the general price level has been rising ... during the past quarter century' (p. 372). Therefore, despite the great gains in productivity afforded by advances in the machine process, gains that could have brought down prices to a fraction of their current figures in Veblen's estimate, prices for the general public are higher than ever. As he reiterates,

a full employment of the available forces of industry regardless of what the traffic would bear ... [would] glut the market and precipitate an irretrievable decline of price-level and concomitantly also a fatal decline of earnings and ... a disastrous liquidation of capitalised intangibles. (p. 373)

The system of absentee ownership, or of highly capitalised corporations, with their pecuniary need to meet fixed charges on securities, thus bars the way to flat-out industrial production to produce cheaper goods and full employment. The result is an inevitable opposition of interests, dividing society, 'a division or cleavage of the people who live under this system of industrial business, whereby the business community ... comes to stand over against the underlying population' (p. 393).

There is, Veblen points out, little that the underlying population can do to meliorate the situation. First, the odds are stacked against the labour unions by the laws defending private property which prevent them taking over idle industrial plant during 'lock-outs'. Secondly, the state agencies – the police, the FBI, the National Guard are employed to defend the property rights of the absentee owners against those of working people. Thirdly, the influence of the absentee owners is ubiquitous through the economy. For by means of such devices as the holding company, the merger, the trust, and interlocking directorates the investment bankers have managed to take over 'the strategic regulation of the key industries and by way of that avenue also the control of the industrial system at large'. They thus constitute 'a General Staff of financial strategy' (p. 338), or 'what may be called the One Big Union of the Interests' (p. 340). Such a massive concentration of financial control is very difficult to counteract, particularly given the collusion of Government. Fourthly, the campaigns for better pay are largely futile, since they are no more than 'a running process of catching up', for 'the general level of prices continues to rise under current conditions of credit capitalisation, and salesmanship' (p. 394). Since these workmen, even if better paid, are also ultimate consumers, their gains will be wiped out in a higher cost of living. The working class is thus caught both ways:

In its dealing with the underlying population the business community buys their manpower and sells them their livelihood. So it is incumbent on the business men in the case to buy industrial manpower as cheap as may be, and to sell the means of living to the ultimate consumer as dear as may be. (p. 400)

To sum up, then, *Absentee Ownership* presents a critique of the modern American economic and social situation that is comprehensive in its sweep and devastating in its unswerving incisiveness. It attempts to do for the era of finance capital what Marx's *Capital* had done for the era of industrial capital. In a nutshell his message is that the cartel of financial institutions and industrial corporations constitutes a threatening concentration and centralisation of economic and social power. Over time this group has hijacked the democratic republic, grabbed its natural resources, commanded its industrial output, bent government policies and government agencies to its ends, and systematically exploited the underlying population first as workers with low wages and then as consumers with high prices. In Veblen's shrewd appropriation and inversion of the terms, American society is not threatened by the IWW, 'the One Big Union', nor by the Russian Soviet, as conservative politicians and the business-funded press would have the American public believe, but by 'the One Big Union of financial Interests' and the 'Soviet of Businessmen's Delegates', *aka* the Republican Administration. And it could not be otherwise, Veblen points out. For unemployment and privation, the restriction of output, and price-inflation are not due to moral failings, to malice or greed, but to the business system's internal logic. Once money-values are accorded primacy over use-values, once net profit is elevated to the primary goal all else follows.

For at the heart of the new order is a fundamental conflict of interest:

It is not that absentee ownership is wrong in principle ... . It is only that its concrete working-out is incompatible with the current state of the industrial arts, and that the material welfare of the civilised peoples is conditioned on the full and orderly operations of the industrial system in which this state of the arts is embodied. (p. 425)

In fact, he suggests, there may well develop such a strain in the system and such a level of hostility from the underlying population as to bring an end to the current, deplorable state of affairs by means of a revolution:

There is always the chance, more or less imminent, that in time, after trial and error, or duly prolonged and intensified irritation, some sizable element of the underlying population, not intrinsically committed to absentee ownership will forsake or forget their moral principles of business-as-usual, and will thereupon endeavor to take this businesslike arrangement to pieces and put the works together again on some other plan. (p. 425)

In general, however, Veblen's prognosis is that things can only get worse, with increasing class conflict and increasing restriction of output either by business or by the workers through strikes. He concludes the book on a note of profound pessimism, reminiscent of Marx's comments on the inevitable immiseration of the proletariat: 'The outlook should accordingly be that the businesslike control of the industrial system in detail should presently reach' a critical point beyond which it 'will result in a progressively widening margin of deficiency in the aggregate material output and a progressive shrinkage in the available means of life' (p. 445). This was to happen, of course, some six years later when the Wall Street Crash saw a catastrophic liquidation of capitalised values, leading to the Great Depression of the 1930s with its mass unemployment.

Absentee Ownership was Veblen's last book on America, bringing to an end a remarkable, coherent *oeuvre*. It is a huge, summative achievement, making many shrewd points such as the dominance of the business corporation in American economic life and the separation of ownership and control it brought with it, points which were to be taken up later, validated and expanded upon by such writers as Adolf Berle and Gardiner Means.[22] It is extraordinary that it has attracted so little commentary, since it represents the culmination of his long-running critique of American economic institutions and of his sustained attack on the complacency and blindness of those who believed in them.

4   Veblen's Reception

Now, they are beginning to pay some attention to me.

Veblen[1]

The first part of this chapter sets out to chart the reception accorded Veblen's theories during his lifetime and posthumously up until the early 1950s, and so to record the debate that went on for fifty years or so concerning them. The second part surveys Veblen's standing from the mid-1950s, when it appears Cold War anti-radicalism led to a diminishing of his reputation, up to the late 1990s, when there has been a marked revival of interest in his work. The purpose of this is to establish the extent and impact of his work and to examine the ups and downs of his reputation, since he has variously been dubbed America's finest social scientist, has been condemned as out-of-date and impenetrable, or simply ignored. His immediate academic discipline was economics and there remains the question of his reputation as an economist. Initially, he gained a considerable following and had some influence, some historians believe, on New Deal economic thinking, but after World War Two his reputation went into decline as economics became more sharply defined and more quantitative, and other economists such as Keynes gained pre-eminence. However, his work ranged far beyond economics as narrowly conceived and had a widespread influence among intellectuals and writers. It is this general reputation as a social analyst, critic and, in a work like *The Engineers and the Price System*, even social prophet, that mainly concerns us here.

His first and most famous work, *The Theory of the Leisure Class* (1899) was widely reviewed. It was criticised in the *Sewanee Review* for containing 'a vicious attack on Christian ideals,' and in the *Journal of Political Economy* was subjected to a lengthy critique by one of Veblen's colleagues, John Cummings, from the point of view of neo-classical economics. Cummings' main points were that Veblen presented a facade of objective analysis while actually engaging in value-laden judgements, and that he failed to acknowledge the individualistic basis of behaviour and thought with his theory of communal habits of thought and generic human traits. Cummings also regarded the dichotomy between industrial and pecuniary pursuits as being invalid, and *contra* Veblen's presentation of businessmen as being engaged in predatory activity, reasserted the conservative celebration of the captain of industry for making a great contribution to economic progress and well deserving of his rich rewards.[2] Veblen replied in an article in the same journal, in which, as Tilman notes, he gives the impression that Cummings simply cannot comprehend the book. And over thirty years later Cummings was to admit that this was the case. He wrote to Joseph Dorfman in 1931: 'My review gives good evidence that I did not at the time fairly appreciate the contribution Veblen was making to our economic and social philosophy. I have often wondered how I could have been so blind.'[3]

In general, *The Theory of the Leisure Class* was very well received, since it tapped the populist, anti-plutocratic temper of the late 1890s, and Veblen became a force among the intellectual radicals. John Dewey and Herbert Spencer sent him compliments; Lester Frank Ward praised it in the *American Journal of Sociology* as 'a mirror in which we see ourselves', and as possessing 'too much truth'.[4] William Dean Howells, the influential editor and the major writer of social fiction, such as *The Rise of Silas Lapham* (1885) and *A Hazard of New Fortunes* (1890) had published an essay, 'Are We A Plutocracy?' in 1894, and an appreciative view of Bellamy in 1898 together with a series of explicitly radical essays and so was highly sympathetic to Veblen's analysis. He devoted the leading article in two successive issues of *Literature* to Veblen's book. In particular, he saw Veblen as having identified a potentially rich subject for American fiction:

> A democracy, the proudest, the most sincere, the most ardent that history has every known, has evolved here a leisure class which has all the distinguishing traits of a patriciate, and which by the chemistry of intermarriage with European aristocracies is rapidly acquiring antiquity. Is not this a phenomenon worthy the highest fiction?[5]

Howells' praise and the publicity he accorded *The Theory of the Leisure Class* helped make it a sensation, and popularised its ideas beyond professional economics. Veblen's phrases, 'conspicuous consumption', 'vicarious leisure', 'conspicuous waste', were immediately in currency on the campuses. As the years went by, it remained so popular that in 1912 the publisher brought out a cheap edition at 50 cents.[6]

The second major work, *The Theory of Business Enterprise* (1904), was also widely and favourably reviewed. Socialists, especially, whole-heartedly approved, given the depth of anti-trust feeling at the time. A long review in the *International Socialist Review* called it 'the most searching analysis of capitalism ever published in the English language', and in a subsequent issue it was described as 'this epoch-making volume' and Veblen was termed 'the revolutionary iconoclast'. It was not only through his publications that Veblen held sway over critical social thought in the early years of the century, but also through his teaching, and as former students of his gained positions in the universities his influence spread, and he was regarded as the inspiration, if not the founder, of a new heterodox school of economics – Institutionalism. This was associated with such figures as Paul Homan, Wesley Mitchell, John Maurice Clark, and John Commons. Wesley Mitchell was a student of Veblen's at Chicago and he was avowedly Veblenian in his work, *Business Cycles* of 1913.[7]

In 1913 Charles A. Beard in *Contemporary American History* praised *The Theory of the Leisure Class* and *Business Enterprise* for the acuteness of the analyses they contained. Veblen's *Instinct of Workmanship and the State of the Industrial Arts* (1914) was extensively summarised and accorded approving commentary by Mitchell in *The Quarterly Journal of Economics*, where he remarked that it 'is a book of inter-pretations written by one with a genius for taking the cosmic point of view'.[8]

He thus sparked controversy, not only in economics, his primary field, but also in the other social sciences as well, and he was becoming an analyst who could not be ignored. Outside academe he was also being widely read and admired. Upton Sinclair read *The Theory of the Leisure Class* in 1903; he influenced Max Eastman; Floyd Dell declared a preference for Veblen over Marx; and Francis Hackett, literary editor of *The New Republic*, repeatedly mentioned and praised Veblen and sought to interest other editors in his work. Patrick Geddes, who coined the term 'conurbation', brought out *Cities in Evolution* in 1915 and acknowledged Veblen's importance. He was the first, Geddes said, to provide a keen analysis of the impact of the machine on society, and so thus 'expresses and explains ... the central thesis of the present volume'.[9]

Both liberal and conservative opinion favoured Veblen's first book in connection with the Great War, *Imperial Germany and the Industrial Revolution* (1916) although, perhaps inevitably, the critique of modern business was overshadowed by the prognosis of Germany's inevitable decline. Graham Wallas in the *Quarterly Journal of Economics* called the book a sociological treatise and labelled Veblen a 'genius'.[10] *An Inquiry into the Nature of Peace and the Terms of Its Perpetuation* came out in the spring of 1917 just as the United States entered the conflict. It was, as Daniel Bell remarks, 'a propitious psychological moment' for the book allowed progressive and socialist intellectuals to justify their switch from an anti-war to a pro-entry position and to hope for the emergence of a rational order after the cessation of hostilities.[11] As a result it was a success and was well reviewed in all the liberal journals. Francis Hackett in *The New Republic* called it 'the most momentous work in English on the encompassment of lasting peace', and the Carnegie Endowment for International Peace bought 500 copies for distribution in colleges and universities. Left-wing reviewers acknowledged the socialist thrust of the argument, which in turn caused concern to conservative reviewers. Floyd Dell in his review in *The Masses* called Veblen 'the most brilliant and perhaps the most profound of American scholars'. Veblen became an international figure and he was in correspondence with people all over the globe. 'Now', he said, 'they are beginning to pay some attention to me.'[12]

In October 1917 Veblen left the University of Missouri for a post with the Food Administration in Washington and then in June 1918 moved to Manhattan as one of the editors of *The Dial*, through which he was able to reach a much wider audience. In 1918 *The Higher Learning in America* appeared to praise from the socialists and liberals, although even *The New Republic*'s reviewer felt that Veblen, though right in his comments about schools of journalism and commerce, was wrong in connection with graduate schools and law schools.[13] *The Theory of the Leisure Class* had been reissued and had been approved by *Vanity Fair*, the magazine of the metropolitan sophisticates. He was also becoming popular, a well-known name in fact. His fame spread to such an extent that in 1919 H. L. Mencken, the satirist, wrote an article, 'Professor Veblen' in *The Smart Set*, in which he acknowledged the ascendancy of Veblen over Dewey as the great thinker in the literary weeklies, and with comic hyperbole bemoaned the spread of Veblen's influence:

In a few months – almost it seemed a few days – he was all over *The Nation*, *The Dial*, *The New Republic* and the rest of them, and his books and pamphlets began to pour from the presses and newspapers reported his every wink and whisper and everybody who was anybody began gabbling about him. ... everyone of intellectual pretensions read his works. Veblenianism was shining in full brilliance. There were Veblenists, Veblen clubs, Veblen remedies, for all the sorrows of the world. There were even in Chicago, Veblen Girls – perhaps Gibson Girls grown middle-aged and despairing.[14]

That year he brought out *The Vested Interests and the State of the Industrial Arts* which was favourably treated in *The Dial* and in the *New York Call* which praised him highly: 'There is none like him and in this book he maintains his prestige as intellectual iconoclast untarnished.'[15]

With these publications and the spread of his ideas his prestige increased. The year 1919 also saw Veblen in *The Dial* discussing President Wilson's betrayal of democratic ideals and attributing it to a clash of interests between the vested interests and the general population. The Lusk Committee of the New York legislature which was clamping down on radical opinion and was responsible for over a thousand arrests, regarded Veblen as a subversive for being one of *The Dial*'s editors, writing such subversive material, and for helping the IWW and the Civil Liberties Union with a pamphlet, 'The Truth About the IWW'. A collection of his essays, edited by three supporters, *The Place of Science in Modern Civilisation* also appeared. The reviews showed different perspectives but it was plain that, though Veblen's general reputation was growing, for orthodox economists he was losing relevance. Frank Knight in *The Journal of Political Economy* wrote that he was 'not a close or clear thinker' and that he could hardly be regarded as a leader in economics.[16]

In February 1921 *The Engineers and the Price System* appeared to a critical reception from even erstwhile supporters. *The Dial*'s reviewer felt that 'the thinker had been swallowed by the propagandist,' and Max Eastman in *The Liberator* condemned 'the Soviet of Technicians' as 'interesting as an intellectual experience but irrelevant to the problem of defining and organising a dynamic force sufficient to alter the essential course of history'.[17] In 1923 Sidney and Beatrice Webb paid considerable attention to and praised *The Theory of the Leisure Class* and *The Theory of Business Enterprise* in their *The Decay of Capitalist Civilisation*. Veblen's last economics book, *Absentee Ownership and Business Enterprise in Recent Times* (1923), was indifferently reviewed, with conservative critics feeling that the prosperity of the 1920s disproved Veblen's arguments and radical critics irritated that he had dismissed 'Socialism and Anti-Socialism' as the terms in which the current economic situation ought to be viewed. The reviewer in *The Liberator*, for instance, wrote that '*Absentee Ownership* borders on Marxian analysis and interpretation. Yet, Veblen insists on steering clear from the scientific values of socialism in his conclusion.'[18] It brought to an end Veblen's project for theorising the economic and social formations of modern America since, apart from a translation of the Icelandic sagas, he published no further books. His appointment at the New School having come to an end, he lived on small stipends supplied by a former student. He was offered the Presidency of the American Economic Association in 1925, but turned it down on grounds of health. He also turned down the offer of a Chair at the University of Oslo. In 1926 he returned to California to live on his ramshackle property in Stanford. [19]

His retirement to a reclusive existence in California and the absence of any further social science publications (his last was in 1925 in the *American Economic Review*)[20] led to a dropping off of interest in him, though some discussions of his ideas did appear throughout the 1920s. In 1924 a volume called *The Trend of Economics* , edited by Rexford G. Tugwell, accorded Veblen an important place and reviewed his work in neutral terms. That year too, Allen and Unwin published English editions of *The Theory of the Leisure Class*, *The Vested Interests*, and *Absentee Ownership* to approving reviews from British left-wing journals. One of these reviewers was the Cambridge Marxist economist, Maurice Dobb, who, though critical of the lack of concrete instances in Veblen's work and of his ponderous style, summarised the main points of *The Theory of the Leisure Class* and praised it as 'a very able, original and interesting study of ideology'.[21]

In 1927 John Maurice Clark published 'Recent Developments in Economics' in which he praised Veblen for moving beyond static neo-classical economics to develop an evolutionary form, but he pointed out that Veblen's analysis was value-laden and not nearly as objective as it claimed to be.[22] The same year Paul Homan, an important commentator on Veblen, published the entry for him in the *American Masters of Social Science* in which he criticised the crudity of Veblen's categorisation of traits and of the phases of prehistory. He also felt that the attack on orthodox economics, though it had considerable impact, was overdone and had its limitations. In the following year in his *Contemporary Economic Trends* Homan also devoted considerable space to him. He pointed out that Veblen was not just a critic of orthodox economics but was also a theorist, supplying an institutional theory based on human instincts and habits of thought and praised his best work for providing an analysis of industrialised commerce.[23]

With Veblen's death in August 1929 however, interest in his work revived markedly, as obituaries and discussions of his contribution to American social thought appeared in leading academic journals such as the *American Economic Review* and *The Sociological Review*. In the latter John Hobson praised him as America's foremost economic thinker and claimed that he should be properly regarded as a sociologist. He had provided, Hobson wrote, 'a far more convincing exposure of capitalist theory than is contained in any of the Marxian or other avowedly socialist treatises'.[24] *Century*'s obituarist ranked him as one of America's most influential and original economic thinkers, and *The New Republic* brought together responses to Veblen in both September 1929 and August 1931. In that issue Lewis Mumford wrote that Veblen was more than just an economic theorist; he summed him up as 'one of the half dozen important figures in scholarship that America has produced since the Civil War', and added that his 'thought should not be confined to economic circles: it should be filtering through and penetrating every pore of our intellectual life. In that process its solecisms would be discovered and thrown aside and its great original contribution would become fundamentally commonplace.'[25]

The 1930s

It was during the 1930s that Veblen's significance became widely recognised and his influence grew, as articles and books both within his formal discipline and in social thought in general engaged with his ideas. One cause of the renewed interest in him was the Wall Street Crash and the ensuing Depression which to many writers on the Left seemed only to confirm the accuracy of his analyses. As the most efficient factories in the world came to a halt and 13 million people were thrown out of work because financial insitutions had failed, Veblen's dichotomy between business and production and his view of the predatory nature of business seemed only too accurate. In the academic journals the first adequate criticism appeared in two articles in 1932 and 1934 in which his thought was set alongside Marx's and their notions of class and social change were compared and contrasted.[26]

In 1932 the first of a number of books devoted solely to him appeared – Richard Teggart's *Thorstein Veblen: A Chapter in American*

Economic Thought – in which Teggart rejected Veblen's claims to be scientific as spurious since he did not provide empirical evidence, also complaining that Veblen over-generalised and was not nearly specific enough, both historically and culturally. Also, he could not accept Veblen's criticism of the price system and his implied wish to see it abolished. Nor could he accept Veblen's view of businessmen as parasitical, since he regarded their entrepreneurial skills and ability to take risks as greatly benefiting American society.[27] However, Adolf Berle and Gardiner Means's volume, *The Modern Corporation and Private Property* appeared, vindicating and expanding upon Veblen's ideas in *The Theory of Business Enterprise* and *Absentee Ownership* on the rise of the corporation and its implications for American society. They do not acknowledge Veblen's influence (there is one footnote reference but he is not listed in the name index), but some of their points derive directly from *Absentee Ownership* some nine years before. They acknowledge the primacy of the corporation as 'the dominant institution of the modern world' (they even invoke Veblen's phrase 'new order') and provide figures to show its rise from being responsible for 66.7 per cent of all manufacturing in 1899 to 87 per cent in 1919. They also point to the concentration of economic power in the hands of a few with just 200 out of 300,000 non-financial corporations controlling nearly half of all corporate wealth in 1930. They develop at length the seriousness and ramifications of the separation of ownership and control, a feature first explored by Veblen. Also they acknowledge the obsolescence of neo-classical economics as derived from Adam Smith in the face of 'the corporate system', concluding: 'In each of the situations to which these fundamental concepts [from Adam Smith] refer the Modern Corporation has wrought such a change as to make the concepts inapplicable. New concepts must be found and a new picture of economic relationships created.' This, of course, was one of Veblen's pet themes as we have seen.[28]

Then, as a result of an article by Howard Scott in *The New York Herald Tribune*, the idea of a technocracy to bring America out of the Depression was revived and struck a popular chord. *The Engineers and the Price System* was recognised as the source of such a notion and press and magazine articles called Veblen 'the founder of technocracy'. Interest in his ideas soared. Between 1 February 1930 and 1 September 1934 approximately five thousand copies of Veblen's books were sold, *The Engineers and the Price System,* reissued, accounting for half that number. The following year a biographical sketch appeared in *Scribner's*, and in 1934 there were a number of popular books in which he was given a prominent place. Lewis Mumford in his *Technics and Civilization* acknowledged his debt to him; James Rorty dedicated his book on advertising, *Our Master's Voice: Advertising* to him; critics of Stuart Chases's *The Economy of Abundance* asked what it contained outside of Veblen; and reviewers of Matthew Josephson's *The Robber Barons* claimed it had its foundations in Veblen.[29]

In 1934 too, *The Theory of the Leisure Class* was reissued in a cheap edition by the Modern Library, and in his introduction Stuart Chase remarked that 'the collapse of orthodox economic doctrine during the years of world depression has vindicated the keenly analytic and prophetic writings of Thorstein Veblen'. This point of view was echoed a year later by of all journals, *Fortune*, which acknowledged that Veblen was achieving fame in the depression years owing to his prophetic insights into absentee ownership and the conflict between pecuniary and industrial interests.[30] Joseph Dorfman's monumental biography and summary of Veblen's work appeared. In addition, Leon Ardzrooni and Wesley C. Mitchell, former students of his, edited respectively his uncollected papers in *Essays In Our Changing Order* (1934) and *What Veblen Taught* (1936). Ardzrooni claimed in his introduction that Veblen was important for his contributions to social science and his influence on his time, and that he possessed a remarkable polemical ability, along with powers of prophetic insight. A contrasting critical view was articulated by Talcott Parsons in a 1935 article in which he provided a detailed analytical criticism of Veblen's economics. That year three articles on Veblen, two by Max Lerner and one by Upton Sinclair, were published in *The New Republic* and a fourth one (by Sidney Hook) in 1936. Across the Atlantic in England, Hobson in *Veblen* (1936) described him as 'one of the great sociologists of our time', whilst, however, also complaining about Veblen's convoluted expression and his exaggeration of the extent of industrial sabotage carried out by businessmen.[31] In the United States, he had long entries in the *Dictionary of American Biography* (1936) and the *Encyclopaedia of Social Sciences* (1938). The pervasiveness and strength of Veblen's influence was confirmed when Malcolm Cowley and the editors of *The New Republic* invited leading American intellectuals to identify the nonfiction authors who had had the biggest effect on them. In the anthology, *Books That Changed Our Mind* (1938), edited by Cowley, Veblen was top of the list with 16 mentions, ahead of Beard, Dewey, Freud, Spengler and Whitehead.[32]

One area of national interest in which Veblen was deemed to have an influence was the New Deal. In November 1932 Franklin D. Roosevelt won the Presidential election for the Democratic Party, which also gained a majority in the Senate and greatly increased its representation in Congress. In March 1933 he was sworn into office, and his administration embarked on a swathe of measures, collectively termed 'the New Deal' to cope with the Depression. The administration's aims were to provide stability for the financial system, stimulus for a stagnating industry, a remedy for the crisis in agriculture, and to alleviate the hardship caused by mass unemployment through creating work. Most historians believe that Veblen had an influence on New Deal thinking and policies, Norman Markowitz claiming that Veblen appeared 'to many to be the patron saint of the New Deal'.[33] Joseph Dorfman believed his impact was wide-ranging and argues that much of the legislation regulating corporations and security markets, such as the Securities Exchange Act (1934) stemmed from the clear implications of Veblen's work. In addition, a number of leaders of the new agencies were strongly impressed with his writings and three important members of the Temporary National Economic Committee – Jerome Frank, Isador Lubin, and Thurman Arnold (author of *The Folklore of Capitalism*, 1937) – were avowed Veblenians. So strong was Veblen's influence on Frank that it was claimed the Securities Exchange Commission's investigation into the house of Morgan was due to Veblen, for the *Christian Science Monitor* reported in February, 1940: 'Truth of the matter is that Morgan lawyers are lawyers, and the SEC lawyers are Veblen readers.'[34]

However, Rick Tilman in his review of the evidence is sceptical about the extent of Veblen's impact in this area. He accepts that Veblen may well have been an intellectual source for the Tennessee Valley Authority, since the public ownership programme of the Authority was partially in keeping with Veblenian doctrine. He also acknowledges that institutional economics, which Veblen founded, achieved its greatest sway over federal policy in the 1930s and shaped the intellectual milieu in which the liberal reformers of the Democrat administration moved. However, other institutionalists such as John R. Commons and Wesley Mitchell were also important, alongside Veblen and, even granting their public standing, Tilman concludes that 'it is doubtful whether a single important New Deal law or policy at its inception can be traced directly to their published work or doctrinal influence.'[35]

More tellingly, as he points out, even though the Department of Agriculture was headed by three men who were familiar with Veblen's views, the administration's farm policies were contrary to Veblen's thinking, based as they were on the artificial cutting of supply to boost prices, or in Veblen's terms on 'sabotaging' production. Also, Veblen would have had little faith in the regulation of business and finance (in which Dorfman sees Veblen's influence at play) for, as we have seen, Veblen believed the modern state to be largely a tool of big business and that no laws would be passed which significantly harmed business interests. The New Deal's objective was not the overthrow of capitalism and the abolition of absentee ownership, but its recuperation and continuation, and to that end Roosevelt's administration 'subsidised the banking system, protected the investment portfolios of savings banks and insurance companies and tried to repair the price system which Veblen condemned'.[36] We may conclude, perhaps, that in undermining classical economics and questioning the myths of business functioning, Veblen had generated an intellectual climate in which new types of economic and legal relationships between the state, business, and the underlying population could be envisaged. As to specific policies, however, it seems impossible to trace their genealogy to Veblen's writings, whose radicalism far outstripped anything the New Deal attempted or achieved.

The 1940s

In the late 1930s and early 1940s the rise of Nazi Germany and indus-trialised Japan were other factors which sent readers back to Veblen with new appreciation. In 1939 *Imperial Germany and the Industrial Revolution* was reissued and in March 1940 Secretary of State Henry Wallace contributed a review article in which he gave Veblen high praise. Drawing the comparison between the First and Second World Wars he emphasised the continued relevance of Veblen's analysis. 'Veblen's study is probably the most acute analysis of modern Germany ever written,' he wrote, for 'nothing that has occurred in the last twenty-five years tends to cast any serious doubt on the cor-rectness of Veblen's penetrating analysis.' He concluded by saying that this book and *The Nature of Peace* should be 'required reading for the statesmen of all the democratic countries', and that Veblen 'is verily a modern Isaiah and as such is without sufficient esteem in his own land'.[37]

Serious, if critical, attention continued to be accorded his economic and social theories. In 1940 an article comparing Veblen with Keynes was published, a book devoted to him appeared in France, and five books surveying the development of social thought that year, and a sixth in 1942, gave extended coverage to his work and theories. One of those authors ranked Veblen as the major theorist of class in early American sociology and praised him for providing 'the most penetrating analysis of the plutocratic control' of American society.[38] Talcott Parsons in his section in the survey volume *Contemporary Social Theory* gave a long critical analysis of Veblen's theory of institutions.

Fleeing Nazism, three major members of the Frankfurt School – Max Horkheimer, Herbert Marcuse, and Theodor Ardorno – settled in the United States to continue the work of the Institute of Social Research. They soon felt impelled to engage with American social thought and to pay Veblen some attention. This they did in 1941 in an issue of the Institute's journal, *Studies in Philosophy and Social Science*. What interested them, as John Diggins points out, was the way Veblen handled the phenomenon of mass society, and how he might offer a key to the possible future of industrial civilisation at that grave juncture when a world-wide Depression had been brought to an end only by global war.[39] Horkheimer in his 'Preface' to the issue pointed to the genesis and significance of their engagement with him: 'It became clear to us that thorough study and careful analysis of Veblen, America's great sociological critic of culture, would help us better to understand the catastrophic change in human nature' that was dramatised for them all by the triumph of National Socialism and the barbarism of World War Two. Horkheimer contributed an article, 'The End of Reason,' which dealt with the irrationality of Nazism, but which did not mention Veblen. Marcuse's contribution, 'Some Social Implications of Modern Technology,' considered Veblen's view of the industrial process and the place of technics in civilisation. He quotes from *The Instinct of Workmanship* and from *The Engineers and the Price System* to bolster his argument about the pervasiveness of technological rationality, and he credits the American thinker with originality in perceiving the impact of industrialism upon ways of thought. 'Veblen was', he writes, 'among the first to derive the new matter-of-factness from the machine process, from which it spread over the whole society.'[40] Adorno contributed a long essay, 'Veblen's Attack on Culture', in which he focuses largely on *The Theory of the Leisure Class*, takes issue with the American on several points, and charges his theory with various shortcomings.[41] Adorno begins by acknowledging Veblen's importance. 'His theory,' he says, 'has been assimilated' and 'is widely and officially recognised.' He then lists the influences on Veblen and makes several criticisms which a familiarity with Veblen's work does not support. 'What Veblen dislikes about capitalism', he writes, 'is its waste rather than its exploitation.' But Veblen mentions exploitation several times in *The Theory of the Leisure Class* and the exploitative nature of business becomes an increasingly central theme of his later works. Adorno next accuses Veblen of 'an overemphasis on the limited sphere of production', but, in fact, Veblen gives most attention to the sphere of consumption, pointing how in a vicarious way it manifests itself in religion, sport, and the role of women. The crux of Veblen's position and of Adorno's critique of it is expressed in this passage from the essay:

> This culture which today takes the form of advertising ... was never anything else to Veblen but advertising, the display of booty, power, and expropriated surplus value. In grandiose misanthropy he neglected everything which goes beyond this display.

He thus charges Veblen with a simplistic notion of culture and with being over-emphatic in linking every aspect of cultural life to the leisure-class canon of conspicuous waste.

There was a growing number of Masters' and Doctoral theses being written on Veblen, and in the mid-1940s Arthur K. Davis published three articles in which he criticised Veblen for seeing only the negative aspects of consumption and emulation and not the beneficial effects in terms of social cohesion.[42] Alfred Kazin in his monumental survey of American prose literature, *On Native Grounds* (1942) devoted a dozen consecutive pages to discussing Veblen, focusing on his style and his quality of being an outsider, an 'alien.' He summed him up as 'one of the most extraordinary and tragic figures in the history of the American imagination'. Richard Hofstadter in *Social Darwinism in American Thought* (1944) also acknowledged Veblen's general intellectual significance and influence. In 1947 Allan Gruchy's assessment of Veblen in *Modern Economic Thought: The American Contribution* was highly favourable. Even Gramsci's posthumous *Historical Materialism and the Philosophy of Benedetto Croce* (1948) includes a short discussion of Veblen in connection with Spencer, Marx, and Henry Ford.[43] The following year *The Theory of the Leisure Class* was translated into Italian and a fierce debate was sparked in Italian journals. Also in

1948 a book linking Veblen and Freud appeared. Louis Schneider's *The Freudian Psychology and Veblen's Social Theory* set out to compare the two contemporaries' theories and to criticise them both for emphasising the repressive and negative aspects of society and ultimately advocating the abolition of social restraints. Though for Schneider there was much that was valuable in Veblen, such as his emphasis on conspicuous consumption, the major defect was a failure to deal adequately with the problem of social order, if current factors in social cohesion such as status emulation were abolished.[44] Most important of all perhaps for extending the spread of Veblen's ideas, *The Portable Veblen* appeared. In the 'Introduction,' Max Lerner detailed Veblen's devastating critique of traditional economic doctrine, emphasising his ideas on machine technology, and putting forward the view that he had been a reformer as well as a theorist. Morton White in *Social Thought in America* continued the serious regard in which Veblen was held by discussing at length his attack on classical economics and its underpinnings in Bentham and Mill, and his own evolutionary approach to institutions. White summed up Veblen's effect on the American mind together with other liberal thinkers, such as Charles Beard and John Dewey, as having been 'enormous, extending from the university to the nursery school, from law courts to political parties'.[45]

In 1950 a book on Veblen's philosophy appeared, which argued that he 'formulated and developed a philosophy that he applied to the analysis of human problems', and in the early 1950s five books on general social thought, including Commager's *The American Mind* and Aaron's *Men of Good Hope*, outlined the main features of Veblen's thought and accorded him the status of a major critic of American business.[46] Then in 1953 the Mentor edition of *The Theory of the Leisure Class* was published with an 'Introduction' by C. Wright Mills in which he called Veblen 'the best critic of America that America has produced', and pointed out that his 'language is part of the vocabulary of every literate American'.

This survey of titles and commentators demonstrates that during his life and in the years after his death, through the 1930s and 1940s into the early 1950s Veblen had an assured place in American social thought, both in regard to his historical importance in the early decades of the century and to the continuing relevance of his ideas in the postwar period.

The 1950s

Veblen, then, had an assured place in American social thought through the early decades of the twentieth century up until the 1950s. Yet, from then on until the mid-1960s there was a shift of approach in which Veblen's significance was repeatedly downplayed. He is ignored altogether, or is marginalised or dismissed as an outdated eccentric of little importance. Whilst there continued to be some favourable comment, Veblen was definitely regarded with increased negativism for about fifteen years.

The 1952 edition of the *Encyclopaedia Britannica* series 'Great Books of the Western World' omits Veblen all together, and David Riesman's *Thorstein Veblen: A Critical Interpretation* (1953) seems to have been instrumental in turning the tide against him in mainstream academia and bringing about a revision of his reputation. In that volume Riesman does not consider the quality or explanatory power of Veblen's theories; rather, he attempts a psychological explanation of them in terms of Veblen's Norwegian and rural background. He argues that Veblen was unable to exorcise his father, had a repressed inner urge to show off, and unconsciously conspired in his own alienation by preferring to remain underpaid and under-ranked. Here is a sample of Riesman's 'cod' analysis:

> Much of Veblen's work may be read as an internalised colloquy between his parents; between one who calls for a hard matter-of-fact, 'Darwinian' appraisal of all phenomena and one who espouses the womanly qualities of peacableness, uncompetiveness, regard for the weak.[47]

In this small-minded, mean-spirited study the major ideas are thus seen as merely generalised extensions of personal idiosyncrasies which possess no objective worth. There is thus no absentee ownership, status emulation, or a parasitic leisure class. All is best in the best of all American worlds!

The attacks on Veblen mounted with H. V. Coals in an article arguing that Veblen pushed his criticism of orthodox economists to extremes, that his contribution to scientific method 'cannot be rated highly', and that his evolutionary method cannot be demonstrated 'on rational grounds'. And Lev Dobriansky in *Veblenism: A New Critique* (1956), was highly critical, claiming that Veblen's work is not particularly profound, that he engaged in disguised moralism, and that his critiques of American society are often unbalanced and contradictory. Veblen's dichotomies were simplistic and the emphasis on habit reduced the significance of rational decision-making in social life. Dobriansky also could not accept the iconoclastic idea that income from capital was unearned and therefore illegitimate, and that certain occupations, 'pecuniary employments' in Veblen's phrase, were wasteful and parasitic. Don Wolfe in his *The Image of Man in America* (1957) devoted a short chapter to Veblen (its brevity being indicative of a low evaluation) in which he focused on Veblen's anthropological stance and was critical and dismissive of Veblen's ideas regarding neolithic humankind's peaceableness and work-manlike propensities.[48]

There were several reasons for this reversal of fortune in Veblen's reputation. Firstly, there were the enormous changes in the American economy brought about by the war, and then the transformation back from a militarised economy to a peacetime (or more accurately, semi-peacetime) one. There was a huge increase in service industries, in the bureaucratic, corporate nature of business, and in the white-collar middle class. It was simply not the same America that had existed in the century's first forty years, but even though the Depression had given way to the postwar consumer boom, this did not necessarily diminish Veblen's relevance, since he had been prescient in his understanding of the role of consumption, as Chapter Five will point out.

Another reason lay in the development of the social sciences themselves as disciplines. The increasing specialisation and frag-mentation in this area made Veblen's wide range difficult to encompass and his overall achievement difficult to grasp. Economics became much more quantitative and Keynesian, and Veblen's ter-minology and formulations appeared vague and of little explanatory value. In sociology Veblen was eclipsed by the European theorists, Durkheim and Weber, and by the leading American social theorist of his generation, Talcott Parsons, whose structural–functional approach was most influential in the 1950s. Parsonian theory viewed societies as self-equilibrating action systems and emphasised stability over change, consensus and coherence over disagreement and con-tradiction. It thus denied the tensions and bifurcations within modern capitalist society posited by Veblen.

Its dominance and Veblen's partial eclipse can be linked to the political climate. The onset of the Cold War and then the Korean War fostered a polarised view of social organisation as being either communist or capitalist. The House Un-American Activities Committee, under Senator McCarthy, through careful media manipulation gained a high public profile in the late 1940s and early 1950s. Its persecution of officials, writers, and intellectuals generated an atmosphere of virulent anti-Communism and extreme conservatism in which no criticism of the 'American Way' would be tolerated.

Christopher Lasch in 'The Cultural Cold War' remarks on the obsession with the so-called Communist conspiracy in the 1950s. This obsession often led to a framing of intellectual choice in terms of a stark binary polarity: either you were pro-American or you were pro-Communist. Middle-of-the-road liberalism was seen as suspect. Irving Kristol, writing in *Commentary* in in 1952 said: 'There is one thing that the American people know about Senator McCarthy: he, like them, is unequivocally anti-Communist. About the spokesmen for American liberalism, they feel they know no such thing.' And Lasch remarks how the anti-Communist hysteria generated a 'cultural vigilantism' which suppressed and denounced any views critical of American society. Veblen, as a sharp critic of American business, became a victim of this vigilantism. Lasch also remarks on the historical break between the decades of the 1930s and 1940s and the decades of the 1950s and 1960s. He points out how American intellectuals in the earlier decades were engaged in a criticism of American life, while in the 1950s and early 1960s they were engaged in a celebration of it. Philip Rahv makes the same point in his contribution to a *Partisan Review* Symposium of 1952 entitled 'American Intellectuals and the Postwar Situation'. He remarks on the absence of 'attitudes of dissidence and revolt' among American intellectuals, and on their 'identification with American life, with its traditions and prospects'. And in the literary culture he notes 'a mood of acceptance' and an 'opportune kind of optimism'.[49]

However, it would be misleading to give the impression that Veblen entirely dropped from view because of this mood of acceptance or that there were only negative responses to him during this period. Serious discussion of his theories and approving commentary continued to appear but not in nearly the same quantity as in previous decades. Robert Heilbroner in his survey of economic thinkers, *The Worldly Philosophers* (1953) devotes a chapter to 'The Savage Society of Thorstein Veblen' in which he summarises his life and work and provides a mixed assessment of him. He criticises him for not recognising the capacity of business to change in the face of new circumstances, but praises him for understanding 'the emergence of technology and science as the leading forces of historic change in the twentieth century'. Rosenberg's *The Values of Veblen: A Critical Appraisal* (1955) analyses at length the main works and compares him favourably to Marx and Weber.[50]

Increasingly, Veblen was attacked by the Marxist Left as articles criticising him and written by such Marxists as Paul Baran and Paul Sweezy appeared in the *Monthly Review*, which, as a mark of the centenary of Veblen's birth, devoted a double special issue in the summer of 1957 to an assessment of Veblen's significance.[51] Arthur K. Davis contributed to this issue with 'Veblen: The Postwar Essays' in which he accorded the iconoclast high praise: 'he looms larger as one of the handful of really great minds of the modern world.' In their general evaluation, perhaps inevitably for them, Veblen succeeded most where he came closest to Marx, and his inadequacies were traceable to his deviations from historical materialism. Davis in a long appraisal in another Marxist journal emphasised (exaggerated, one has to say) Veblen's 'intellectual kinship' with Marx, and criticised him for the utopian anarchism that permeated his thought, while acknowledging *The Theory of the Leisure Class* to be 'a landmark in American social science', and rating only Keynes as being comparable in modern times to Veblen.[52] What the Marxists particularly praised was the way Veblen drew attention to the linkage between economics and politics, as well as to the rise of monopoly or oligopoly capitalism before other economists. One can see the legacy of the later Veblen in Baran and Sweezy's *Monopoly Capital* (1966), in which they point to the concentration of economic power in the hands of a few huge corporations and expand in Chapter Five on Veblen's point about the extent of the resources devoted by corporations to salesmanship and advertising.

Also to mark the centenary of his birth, *Thorstein Veblen: A Critical Reappraisal* was published and the editor, Douglas Dowd, claimed that Veblen 'was and remains the most eminent and seminal thinker in the area of social analysis yet to emerge in America', and that his ideas retained contemporary relevance. One of the contributors argued, *contra* Davis and the other Marxists, that Veblen's importance did not depend on being assimilated to Marx, but on being recognised as having superseded him, that 'in a real sense, Marxism became Veblenism'. John Kenneth Galbraith in *The Affluent Society* (1958) portrayed Veblen's unique position in American economics and echoed Veblen in his ironic references to 'the conventional wisdom' in economics, in his attention to the role of advertising and salesmanship, and in his emphasis on the role of conspicuous consumption in a system of emulation: 'Moreover, wealth has never been a sufficient source of honor in itself. It must be advertised, and the normal medium is obtrusively expensive goods.' The following year, the major Veblen scholar, Joseph Dorfman, published *The Economic Mind in American Civilization 1918–1933* in which he discussed Veblen's later writings and argued that many of his ideas had exerted a profound effect on later thinkers. The popular sociological works of Vance Packard, *The Hidden Persuaders* and *The Status Seekers,* though making only a few direct references to Veblen, were both underpinned by his insights into the roles of salesmanship and of status emulation, and were a fleshing out of those insights with empirical evidence from 1950s America.[53]

The 1960s

At the beginning of the 1960s an article by Riesman that is generally unsympathetic to Veblen and finds contradictions in his work seems to presage a further period of negative assessment, but this is not borne out by subsequent commentary.[54] There seemed to be a revival of interest in Veblen in the 1960s, linked to the mood of disillusionment with the direction American society was taking. In 1963 *The Engineers and The Price System* was reissued in a paperback edition with an 'Introduction' by Daniel Bell. While noting various shortcomings in Veblen's analysis in that book, such as his ignoring the role of bureaucracy in modern society and his failure to understand the political dimension of any radical movement, Bell summed it up as being 'surprisingly accurate and relevant to the present-day economy'. He cited the 1958 Kefauver Committee reports on 'administered prices' in the steel and automobile industries as supporting Veblen's opening chapter which deals with 'sabotage' or the deliberate restriction of production by business in order to maintain profitable prices, and he pointed to the huge increase in marketing since Veblen's day as giving his remarks on the cost and wastefulness of 'salesmanship' continuing 'telling bite'. Bell also published 'Veblen and the New Class' and continued to invoke Veblen in his writings, although as Rick Tilman points out he tends in general to try and defuse Veblen's attack on modern American capitalism by labelling it 'utopian'.[55] Veblen was certainly egalitarian and he was cynical about an Executive he considered to be in the pocket of big business, but this did not make him an 'utopian'; it simply confirmed him in the tradition of the revolutionary democratic republic of 1776 founded on the dictum that 'all men are created equal'. Veblen's general point was that the liberty and equality promised by the new nation-state had been stifled not by the state *per se*, nor by industrialism *per se*, but by a corporate capitalism which used the state as an instrument to further its own interests, used industrialism to provide profits, and then devised stock and bond issues to secure massive gains for the financiers at the expense of the 'the underlying population', the American people at large.

To continue the survey: Clarence Ayres in *Institutional Economics* (1964) assessed the importance of Veblen's legacy and came to the conclusion that history had largely confirmed his insights. Two previous writers on our subject added more volumes to the Veblen bibliogrpahy, one a selection of his writings edited by Rosenberg, and a general introduction to his ideas published by Dowd. There was also a volume of essays sympathetic to him and assessing his contribution published in connection with the centenary of Carleton College, where Veblen first began his higher education.[56] Also, Veblen had by now become a standard inclusion in histories of thought in the social sciences with entries on him in *The Encyclopaedia of Philosophy*, *The International Encyclopaedia of the Social Sciences*, and *Masters of Sociological Thought*. Interestingly, he even became the subject of drama in 1966 when a play based on his life was published. John Kenneth Galbraith's *New Industrial State* appeared, showing considerable similarity with Veblen's 'New Order' of *Absentee Ownership*. In both absentee ownership flourishes, and both writers portray society as being ruled by big business, and emphasise the growth of technological knowledge. In 1968 Stephen S. Conroy argued that Veblen had had a major influence on the popular sociology of David Riesman, William H. Whyte, and C. Wright Mills.[57]

Nonetheless, although by the late 1960s Veblen seems to have been accepted as a central historical figure, the New Left largely ignored him, and he still suffered some notable omissions from interpretations of the early modern period. Christopher Lasch's *The New Radicalism in America 1889–1963* (1965), for instance, surely a likely place to find an extended treatment of this influential radical thinker, has not a single reference to him, even though one long chapter is devoted to *The New Republic* which frequently publicised Veblen and to the Great War, about which Veblen wrote two highly regarded books. According to Lasch's version of American radicalism, Veblen had simply never existed, let alone had widespread influence. By such means Veblen was almost written out of American cultural history.[58]

The 1970s

In the 1970s the debate on his significance continued. Daniel Bell in *The Coming of Post-Industrial Society* (1973) devoted some space to Veblen in connection with technocracy, pointing out how his hope for a soviet of technicians had been misplaced, although his ideas had resurfaced in the France of the 1960s through Serge Mallet's *La Nouvelle Classe Ouvrière* (1963). Then, there were two critical assessments, one in an article in *Daedalus* (1974) which argued that Veblen was out of date and that his books had not lasted, and the second, a book by David Seckler, *Thorstein Veblen and the Institutionalists* (1975) which argued that Veblen had been ruled out of both economics and social philosophy and that his type of grand theorising was out of vogue.[59]

It is in the second half of the 1970s that Veblen comes to be acknowledged not as a merely marginal figure but as someone central to any account of the development of American social thought. William Akin's *Technocracy and the American Dream* describes Veblen's profound influence on the technocracy movement, and John Kenneth Galbraith in *The Age of Uncertainty* describes Veblen's life and times and considers his enduring achievement to have been in sociology. A few years later in his autobiography Galbraith was to employ Veblen's distinction in *The Higher Learning* between esoteric and exoteric, i.e. useful, knowledge, and to acknowledge Veblen's impact on him. Speaking of his youthful years at Berkeley, he wrote, 'after Marshall, the major influence on me from those years was Thorstein Veblen', and later, considering Veblen's scepticism, he notes that it might have made one dismissive of the hope of any reform, but though he has resisted that tendency 'in other respects Veblen's influence on me has lasted long'. He sums him up as 'the most interesting social scientist the United States has produced', and one who still has 'a substantial and appreciative audience'.[60]

Leonard Dente's *Veblen's Theory of Social Change* (1977) and John Diggins' *The Bard of Savagery: Thorstein Veblen and Modern Social Theory* (1978) gave long and serious consideration to Veblen's ideas. Dente's is a systematic study in comparative theory which begins by examining Veblen's theories of economic growth, business cycles and social change, and stresses the unity of his system. Next, it sets

Veblen's perspectives against those of Von Neuman, Schumpeter, and Marx, in order to reveal Veblen's essential contribution to the theory of economic growth. He sees Veblen comparing 'most favorably' with these other economists and identifies Veblen's contribution as being a theory of waste, a theory that allows us to understand the development of industrial nations. In his final chapter, 'An Evaluation of Veblen's Theory' he sums him up as demonstrating 'that economic stagnation is a constant threat to capitalism, because of the property relations that exist within this society' and as showing 'the importance of political, social, cultural, and psychological elements' in social change. Diggins also takes a comparative approach putting Veblen in the company of Marx, Durkheim, and Weber for achieving 'new and important insights into the nature of society', and he remarks that 'like the novelist of manners he illuminated the deeper meaning of social behavior with imperishable perceptions'.[61]

The following year Arthur K. Davis who as we have seen wrote on our man in the mid-1940s and mid-1950s published his 1941 PhD thesis, *Thorstein Veblen's Social Theory*, and in an added preliminary chapter, 'Veblen Once More: A View from 1979,' gave his revised perspective on the theorist. He now wanted to emphasise more than he had done so in the thesis the Marxian character of Veblen's work (an emphasis we have seen in his 1957 *Science and Society* article), and to defend Veblen's criticism of orthodox economics. He also now evaluated *Absentee Ownership* and *Essays in Our Changing Order* as the most significant of Veblen's works, for they were, 'still pregnant with insights into the terminal disease of the United States of America. The name of the disease? DEMENTIA PRAECOX.' He thus deliberately echoes the title of one of Veblen's most outspoken articles published in *The Freeman* some 57 years before, and goes on to say how this piece 'still carries much valid insight'.[62]

The 1980s Onwards

In 1981 Jean Baudrillard published *For a Critique of the Political Economy of the Sign* in which he showed an appreciation of Veblen's insights into consumption and its role in social domination, and he concluded:

Critical theorists of the political economy of the sign are rare. They are exiled, buried under the Marxist (or neo-Marxist) terrorist analysis. Veblen and Goblot are the great precursors of the analysts of class. [63]

In the academic journals in the 1980s interest in him was even greater than the decade before, for of the 21 articles collected in Mark Blaug's volume of 1992, two-thirds date from that period. An incomplete bibliography of secondary material was published in 1985, and as consumerism became a growing object of study so Veblen was invoked the more. Titles such as *Showing off in America: From Conspicuous Consumption to Parody Display* and *Conspicuous Consumption: A Study of Exceptional Behavior* demonstrate the continuing currency of Veblenian vocabulary as writers built on his ideas and acknowledged that his understanding of modern social behaviour provided the basis for further analysis.[64] Jackson Lears in a 1989 piece, 'Beyond Veblen: Rethinking Consumer Culture in America,' acknowledges Veblen's importance, remarking that he anticipated Gramsci with his notion of the cultural hegemony of dominant groups, although he then criticises the limitations of Veblen's puritan view of consumption.[65] Interestingly, Veblen was now included in the 1990 edition of the *Encyclopaedia Britannica* series 'Great Books of the Western World' with a volume that carried long extracts from *The Theory of the Leisure Class* alongside extracts from Tawney and Keynes. In 1992 there appeared Rick Tilman's *Thorstein Veblen and His Critics* which covers some of the same ground as this chapter but which also organises reactions to Veblen up until 1963 according to three positions on the political spectrum: conservative, liberal and radical.[66]

In the late 1970s his stature as a thinker came to be recognised, but even recent histories of American thought do not fully acknowedge that stature. Dorothy Ross in *The Origins of American Social Science* (1991) places Veblen in his context and discusses his influence on Mitchell, Hoxie, and Davenport, but devotes only 14 pages to him in a work of 476 pages, a proportion that is far from commensurate with his impact on American social thought. Even though her focus is on Veblen as an economist she completely ignores his major, summative work, *Absentee Ownership*, and so fails to appreciate his contribution to an understanding of the rise of the corporation and the significance of the separation of ownership and control (which Berle and Means were to pick up on in *The Modern Corporation and Private Property* as noted earlier in this chapter). Douglas Tallack's impressive *Twentieth-Century America: The Intellectual and Cultural Context* (1991) refers to Veblen several times, quotes from *The Theory of the Leisure Class*, and employs a number of Veblen's insights, but does not mention any of Veblen's other works and fails to accord him the significance within the intellectual and cultural context of early modern America that he deserves.[67]

Later in the 1990s, however, it does seem that the wry iconoclast was finally receiving the kind of historical recognition owed him. The restoration of his family home near Northfield, Minnesota was begun in 1992 and completed in 1996. The International Thorstein Veblen Association met for the first time in February 1994 and has held regular conferences. Through the decade over 50 articles devoted to him, ranging from his intellectual debts to comparative studies to reassessments, appeared in journals with 1997 being the peak year with 12. Rick Tilman brought out *The Intellectual Legacy of Thorstein Veblen* in 1996; a survey of American social thought which was focused on him appeared in 1997; and a collection of essays on his work came out in 1998, as well as a comparative study with Dreiser. John P. Diggins reissued his earlier work under the title *Thorstein Veblen:Theorist of the Leisure Class* as a paperback in 1999, the same year as a new biographical study, *Thorstein Veblen: Victorian Firebrand* by Elizabeth Watkin and Henry Irving Jorgensen, appeared, as well as a study linking Veblen and Dreiser as 'saboteurs of the status quo'.

Veblen then continues to provoke interest and generate commentary.[68] What can we learn from a survey across the decades of the debate on Veblen? A study of the varying fortunes of Veblen alerts us to the continual need to return to primary sources and contemporary commentaries and not to allow later assessments and their historically determined emphases and blind spots to become our emphases and blind spots. It is incontrovertible, as established earlier, that to his contemporaries Veblen was a key influential figure, but in postwar commentaries that importance was diluted and negative assessments of both his past significance and of his contemporary relevance multiplied. This was due to a preoccupation with communism (*vide* HUAC and Aaron's *Writers on the Left*) at the expense of other sources of radical thought, and was part of the 'mood of celebration' and 'end of ideology' consensus in which oppositional strands even within native American thought were denied or glossed over. Further it was symptomatic of the 'one-dimensional' character of consumer capitalism highlighted by Herbert Marcuse that alternative ways of constructing social life could not be accommodated within an interlocking system of categories that validated the bourgeois *status quo* as the natural, the best, and the totality.[69]

5 Veblen and Consumerism

America was going on the greatest, gaudiest spree in history and there was going to be plenty to tell about it. The whole golden boom was in the air.

F. Scott Fitzgerald

Years ago a person, he was unhappy, didn't know what to do with himself – he'd go to church, start a revolution – *something*. Today, you're unhappy? Can't figure it out? What is the salvation? Go shopping.

Arthur Miller, *The Price*[1]

That contemporary American society is dominated by mass consumerism is accepted by every commentator, but opinions vary on the historical timing of the emergence of a distinctively modern form of consumption-oriented economy. Some elements, such as the department store and newspaper advertising, were present by the end of the nineteenth century, but the economic indices point to the the 1920s as being the period when consumerism became established as a way of life with its attendant ideologies.

Using data drawn from a large number of sources, Louis J. Paradiso made the important observation that the average propensity to consume over the period 1900–1920 did not continue into the 1920s and 1930s but took an abrupt upward turn. Consumer expenditures for the same amount of disposable income were generally about $5 billion higher in the years after 1920 than before. He also found that the ratio of savings of individuals to their disposable income declined from an annual average of 16 per cent in the period 1910–20 to an annual average of 9 per cent in the period 1921–40. Also, H. T. Oshima has shown that in the American economy of the post-World War One period producer or fixed-asset production ceased to dominate the total production of durables and structures, and was replaced as the leading characteristic of the economy by the formation of consumer assets, i.e. the purchase of dwellings and durables by households corresponding respectively to the purchase of factories and machinery by business. In his conclusion he propounded the view that this development of the consumer sector was 'a natural outcome of the maturation of the business sector of the capitalist economy', and marked a new phase of capitalism. Walter Rostow also sees a structural change occuring in the American economy at this time. He sees the shift from the phase of 'the drive to maturity' to the phase of 'high mass consumption' as having happened around 1920, and regards the cheap mass automobile as the decisive element.[2]

The turning point in the automobile industry's development was Henry Ford's moving assembly line of 1914, which produced the Model T, the first cheap, mass-produced car, and as such the first significant consumer durable. Ford, then, was one of the initiators of the consumer phase of the American economy and in his attitudes as a businessman he heralded a whole new approach. 'Industry,' he told the Press, 'must manage to keep wages high and prices low, otherwise it will limit the number of its customers. One's own employees should be one's own best customers.'[3] He cut the factory day from nine to eight hours and raised the daily wage to five dollars (twice the highest common labour wage) in 1914, a policy that was in marked contrast to that of other employers who paid as little as possible and kept their employees near to subsistence level. Employers still mainly viewed the worker as a producer, but Ford viewed him as also as a consumer and realised from the start that, industrial as his enterprise was, it was a different kind of industry, one that sold its commodities not to other businessmen, but to the ordinary public.

Mass production demanded and brought into being the mass market. Through the efforts of Ford and his main rival, General Motors, the mass ownership of cars became one of the distinctive features of the 1920s. Factory sales rose from a mere 4000 in 1900 to nearly a million in 1918, doubled in the next two years, and climbed steadily through the decade to reach a peak of 4.5 million in 1929, a record that was not equalled until 1946.[4]

Not only cars but every other type of consumer durable came to be produced and sold on a massive scale during the 1920s. Sales of radios and electrical equipment, for instance, rose from $28 million to over $388 million between 1922 and 1929. According to Rostow 'that decade is ... to be understood as the first protracted period in which a society absorbed the fruits and consequences of the age of durable goods and services', and in the view of Peter d'A. Jones much that is typical of the American consumer economy came into being in the 1920s.[5]

As part of this economic transformation the 1920s saw massive increases in both productive capacity (GNP rose 40 per cent from 1919 to 1929) and in worker productivity.[6] There seemed to be no limit to how much the nation could produce. As the distinguished group of social scientists who composed the Committee on Recent Social Changes commented in their report *Recent Economic Changes* (1929), 'never before has the human race made such progress in solving the problem of production'.[7] The result of such advances, however, was to raise the spectre of chronic overproduction.

The Brookings Institute report, *America's Capacity to Produce and America's Capacity to Consume* (1933) revealed that available plant worked at only 80 per cent capacity from 1925 to 1929, and its contributors observed that 'if each industry would run to its full capacity huge surpluses of some goods would no doubt soon pile up'.[8] The problem facing the 1920s was to create new techniques of mass consumption to meet the new techniques of mass production. A far-reaching alteration in the character of capitalism had taken place. Whereas the traditional problems of economics had been related to scarcity, those facing the age of 'high mass consumption' were related to abundance and, whereas the phase of industrial capitalism had faced the challenge of production, the phase of consumer capitalism faced the new challenge of maintaining aggregate demand. But how was aggregate demand to be maintained? How were hardheaded, thrifty Americans to be induced to spend money on goods they did not really need? This need to maintain or increase market demand led to a heavy focus on selling, and the closely related need to overcome consumer resistance. Three main strategies were adopted to promote consumption: product innovation, consumer credit, and intensive advertising.

The automobile industry set the pattern for all other consumer durable industries by pioneering these strategies. In 1928 Ford brought out his Model A in order to counter the drop in sales of his Model T but, whereas the first model had remained in production for 15 years, the Model A lasted only five. Ford's competitors, General Motors and Chrysler, made it obsolete, not in performance but in appearance.[9] They modified and elaborated the visual appeal of their models, while Ford, with a farm mechanic's functional view of machinery, found it difficult to adapt to the rise of fashion in the world of car manufacture. Unnecessary product innovation or planned obsolescence was early adopted by the big car makers (later to include Ford) to maintain demand as each year new models appeared in the showrooms and rendered the previous models out of date. Owning the newest type of car became one of the main ways in which people could trumpet their financial success. Other consumer industries adopted the same strategies, as radios and electrical goods soon came to sport style-features in order to emphasise the age and unattractiveness of earlier models.[10]

Consumer credit or hire purchase also made its appearance in the 1920s through the efforts of the motor industry. In 1925 General Motors financed a study, *The Economics of Instalment Selling*, to test the soundness of consumer credit, and on the basis of its findings set up a credit agency to facilitate the purchase of its products.[11] This was so successful it was adopted by other consumer industries such as electrical goods and it constituted a major factor in making mass consumerism possible. In 1929 it has been estimated that instalment sales approximated to some $7 billion. A related development that also encouraged consumer habits was the growth of the chain department store, the number of which rose from 29,000 in 1918 to 160,000 in 1929.[12]

A further important factor in maintaining aggregate demand that was quickly exploited by the motor industry was advertising. Money spent on periodical advertising by the car manufacturers rose from $5 million in 1915 to $23 million in 1929. Other consumer industries soon followed suit and mounted their own intensive advertising campaigns, bringing about a growth in the total volume of advertising from $1.5 billion in 1918 to nearly $3.5 billion in 1929.[13] Advertising had been common in American newspapers since they began, but it had largely been of straighforward, informative character with little irrational impact since pictorial display was either prohibited or discouraged.[14] But a marked qualitative change accompanied the huge quantitative increase in advertising in the 1920s. Advertisers increasingly resorted to irrational appeals and drew upon J. B. Watson's behavioural psychology to manipulate the subconscious needs of the consumer. Watson himself left Johns Hopkins University to become vice-president of an advertising agency.[15]

Closely associated with advertising, public relations also rose to prominence in the 1920s. Many of the men who set themselves up as public relations counsellors received their training in manipulating opinion in George Creel's Committee on Public Information, which was responsible for the anti-German propaganda aimed at Americans during the First World War.[16] Companies that were aware of the importance of 'image' began to hire these counsellors, as the Rockefellers hired Ivy Lee, to improve the impression the public had of them. Standard devices were favourable news releases, articles planted in ostensibly independent magazines, and advertisements that did not sell a product so much as promote a quality (such as size or progressiveness) that the company wished to project. Such expensive efforts to influence public opinion were a far cry from the 'public-be-damned' attitude of William Vanderbilt and the other aggressive, individualistic entrepreneurs of the nineteenth century, but in a consumer economy companies depended upon customer approval for the sale of their products as well as for forestalling any hostile legislation which might be enacted.

The structural change in the economy augmented by these selling strategies led to a massive growth in personal consumption comparable only with the 1950s and 1960s. As well as the spectacular increase in cars, telephones increased from 13 million to 20 million between 1920 and 1929; the number of families with a radio rose from 60,000 in 1922 to 10 million in 1929; annual sales of vacuum cleaners amounted to $40 million in 1925, of electric cookers to $20 million in 1927, and of refrigeration equipment to $167 million in 1929. Estimated expenditure on recreation also doubled in the decade with mass entertainment such as movies and records showing a great increase.[17]

The shift into a consumerist economy manifested in the 1920s was largely arrested during the Depression and war years but resumed with greater intensity in the postwar consumer boom. During the war average incomes rose considerably, but there were few consumer durables to spend them on since most industries had been converted to the production of war matériel. As a result savings reached the record level of $100 billion during the years 1942–44, and it was widely expected that this pent-up spending power would boost consumerism when the war ended and the economy reverted to peacetime production. 'The end of the war will inaugurate the most gigantic sales program in all of our history', a contributor to a symposium on consumption economics prophesied in 1945. 'There is reason to believe', another contributor confidently remarked, 'that high-level consumption may well become the permanent characteristic of our economy.'[18]

As predicted, the sales of consumer durables expanded at an enormous rate during the period 1946 to 1956. In 1946, 69 per cent of the houses wired for electricity possessed electric refrigerators, while ten years later the proportion had risen to 96 per cent. The increase was similar for other electrical goods. Television, for instance, was installed in 86 per cent of homes by 1956. In 1946 the sale of cars reached the 1929 level and the proportion of families owning their own car rose from 54 per cent in 1948 to 73 per cent in 1958.[19] In the five-year period 1953–57 the purchase of major consumer durables amounted to $150 billion and residential construction to $88 billion, a total of $238 billion. This was 120 per cent of the total purchase of equipment and construction by business during this period. Consumer asset formation, which had shown a marked rise during the 1920s, had thus come to exceed capital asset formation by a substantial margin in the 1950s.[20]

Once the war-time savings were spent, the still rapidly increasing consumption was financed more and more by consumer credit. In the earlier post-war period from 1947 to 1950 annual instalment credit amounted to 69 per cent of all consumer goods purchased, but for the later period of 1960–63 this proportion had risen to 88 per cent. The consumer economy, it was evident, was increasingly financed by debt.[21]

'Down through the ages in most places the dominant economic problem has been production,' Dexter M. Keezer remarks, but 'in an economy of abundance such as that which has been created in the United States successful selling is a key ingredient of successful performance.'[22] To help them sell successfully manufacturers resorted more and more to advertising to bolster aggregate demand, causing the amount spent on it to multiply three-fold during this period from over $3 billion in 1946 to over $10 billion in 1957. Not only was there a quantitative increase but also a qualitative change as depth psychology was extensively employed to manipulate people's responses to consumer goods. Advertising also penetrated the home a great deal more through the sponsoring of radio and television programmes and the use of 'commercial breaks' between programmes.[23]

The economic phase of distribution and selling had thus emerged as dominant over the productive phase, its particular demands ramifying back through the organisation to affect the entire mode of production:

A major change in thinking is now making itself felt. Today, the orientation of the manufacturing companies is increasingly toward the market and away from production. In fact, this change has gone so far in some cases that the General Electric Company, as one striking example, now conceives itself to be essentially a marketing rather than a production organization. This thinking flows back through the structure of the company, to the point that marketing needs reach back and dictate the arrangement and grouping of production facilities.

The classic pattern of industrial organisation in which production was the key, had given way to a pattern in which the imperative of selling was saturating every aspect of the industrial process. 'The business problem shifts from being one of production to one of marketing, distributing and selling.'[24]

Thus, in the 1920s a revolution in the texture of everyday material culture took place as the consumerist economy developed, and Veblen was prescient in his understanding of some of the social bases of consumerism and of the origins of the consumerist ideology that accompanied this economic shift. As Norman O. Brown, one of the few in the 1950s to reassert the accuracy of Veblen's ideas wrote: 'When the core of the economic problem becomes not production but consumption, when the core of the sociological problem is the jungle pattern of irrational human demands, Veblen is the pioneer.' Dorothy Ross also accords him historical priority in focusing on this field: 'In focusing on emulation, Veblen was, along with Simon Patten, one of the first American economists of his generation to sense the growing importance in modern capitalist society of consumption and its conventional character.'[25] For Veblen was the first to identify the irrational factors that governed acquisition, that is to say the manner in which goods within a system of invidious emulation became status symbols, fulfilling subjective needs for social esteem.

Influential commentators on American culture agree that the development of a consumerist ideology originating in the 1920s and continuing in the post-Second World War period has occurred. David Riesman and his collaborators claim that there was a revolution taking place in the United States, 'a whole range of social developments associated with a shift from an age of production to an age of consumption', and William H. Whyte sees a major change in the decline of the Protestant Ethic and the rise of 'the Social Ethic'.

David M. Potter regards American society as having been reoriented from a producers' into a consumers' culture, and Daniel Bell argues that in the 1920s 'a consumption society was emerging, with its emphasis on spending and material possessions, and it was undermining the traditional value system with its emphasis on thrift, frugality, self-control, and impulse renunciation'. Bell points out that, though there was an intellectual attack on traditional values, it was capitalism itself which sent them into decline by means of advertising, the instalment plan and credit card. Mass consumption, in his view, led to the eclipse of Puritanism and the Protestant Ethic and the rise of a consumer hedonism which propagated the idea of pleasure and gratification as a way of life.[26] As F. Scott Fitzgerald commenting on the period put it succinctly: 'A whole race going hedonistic, deciding on pleasure.'[27]

As Raymond Williams pointed out, in any cultural situation of change there are residual, dominant, and emergent elements.[28] The traditional Protestant American values did not, of course, disappear overnight, but persisted in the 1920s in conflict with an emergent consumer hedonism. The success of the Anti-Saloon League in securing nationwide Prohibition through the Eighteenth Amendment in 1920 illustrated the continuing vitality of Puritan moral values. In 1935, for instance, the Lynds found that there was still a strong emphasis on the Protestant ethic and *laissez-faire* individualism in the Midwestern city of Muncie, Indiana that formed the subject of their famous study.[29] It was not until the 1950s that hedonistic values of consumerism became dominant, and during the transition period of the 1920s the two ideologies coexisted uneasily in the national culture. This state of affairs was summed up in 1933 by the President's Research Committee on Social Trends:

The lingering Puritan tradition of abstinence which makes play, idleness and free spending sin; and the increased secularization of spending and the growing pleasure basis of living.

The tradition that rigorous saving and paying cash are the marks of sound family economy and personal self-respect; and the new gospel which encourages liberal spending to make the wheels of industry turn as a duty of the citizen.

The deep-rooted philosophy of hardship viewing this stern discipline as the inevitable lot of men; the new attitude toward hardship as a thing to be avoided by living in the here and now, utilizing instalment credit and other devices to telescope the future into the present.[30]

The coexistence of two conflicting ideologies was also identified by Malcolm Cowley in his memoir of the twenties, *Exile's Return* (1934). He identified, firstly, a set of conservative attitudes, 'the business-Christian ethic'. 'Substantially,' he wrote, 'it was a *production* ethic. The great virtues it taught were industry, foresight, thrift and personal initiative.' This ethic had been congruent with the young and expanding economy, but with the end of the First World War a major change had occurred.

> Our industries had grown enormously to satisfy a demand that suddenly ceased. To keep the factory wheels turning, a new domestic market had to be created. Industry and thrift were no longer adequate. There must be a new ethic that encouraged people to buy, a *consumption* ethic.[31]

From where did this consumption ethic come? While advertising helped undermine the Puritan thrift and abstinence which inhibited consumer demand and propagated values and a lifestyle based on personal consumption, it did not create those values or that lifestyle. Cowley argues that one important source for consumer values was the subculture of New York's bohemia:

> It happened that many of the Greenwich Village ideas proved useful in the altered situation. Thus, *self-expression* and *paganism* encouraged a demand for all sorts of products, modern furniture, beach pyjamas, cosmetics, colored bathrooms with toilet paper to match. *Living for the moment* meant buying an automobile, radio or house, using it now and paying for it tomorrow. *Female equality* was capable of doubling the consumption of products formerly used by men alone.[32]

As a member of that subculture, Cowley accords it more influence on popular attitudes than it really enjoyed. Intellectuals did indeed lead the attack on Puritanism with Van Wyck Brooks's *America's Coming of Age* (1915) and Harold Stearns's *America and the Young Intellectual* (1921), but it was not the criticisms of the culturally progressive which had a mass effect on the decline of traditional values. Rather, the origin of a consumption ethic in a society dominated by Protestant values of work and thrift and a scarcity psychology can be traced to two sources, both first commented on by Veblen, namely, the motive of gaining social esteem through the display of economic success, and the rise and influence of a new hegemonic group, the leisure class, whose historic function it was to be model consumers, to educate America in the meaning of abundance and make acceptable hedonism, personal consumption, and status rivalry.

A Society of Pecuniary Emulation

As early as 1892 Veblen had pointed to the importance of social esteem and to the striving of men and women for public approval. In a pecuniary society such esteem was largely gained through financial success, but in the mobile, anonymous environment of the modern town or city it was necessary to put that success on show. 'To sustain one's dignity – and to sustain one's self-respect,' he wrote, 'under the eyes of people who are not socially one's immediate neighbours it is necessary to display the tokens of economic worth.'[33] Dress, and other publicly viewed possessions, thus came to play a key role in gaining the respect of others and so enhancing one's sense of self-worth. Dreiser dramatises this point in *Sister Carrie* when Carrie first encounters Drouet, the travelling salesman, or 'drummer' on the train:

> His suit was of a striped and crossed pattern of brown wool, new at that time, but since become famous as a business suit ... . His fingers bore several rings – one, the ever-enduring heavy seal – and from his vest dangled a neat gold watch chain, from which was suspended the secret insignia of the Order of Elks. The whole suit was rather tight-fitting, and was finished off with heavy-soled tan shoes, highly polished, and the grey fedora hat.[34]

The process of emulation that is set in motion, Veblen points out, is only likely to intensify since society is becoming more and more mobile and since it is based not on absolute worth but on the perception of relative worth. Once a general level of comfort or display is achieved, then some will seek to better themselves relative to that level, to become 'superior' to it. The others, on seeing the new level attained with the esteem attached to it, will then strive to catch up until a certain equalisation is attained and then the whole process sets off again.

Possessions, then, commodities, are bought not only for their use value, but for what economists term their 'nonfunctional utility,' their role as indicators of economic success. In *The Theory of the Leisure Class* Veblen wrote of the symbolic function of goods: 'The human proclivity to emulation has seized on the consumption of goods as a means to invidious comparison and has thereby invested consumable goods with a secondary utility as evidence of relative ability to pay.'[35] Objects thus become signs that can be read or interpreted by those who are literate in that particular symbolic system. Within this system the normal logic of the market that a lower price will lead to increased demand is turned on its head, since it is items which are expensive which become the most desirable. In 1950 Harvey Leibenstein coined, along with two other terms, the term 'Veblen effect' to describe one of the interpersonal factors that affect consumers' behaviour. This, he wrote, 'refers to the phenomenon of conspicuous consumption, to the extent to which demand for a consumers' good is increased because it bears a higher rather than a lower price'. 'Veblen effect' became a standard marketing term into the 1970s, and is plainly at work in the consumption of such items as perfumes and wristwatches.[36]

Another point Veblen makes is that, since conspicuous consumption is indefinitely expansible, increased industrial productivity will not lead to less working time and more leisure for ordinary people as envisaged in such utopias as Bellamy's *Looking Backward*. Rather, working time will be maintained in order that the increased surplus of income over subsistence will be employed in conspicuous expenditure:

> As increased industrial efficiency makes it possible to procure the means of livelihood with less labor, the energies of the industrious members of the community are bent to the compassing of a higher result in conspicuous expenditure, rather than slackened to a more comfortable pace.[37]

This was remarkably prescient, for Gary Cross has documented how, indeed, American workers in the 1920s chose to forego campaigning for a shorter working week or opportunities for more time off in favour of higher wages, so that they could increase their scale of consumption. His conclusion is that 'the triumph of consumerism meant a rejection of the progressive reduction of worktime and of "democratic leisure". It realised instead the dominance of a work-and-spend culture.'[38]

As we saw in Chapter Two, Veblen pinpointed the social and ideological significance of the *nouveaux riches*, produced by the rapid capital accumulation of the late nineteenth century, in his most famous book. The leisure class set the standards followed by every level of society and, indeed, largely instigated the whole system of stratification based on status. It 'stands at the head of the social structure in point of reputability; and its manner of life and its standards of worth therefore afford the norm of reputability for the community'. Consequently, 'its example and precept carries the force of prescription for all classes below it'.[39] As the son of an artisan-farmer, Veblen had imbibed the production-oriented values of thrift, self-reliance and industry and hence was especially alert to the leisure class's establishment of values antithetical to the Protestant ethic.

First, its members rejected the practice of thrift and industry, for 'the substantial canons of the leisure-class scheme of life' were 'a conspicuous waste of time and substance and a withdrawal from the industrial process'. Secondly, they rejected the sober, restrained lifestyle of the typical nineteenth-century entrepreneur. 'The duty of the man of Wealth', Carnegie, the steel king, had written, was 'to set an example of modest unostentatious living, shunning display or extravagance', for 'whatever makes one conspicuous offends the canons [of good taste]'.[41] However, the American rich shifted from a code of inconspicuousness to one of ostentatious display or 'conspicuous consumption' because 'in order to gain or hold the esteem of men it is not sufficient merely to possess wealth or power'; they 'must be put in evidence, for esteem is awarded only on evidence'. Wealth, previously regarded in the Protestant scheme as the just reward for abstinence and struggle, had become respectable in itself and 'by further refinement, wealth acquired passively by transmission from ancestors or other antecedents presently becomes more honorific than wealth acquired by the possessor's own effort'. Hand in hand with this exaltation of inherited wealth went a corresponding denigration of work and occupation. The life of conspicuous leisure, far from being a subject for moral condemnation, became elevated to high status since 'conspicuous abstention from labor' became 'the conventional mark of superior pecuniary achievement'. The example of the leisure class thus severely undermined Protestant values and generated attitudes towards leisure and luxury which came to constitute a consumption ethic. Also, by inaugurating the system of status and 'pecuniary emulation' the leisure class enabled manufacturers and advertisers to exploit the desire to emulate and the need for approbation by marketing consumer products as indicators of social position, as 'status symbols'.[41]

Of course, many members of the bourgeoisie in the early decades of the century still engaged in manufacturing and commerce and led a life of sobriety and industry as Protestant values taught them. The emergence of the leisure class took several decades and the validity of Veblen's observations gained with time. Evidence of a leisure class was available in the East as early as the mid-1890s, as confirmed by James Bryce, but in the Midwestern city of Muncie, Indiana such a group did not form until the 1930s. Until then the few wealthy families of the city had avoided ostentation and had merged themselves into the general business class, but the second-generation wealthy had begun to mark themselves off as a distinct social stratum through the exhibition of conspicuously leisure pursuits involving horses and private aircraft.[42]

The Spread of Consumer Hedonism

Accompanying the development of localised leisure-class groups such as that at Muncie, was the formation during the 1920s and 1930s of a national leisure class. This was composed not only of the hereditary rich but also of the new rich such as millionaires created by the boom in manufactures during the First World War, stock market and property speculators, and Hollywood film stars. These social developments greatly disturbed national values as a large section of the ruling class publicly abandoned the Protestant ethic and generated in tension with it a consumer hedonism that was propagated throughout society. This change was felt all the more acutely in the 1920s because the war acted as a watershed between the old and the new and the economic boom of the 1920s brought the leisure class into great social prominence. In addition, the 1920s saw the emergence of a distinctive youth culture which, influenced by the leisure class and advertising, was heavily consumerist in character.[43] Leisure-class tastes and lifestyle were impressed upon the public through the newspapers, glossy magazines and the movies. The activities of the rich, particularly the young rich, made good copy, and the impression to be gained from their typical behaviour as retailed in the popular media was of wealth acquired without effort and used without responsibility. As F. Scott Fitzgerald expressed it: 'A whole race going hedonistic, deciding on pleasure.'[44] The display of wealth on such a lavish scale without moral restraint and the threat to traditional values that it posed led some commentators to view the institution of the leisure class as a problematic phenomenon.

There was some contemporary discussion of the social role of the leisure class and of the implications of leisure in general. In 1911 Frederick Townsend Martin had published *The Passing of the Idle Rich* in which he described the feverish search of the wealthy for some new sensation to be had only at immense cost and by the most fantastically conspicuous waste. Parties at which guests sat between monkeys, and lighted cigarettes wrapped in new dollar bills, exemplified desperate efforts to outdo friends in ostentation. However, Martin went on, this belonged to a past era for, with the widening gap between rich and poor, the idle rich must reform or be swept aside in a social revolution. 'The grim truth is that we as a class are condemned to death. We have outlived our time ... . We are charged openly with being parasites and the mass of evidence against us is so overwhelming that there is no doubt whatever about the verdict of history, if indeed it must come to a verdict.' Martin concluded by insisting that reform and adjustment long overdue must be forthcoming in business no less than in government if cataclysmic revolution was to be averted.[45]

Herbert L. Stewart in 'The Ethics of Luxury and Leisure'(1918), quoted defences of the English aristocracy and gave qualified approval to the view that the rich acted as reservoirs of culture and taste. He thus echoed in part James Russell Lowell, one of the Boston Brahmins, who in 1884 in his 'Democracy' address had defended hereditary wealth as an institution which could preserve culture in a democracy. This positive value assigned to the rich was being attacked by the early 1930s by C. D. Burns, who argued that the most significant change in the social system was 'the displacement of the leisured class as the preservers and promoters of culture'. For Stewart any beneficial effect exercised by the American rich was offset, first, by their lifestyle of conspicuous consumption which he castigated with a Puritan fervour, and secondly by their conspicuous idleness which he condemned by appealing to the Protestant work ethic:

The legitimacy of the leisured and luxurious life can never be admitted in any sense which would conceal the eternal principle that some form of useful, strenuous, even exhausting work is both the duty and privilege of every man and woman in good physical and mental health.

If Stewart's response can be regarded as representative, it is evident that the rise of the leisure class called forth dual feelings of approbation and condemnation from the middle class, reflecting a tension between their Protestant values of work and thrift and the consumerist hedonism which the leisure class represented.[46]

American capitalism in its phase of high mass consumption required contrasting behaviour to that demanded in the phase of production. People were now required not to save, but to spend and get into debt; not to deny themselves possessions and comforts, but to gorge themselves on consumer items; not to work long and hard, but to enjoy themselves in marketed leisure-time activities. Max Weber's 'worldly asceticism' of the Protestant ethic was to be replaced by a worldly hedonism in which pleasure and gratification formed the basis of living.

In conclusion, then, it is Veblen to whom one must turn for an understanding of how mass consumerism was able to establish so dominant a position in a society where this ethic of denial and hard work had reigned supreme. He was the first to perceive that commodities could become signs and so operate by virtue of their differences as a semiotic system. Baudrillard was to expand upon this facet much later in *Consumer Society* (1970). 'In this field of connotations the object takes on the value of a sign', he writes. 'In this way a washing machine *serves* as equipment and *plays* as an element of comfort or of prestige, etc.' He goes on: 'Consumer behaviour which appears to be focused and directed at the the object and pleasure in fact responds to quite different objectives: the metaphoric or displaced expression of desire, and the production of a code of social values through the use of differentiating signs.' He concludes, 'In this sense consumption is a system of meaning, like language, or like the kinship system in primitive societies.' Also, as Baudrillard points out, neo-classical economics fails to understand consumption since it operates with a naive view of consumer rationality and sovereignity, with what in effect is a 'mystification'.[47] An example of this is provided by just such an apologist for consumerism as George Katona, who could assert: 'A study of empirical evidence will show that most consumers though they are not ideal "rational men", are circumspect and sensible,' and who could therefore argue that marketing and advertising had very little influence on generating consumer desire.[48]

In addition, Veblen established that a status hierarchy based on invidious comparison would endlessly fuel personal consumption and product innovation, as each stratum sought both to catch up with the group above and to differentiate itself from the group below. Vance Packard in *The Status Seekers* was to develop this point at length, noting how houses and personal possessions became important indicators of social position: 'The vigorous merchandising of goods as status symbols by advertisers is playing a major role in intensifying status consciousness.'[49] It is also Veblen to whom we must turn to understand the contemporary proliferation of advertising (the top 100 US advertisers spent more than $50 billion in 1995 alone)[50], the shopping mall, the massive department store, and shopping not as a necessary duty but as a leisure pastime. As Jackson Lears points out, Veblen 'was one of the first theorists to move away from the producer orientation of nineteenth-century economics and focus on consumption as an important category of social and economic behaviour'. And 'the ideas of the celebrated iconoclast have become part of the conventional wisdom about American society and conspicuous consumption'.[51] However, Lears goes on to argue that Veblen's approach is too restrictive because it relies on a unidirectional 'trickle down' of tastes from the top of the hierarchy to the bottom, while in reality other influences are also at work, but Andrew Trigg, refining Veblen's theory with Pierre Bourdieu's distinction between economic and cultural capital, successfully defends Veblen against this criticism. Other, newer theories about consumption which emphasise 'lifestyle choice,' or 'status drift' have also sought to displace Veblen's theory but Yngve Ramstad in his review of these perspectives comes to this conclusion: 'No, Veblen has not been shown to be wrong. Yes, pecuniary emulation, as Veblen conceived it, by all signs continues to be a central element of human nature.'[52] Veblen, then, remains a prescient analyst of modern American consumerism.

6 Veblen and Modern American Fiction

It is the supreme opportunity of the American novelist.

W. D. Howells[1]

Veblen's ideas, then, as we have seen in Chapter Four, whilst recognised in his own academic field – Stuart Chase described him as being responsible for 'one of the boldest interpretations in the history of economics' – also spread through the literary weeklies into general thought and parlance.[2] Howells had entitled his two-part essay on *The Theory of the Leisure Class* 'An Opportunity for American Fiction', and had suggested that 'the material of the great American novel' could be found in Veblen's treatment of the 'artistocratization' of a democratic society by old-world values of luxury and idleness. And, I would argue, Veblen's ideas did inform and underpin some significant American novels between the wars.

This is not the conventional view. Most histories of modern American fiction do not mention Veblen at all, and even literary critics with an avowed socio-historical perspective from Walter B. Rideout to Eric Homberger pay him little attention.[3] Even Alfred Kazin in his comprehensive survey, *On Native Grounds*, made only a passing connection between him and Dos Passos and did not link him to any other writer, despite devoting a dozen consecutive pages to discussing Veblen as a writer. There have been a few short studies but there seems to have been no extensive exploration of his influence.[4] Any such exploration must acknowledge, of course, that he was not the only critical analyst of American social life in this period, nor the only source of radical ideas and perspectives. Marx and communism were powerful influences, as documented by Daniel Aaron, and during the Progressive era there was widespread distrust of, and many attacks on, the practices and ethos of big business.[5] The rise of an American plutocracy (as concerned Howells), corruption in economic and political life, the growth of monopolies, and the brute power of money to override all other considerations were the concern of many, and inasmuch as the novelists discussed here articulate those concerns, they shared the general critical temper of the time. However, these writers expressed more than a vague dislike of capitalism or a distaste for materialism; their texts, I hope to demonstrate, are informed by a specifically Veblenian perspective.

There are several reasons why Veblen especially should exert a literary influence in this period *entre deux guerres*. With the 1920s the United States economy, as we have seen in the previous chapter, entered a phase of mass consumerism and the leisure class gained in prominence. It acted as the ultimate arbiter of status and as the hegemonic group that embodied the consumerist ideology of unending personal consumption, leisure, and hedonism. Then, in October 1929 with the collapse of the stock market and the ensuing Depression the instability and contradictions of capitalism manifested themselves on a global scale. Veblen's reiterated point about the predatory relationship of business to production took on especial force as the most efficient factories in the world lay idle and silent because the much-vaunted financial credit system had failed.

Further, with the demise of Social Darwinism in the first decade of the century and the decline of its associated literary Naturalism there was no longer any intellectual system and set of categories (other than Marxism) which American writers could employ to describe and comment upon contemporary social life. Veblen's project of theoretising economic behaviour and relations as articulated through his books filled that gap. Native in origin, it provided an oppositional stance, a conceptual framework, a set of structural dichotomies, and a vocabulary current in radical circles, all of which shaped how writers of critical social fiction perceived the life around them and how they represented that life in their fictive constructions of American society. Veblen had reshaped the critical discourse of American social life and no participant in that discourse, such as Sinclair Lewis, Theodore Dreiser, Willa Cather, F. Scott Fitzgerald, and John Dos Passos, could fail, either knowingly or unknowingly, to be affected.

Like Veblen from Minnesota in the rural Midwest, Sinclair Lewis adopted a critical distance towards the urban business class he encountered and wrote about its rituals and status system with sardonic humour. He once joined the Socialist Party and spent some time at Upton Sinclair's cooperative experiment at Helicon Hall. He had considerable sympathy, therefore, with radical critiques of American society, and Veblen has an undeniable presence in his

work. In his 1920 bestseller, *Main Street*, the satire of the quintes-
sential small town, Gopher Prairie, is directed against the middle
class which is portrayed as Puritan and provincial, philistine and
materialist. The story charts the outsider Carol Kennicott's education
in the mores of the town, her initial rebellion against them, and her
final acquiescence. As part of his characterisation of Carol as a non-
conformist, Lewis shows her reading Veblen, and the only radical in
the town, Bjornstam, uses the term 'leisure class' and has Veblen on
his bookshelves. Veblen is thus utilised in the novel as a marker for
an independent, oppositional stance.

Further than that, Lewis's critical thrust against the complacency
and self-importance of the small-town businessmen he sketches is
informed by Veblen's dichotomy of interests between the town and
the country first laid out in his farm labour articles (e.g. the long
note appended at the end of *Imperial Germany and the Industrial
Revolution*). This dichotomy would be echoed a little later in the
chapter, 'The Country Town' in *Absentee Ownership*. Veblen identifies
in the small town the roots of the capitalist attitude and sees at work
the 'predatory' and 'prehensile' spirit of business, which does not
produce but which is quick to discern a profit and greedy to grasp it.
In Lewis's novel the town, we are told, lives on the farmers and its
inhabitants are 'parasites', for the businessmen there do not produce
but act as middlemen, cloaking their exploitation of the rural
producers by a hypocritical assertion of 'service'. As Carol remarks,
'We townies are parasites.' The town is founded on exploitative com-
mercialism, and both its social sterility and its physical ugliness
proclaim the dispiriting triumph of business values.[6]

In their 1920s study of Muncie, Indiana, *Middletown,* the Lynds
observed that: 'Never was there more pressure in the business world
for solidarity, conformity, and wide personal acquaintance than
exists today'; and 'Standardized pursuits are the rule; with little in
their environment to stimulate originality and competitive social
life to discourage it, being "different" is rare even among the
young.'[7] And in his next novel, *Babbitt* (1922), Lewis keenly satirises
the relentless pressure for conformity and the tedious standardisation of business life that characterise the middle-sized town of
Zenith, which is meant to stand for middle-sized American towns
everywhere. There is no real plot, the only unifying thread being
provided by George F. Babbitt's progression, through a series of
dramatised episodes, from acceptance to rebellion to compromise.
The documentary accuracy of Zenith is attested to by its similarity

with the real-life Muncie, Indiana. Both share such features of consumerism as advertising, the prevalence of electrical goods, and dominance of the claims of business over everything. Veblen's perspective again underlies this treatment, for as Lewis's biographer, Mark Schorer, suggests, *Babbitt* can be read as a dramatisation of the divorce between industry and business and of the loss of independence and individualism in an era of mass culture. He further suggests that Lewis's major contribution was to popularise certain leading ideas of Veblen regarding the leisure class and business enterprise.[8] Veblen, as we saw in the previous chapter, was among the first to point to the significance of consumer durables in the status system, and Lewis follows him in his characterisation of Babbitt who is shown immersed in the world of commodities. Advertising shapes his tastes and objects dominate his life, supplying him with reassurance and an identity. We are told:

> The large national advertisers fix the surface of his life, fix what he believed to be his individuality. These standard advertised wares – toothpastes, socks, tyres, cameras, instantaneous hot-water heaters – were his symbols and proofs of excellence; at first the signs, then the substitutes, for joy, passion and wisdom.[9]

His backyard was 'the neat yard of a successful business man of Zenith, that is, it was perfection, and made him also perfect'. His office water cooler and expensive ties confirm him in his sense of social superiority. Lewis, therefore, provides a poignant portrait of a man who has surrendered all sense of self-worth to a status system based on conspicuous consumption and invidious emulation.

Another novelist of the Midwest, Willa Cather is not usually associated with the wry iconoclast, but her *The Professor's House* (1925) is, I suggest, even if not informed by Veblen (none of her biographers mention him), still a fruitful text for analysis in terms of Veblenian dichotomies. The ideological tension in the novel is conventionally seen as operating between traditional ideals and modern materialist values,[10] but we can render it with greater specificity by recasting it in terms derived from Veblen. Moreover, it is a parallelism of Veblenian dichotomies which renders the *nouvelle* of the inserted narrative, 'Tom Outland's Story,' thematically apposite to the *roman*, or narrative centred on Professor Godfrey St Peter which frames it.

In his chapter 'The Conservation of Archaic Traits' in *The Theory of the Leisure Class*, Veblen, as we have seen, sets out a Darwinian model of historical development in which a 'peaceable' phase gives way to a 'predatory' one. The first human societies, he proposes, were peaceful and sedentary and generated character traits, certain of which survive into the modern period – 'that instinct of race solidarity which we call conscience, including the sense of truthfulness and equity, and the instinct of workmanship in its native, non-invidious expression'. These societies, however, gave way to nomadic groups that established 'the predatory culture, the regime of status, and the growth of pecuniary emulation'. The predatory barbarian supplanted the peaceable savage. The effect of this was to change the character of the struggle for existence from a 'struggle of the group against a non-human environment to a struggle against a human envirnoment'. And it is the leisure-class scheme of life which preserves the predatory traits.[11]

In 1915 Willa Cather had visited the Mesa Verde in Colorado National Park and been impressed with the 'Cliff Palace', the remains of an extensive ancient native American town discovered by a cowboy, Richard Wetherill, in the cliffs there. This encounter became the source for 'Tom Outland's Story' which tells of the accidental discovery by two cowboys of a remote mesa town and their response to it. The mesa civilisation they discovered was obviously of the sedentary, peaceable type, for they had 'developed considerably the arts of peace,' we are told, and with their achieved harmony of use and beauty, their good design, they manifested, in Veblen's phrase, 'the instinct of workmanship'. The mesa people mysteriously disappeared a long time in the past, presumably wiped out by a nomadic horde that established the predatory culture.

Tom Outland is an idealised figure, who carries the archaic traits of the peaceable phase; he is an embodiment of 'the instinct of workmanship', of productive activity, intellectual as well as practical, carried out for motives other than financial ones. His wide-ranging, disinterested curiosity is stressed; as an engineer he invents a revolutionary engine; he is a figure of complete independence and moral integrity; he volunteers to fight in First World War (in which he is killed) because of his 'race solidarity'; and it is emphasised that his interest in the mesa cliff-dwellers has nothing to do with personal profit. 'There never was a question of money with me where the mesa and its people were concerned,' he tells his uncomprehending friend, Blake.[12] His lack of motives of pecuniary emulation and of engagement in the unproductive activities of the leisure class, together with his success as a scientist in dealing with the non-human environment, mean he does not possess the traits of the predatory culture and therefore is unfitted (in the Darwinian sense) to struggle against the human environment of the Washington bureaucracy which he vainly tries to interest in his remarkable find.

The extinction of a culture based on 'the instinct of workmanship' is paralleled in the *roman* set in the 1920s and centred on the Professor by the predominance of leisure-class pecuniary values. Louie Marsellus represents business enterprise. His pretentious Norwegian manor house on the lake shore and his wife's conspicuous consumption, what the Professor refers to as 'an orgy of acquisition', demonstrate the triumph of pecuniary emulation over the values of production. Louie takes Outland's engine and turns it into profit; he takes Outland's name and attaches it to a status symbol, the lakeside house. The 'story' then functions as a fable for the larger narrative, and *The Professor's House* thus dramatises a two-fold process of appropriation and displacement in which non-pecuniary motives and achievements (Outland's engine and the mesa civilisation) are first taken over and then absorbed by an ideological system whose fundamental premise is the primacy of acquisitive self-interest and whose symbols of the honorific owe nothing either to the scientific or to the aesthetic but to the predatory traits preserved by the leisure-class scheme of life.

Bringing Veblen to bear also throws new light on the enigmatic dead woman discovered in the mesa city. Hers is the only body to be found and the naming of her as 'Mother Eve' immediately appropriates her into the Judaeo-Christian moral framework as well as into its narrative of human origins – an Edenic state of innocence corrupted by disobedience, betrayal, and punishment. So, when Tom asks the priest for an explanation of the woman being there, he is told:

> Perhaps when the tribe went down to the summer camp, our lady was sick and would not go. Perhaps her husband thought it worth while to return unannounced from the farms some night, and found her in improper company.[13]

In other words, he is given a narrative which places the woman in a patriarchal, monogamous society, in which sexual transgressions, particularly by women, would be punished by death. Yet, there is no evidence to support the priest's 'reading' and the function of it in the novel I would suggest is to highlight the dangers of attributing to culturally specific frameworks, particularly our own, mythic qualities of immutability and universality. This is very much a Veblenian perspective, for what his studies of Lewis H. Morgan and others had demonstrated was that institutions change through time. In addition, in Veblen's view such peaceable early societies were matrilineal, not patrilineal, worshipped fertility goddesses, and lived communally with no sense of private property. The mystery woman was labelled an 'adulteress' because a patriarchal, mysogynistic discourse could find no other way of 'framing' her. She was more likely to have been killed by the predatory horde that wiped out her people, or, alternatively, have been a sacrifice to some deity in order to ameliorate the disaster – drought, for instance – that was bringing the mesa civilisation to an end. But these other 'readings' cannot be heard because only the dominant discourse is given a voice. Cather's novel is more subtle and profound than it is usually given credit for.

Theodore Dreiser's *An American Tragedy* of the same year contains a heavily detailed rendition of a medium-sized industrial town, Lycurgus, and it is into this social and ideological context that the protagonist, Clyde Griffiths, is projected. In his early adolescence Clyde is keen to achieve success by means of the Protestant virtues: 'He would work and save his money and be somebody.' However, from the very beginning his adoption of that programme is undercut both by his motivation and by the content with which his milieu endows the notion of success. His milieu is dominated by consumerism and the acquisition of the requisite status symbols. At the drug store where he works as a soda jerk he observes that it requires an expensive style of dress to win girls:

> Very often one or another of these young beauties was accompanied by some male in evening suit, dress shirt, high hat, bow tie, white kid gloves and patent leather shoes. ... No good-looking girl, as it then appeared to him, would have anything to do with him if he did not possess this standard of equipment.

His social ambition is thus fuelled initially by sexual desire and his conception of advancement is coloured by consumption and display. He moves to work as a bell-hop at the Green-Davidson Hotel in Kansas City where his Protestant belief in work is subverted by the generous tips he receives for doing very little. The money he earns he does not give to his needy family but spends on smart clothes for himself or his girlfriend. The hotel also acquaints him with a hedonistic, leisure-dominated lifestyle:

> The talk and the palaver that went on in the lobby and the grill … were sufficient to convince any inexperienced and none-too-discerning mind that the chief business of life for anyone with a little money or social position was to attend a theatre, a ball-game in season, or to dance, motor, entertain friends at dinner, or to travel to New York, Europe, Chicago, California.

This is a lifestyle Clyde and the other bell-hops seek to imitate and which he meets again in Lycurgus, to which he moves when his uncle gives him a job in his factory.[14]

The town, we are told, has a 'fast set' led by the Cranstons and Finchleys who are 'given to wearing the smartest clothes,' and 'to the latest novelties in cars and entertainments', and whose characteristic pursuits are dancing, cabareting, parties, car-rides and watersports. In Dreiser's representative social image they thus exemplify Veblen's 'substantial canons of the leisure-class scheme of life', namely 'a conspicuous waste of time and substance and a withdrawal from the industrial process'. Since too, according to Veblen, the leisure class's 'example and precept carries the force of a prescription for all classes below it', its local embodiment in Lycurgus provides Clyde with a model of behaviour which is both honorific and pleasurable and to which he aspires.[15] He also, rather like Jay Gatsby, suffers a conflation of social and sexual desire in the figure of a leisure-class female, by becoming attracted to one the 'fast set', Sondra Finchley.

However, despite being the nephew of the factory owner, Samuel Griffiths, and therefore tantalisingly close to wealth, Clyde is poor and a worker and is expected to abide by a Protestant code of labour and denial. Yet, Clyde is a product of that youth subculture of consumerism represented in records, dancing, movies, parties, joy-rides in cars, pleasure parks and fashionable clothes which first flowered in the 1920s.[16] He has lost the discipline for the long, gruelling climb through the factory hierarchy offered by his uncle, and comes to rely on a male version of the Cinderella myth in which Sondra, cast as a Princess Charming, will spirit him by marriage into the ranks of the rich. Yet, for this to occur he must dispose of his pregnant working-class girlfriend, whom he drowns (or at least allows to drown) in a lake. Dreiser emphasises the contrast between the productive work of the industrial process that Clyde is tied to and the consumer hedonism of the town's leisure class, and he demonstrates with deterministic inevitablity that caught between these contradictory values Clyde can only suffer a peculiarly *American* tragedy.

It was the rise of the American leisure class and its huge cultural and political influence that Howells saw as 'the supreme opportunity of the American novelist'. If two writers of the mid-1920s, Cather and Dreiser, partially seized that opportunity, a third was to seize it and make it wholly his own, depicting the corrosive effect of the elite's pecuniary canons upon both individual and social values. Howells expanded on his point thus:

> It is far the most dramatic social fact of our time, and if some man of creative imagination were to seize upon it he would find in it the material of that great American novel which after so much travail has not yet seen the light. It is, above all our other facts, synthetic; it sums up and includes in itself the whole American story: the relentless will, the tireless force, the vague ideal, the inexorable destiny, the often bewildered acquiescence.[17]

Howells also pointed to the prerequisite of distance for any chronicler of the leisure class: 'The observer must have some favorable position on the outside and must regard it neither "with a foolish face of praise" nor with satiric scorn.' F. Scott Fitzgerald was to be the 'man of creative imagination' who enjoyed both an entrée to the rich and yet an outsider's perspective, and who was to make the leisure class his own literary territory.

F. Scott Fitzgerald

In 'The Diamond as Big as the Ritz' (1922) he created an imaginary fable about the baronial arrogance and ruthlessness of the very wealthy, and one of the opening paragraphs of his short story 'The Rich Boy' provides the template for most of his fiction:

> Let me tell you about the very rich. They are different from you and me. They possess and enjoy early and it does something to them, makes them soft where we are hard, and cynical where we are trustful in a way that unless you were born rich, it is difficult to understand.[18]

Here, concisely expressed and in close conjunction are some of those elements that contribute to his novels' fullness and seriousness of effect: the knowing tone of authoritative experience; the distanced assessment; the attempt at definition of this social group; and, most important of all, his adopted stance of intermediary, interpreting one section of American society – the leisure class – to another section – the middle class. This, of course, is very much the stance of Nick Carraway, the narrator, in *The Great Gatsby* (1925), but before that major novel Fitzgerald published two others, relatively minor, which dealt also with the phenomenon of the leisure class. In *This Side of Paradise* (1920) the protagonist, Amory Blaine, expresses the sensuous and prestigious appeal of the leisure class. 'I think of Princeton', he says, 'as being lazy and good-looking and aristocratic', and he reverses traditional moral values by exclaiming his contempt for the poor and asserting that 'it's essentially cleaner to be corrupt and rich than it is to be innocent and poor.' He gives up his job writing copy for an advertising agency (Fitzgerald's own occupation at the time) and in his new state of social desperation expounds socialism to a rich man who belongs to 'the class I belonged to until recently; those who by inheritance or industry or brains or dishonesty have become the moneyed class'.[19]

His second novel, *The Beautiful and the Damned* (1922) neatly encapsulates the ambivalence the middle class felt towards the leisure class (an ambivalence laid out in greater detail in Chapter Five). It presents the rich as a bewitching combination of glamour and corruption, as, enviably, the physically blessed on earth, and, comfortingly, the morally degenerate who will suffer in the hereafter. The protagonist, Anthony Patch, is a thoroughgoing member of the leisure class, in line for an inheritance from his grand-father of $75 million, generated from speculation on Wall Street. He

> drew as much consciousness of social security from being the grandson of Adam J. Patch as he would have had from tracing his line over the sea to the crusaders. This is inevitable; Virginians and Bostonians to the contrary notwithstanding, an aristocracy founded sheerly on money postulates wealth in the particular.

As an expression of this aristocratic consciousness engendered by inherited wealth, Anthony prefers to live off his bonds and make a desultory attempt at writing a history of the Renaissance popes rather than take on a job of work. When his funds are exhausted and he is forced to try several jobs, he finds that his nature is too indolent to be capable of sustained effort and they are abruptly terminated. His final words: 'It was a hard fight, but I didn't give up and I came through', express his pride, as he sails for Europe, a rich man once more, in remaining loyal to the values and behaviour of the leisure class during the long legal battle over Adam Patch's fortune.[20]

These first two novels had relied on the traditional narrative strategy of an external, omniscient narrator to render the action but in *The Great Gatsby* Fitzgerald adopted the most effective and economical technique for conveying the tension in his own perspective on the wealthy – a narrator-participant who would evoke both the sensuous attraction of a gilded life as well as bring a moral consciousness to bear on the waste and corruption involved. Nick Carraway, a young man like Fitzgerald from the Midwest, brings an openness as well as a sense of decency to bear on his story of his summer of 1922 on Long Island when he encounters his distant leisure class relatives, Tom and Daisy Buchanan, and a self-made millionaire, Jay Gatsby. Tom was born rich and his palatial home, polo ponies, wedding gift to Daisy of a $350,000 pearl necklace, and conspicuous leisure all attest to his established position in the leisure class. Gatsby with his mansion and automobiles and lavish parties and dubious wealth (to echo Amory Blaine, he is 'corrupt and rich' and so 'cleaner') partakes of both the glamour and corruption of the leisure class of the 1920s when bootlegging and speculating, not industry and thrift, were the most effective ways to wealth. The tone of distaste for Gatsby would have been all the more forceful had Fitzgerald entitled it 'Trimalchio' as he subsequently wished he had.[21] The extended comparison of Gatsby with the vulgar, upstart emperor of Petronious's *Satyricon* would have considerably added to the disapproval extended to this glamorous criminal. As the novel stands with only the residual reference,[22] Carraway easily disengages him from his sordid milieu and clothes him in the imagery of fairy tale as a knight in quest of the princess in the tower.

Gatsby's pursuit of Daisy Buchanan, who represents the powerful integration of both sexual possession and class advancement to a poor boy, is romanticised into a complex cultural symbol for the discrepancy between the great promise of America and its latter-day realisation in the lifestyle of the leisure class. Gatsby is redeemed in Carraway's eyes because in the midst of corruption he maintains 'an incorruptible dream'. For all his parties and his money are but a means to the consummation of his early romance with Daisy and that consummation can take place only when he has proved himself her social equal. Showing her his mansion and displaying his many shirts constitutes the ritual presentation of his credentials for membership of the leisure class, and hence for socially legitimate possession of her:

> He took out a pile of shirts and began throwing them, one by one, before us, shirts of sheer linen and thick silk and fine flannel, which lost their folds as they fell and covered the table in many coloured disarray. ... Suddenly, with a strained sound, Daisy bent her head into the shirts and began to cry stormily.

Daisy's oddly emotional response to this display of conspicuous consumption betrays her recognition that Gatsby has overcome the social barriers that separated them and is now directly asking for her favour. That Gatsby's dedication is misplaced is made evident in the remainder of the novel, and Carraway's damning verdict on the Buchanans is that they are 'careless people'. One reason for Gatsby's emotional misplacement is his lack of awareness that, although he has accumulated the material capital necessary to claim access to the leisure class, he has not had the leisure (despite his year in Oxford) to accumulate the cultural capital, namely the learning, the taste (*vide* his pink suit), the manners, to gain full acceptance.[23]

The delineation of the nature of the 'difference' between the very rich and the rest of us, begun with Anthony J. Patch and continued with the Buchanans, was developed at greater length and with greater surety and subtlety in the picture of the 'feudal' Warrens contained in *Tender is the Night*, the novel Fitzgerald began in 1926 but could not complete until 1934. And it was Veblen who supplied the perspective and vocabulary of so much of the book. The background to the action of the novel, Fitzgerald wrote in 1932, was to be 'one in which the leisure class is at their truly most brilliant and glamorous'.[24] This is the effect aimed for in the stages of the novel that are presented through the eyes of Rosemary Hoyt. The Divers, to her, are exemplars of the civilised life, and externally, Fitzgerald assures us, they represented the 'exact furthermost evolution of a class'. Rosemary is imbued with the middle-class values of work and thrift, but Nicole Diver(formerly Nicole Warren) is the romantic epitome of the leisure-class woman. As such, her characteristic activity is conspicuous consumption:

Nicole bought from a great list that ran two pages, and bought the things in the windows besides. ... She bought coloured beads, folding beach cushions, artificial flowers, honey, and a guest bed, bags, scarfs [sic], love birds, miniatures for a doll's house ... a dozen bathing suits, a rubber alligator, a travelling chess set of gold and ivory, big linen handkerchiefs for Abe, two chamois leather jackets of kingfisher blue and burning bush from Hermes ... [25]

Dick Diver, the psychiatrist protagonist Fitzgerald laid down in his 1932 outline for the novel, was to be 'a natural idealist, a spoiled priest, giving in for various reasons to the ideas of the *haute bourgeoisie*, and in his rise to the top of the social world losing his idealism, his talent and turning to drink and dissipation'.[26] He is taken up by the Warrens as a doctor for the mentally sick Nicole, adapts to the lifestyle of leisure and hedonism, and loses, in Veblen's phrase, his 'instinct of workmanship', his pursuit of intellectual goals for non-financial motives. In the final stages of the novel Nicole transfers her affection to Tommy Barban, a fully fledged member of the leisure class, his name deliberately suggesting 'barbarian', and his occupation as a mercenary of waging war being in Veblen's words 'chief among the honourable employments in any feudal community'.[27]

John Dos Passos

Whilst *The Theory of the Leisure Class* certainly informed Fitzgerald's representation of the extremely wealthy in *The Great Gatsby* and *Tender is the Night*, to his contemporary John Dos Passos it was not nearly so important as other works in Veblen's *oeuvre,* which contain his dichotomy between business and production and emphasise the polarisation of American society. Dos Passos was closely associated with the *New Republic* group of intellectuals, like Francis Hackett, who championed Veblen; he read Dorfman's 1934 biography and wrote to Edmund Wilson on 24 September 1934 that he had been reading 'a good deal of' Veblen, and continued, 'I shouldn't wonder if he were the only American economist whose work has any lasting value', citing *The Vested Interests*, *The Nature of Peace*, and *Business Enterprise*, and adding 'I think *The Leisure Class* is more or less a side issue'.[28] He drew on the Dorfman study and one other source for a biographical sketch which he published in 1935 in *Esquire*, at the same time as he was writing the third volume of his *U.S.A.* trilogy, *The Big Money* (1936).

Veblen's best-known work does indeed make an appearance in both the second (*Nineteen Nineteen*) and third volumes of the 1938 trilogy in scenes evoking its status as an influential book of the time. In the former, in the 'Daughter' narrative, we are told that a Columbia sociology student, Edwin Vinal, was 'quoting all the time from a man named Veblen' to 'Daughter' at their first meeting, and that the next day he brings her a copy of *The Theory of the Leisure Class*. In *The Big Money* in the early stages of the Mary French narrative which details and dramatises radical involvement in some of the key *causes célèbres* of the American Left we are told that her mother wants the family to conform to the leisure-class life that her inherited wealth provides and demands: 'Mrs French was feeling fine and talking about how Mary ought to make her debut next Fall. "After all you owe it to your parents to keep up your position, dear."' Mary, however, is increasingly alienated from the bourgeois values she sees around her and Veblen is identified as one of the intellectual influences behind this development : 'Talk like that made [her] feel sick in the pit of her stomach. When they got back to the hotel she said she felt tired and went to her room and lay on the bed and read *The Theory of the Leisure Class*.' [29]

In the first volume of *U.S.A., The Forty-Second Parallel*, Dos Passos, as part of his disruption of the traditional novel form, had introduced three devices – the Newsreel, the Camera Eye, and the biographical portrait, a series documenting real people, and 'interlarded in the pauses in the narrative because their lives seem to embody so well the quality of the soil in which Americans of these generations grew'.[30] In *The Big Money* the first two portraits are of Frederick Taylor and Henry Ford. Taylor founded scientific management and 'Taylorism', the improvement of efficiency by breaking down manufacturing skills into simple, repetitive tasks. It was Ford who put it into practice in his automobile factories, and so between them they revolutionised industrial production. Then, some seventy pages into the novel, we come to the portrait of Veblen which appeared in *Esquire* and which is the longest biography in the trilogy. Entitled 'The Bitter Drink' in an allusion to Socrates it focuses on Veblen's later works, the dichotomies highlighted therein, and the vision of an America polarised between 'the vested interests' and 'the underlying population', dichotomies and polarisations which thoroughly inform the conception of society in *The Big Money* and partly account for the shift of tone from the previous volumes.

Through *The Theory of Business Enterprise, The Instinct of Workmanship*, and *The Vested Interests and the Common Man*, Veblen, Dos Passos says:

> established a new diagram of society dominated by monopoly capital
> etched in irony
> the sabotage of production by business
> the sabotage of life by blind need for money profits. (p. 812)

As for Veblen's radical hope that the worker-technicians would take over production and run it for use and not profit, 'War cut across all that: under the cover of the bunting of Woodrow Wilson's phrases the monopolies cracked down. American democracy was crushed.' This, the destruction of democracy by monopoly capital, constitutes the politico-economic theme of *U.S.A.*, orchestrated through all the different formal elements of 'Newsreel', 'Camera Eye', biographical portrait and fictional narrative.

Dominating the early part of *The Big Money* is the narrative of Charley Anderson, a character Dos Passos strongly associates with the world of production. 'The pilot's nothin' without his mechanic, the promoter's nothin' without production', Charley says. 'You and me, Bill, we're in production'(p. 905). Veblen's thematically central portrait is inserted into Charley's narrative just as he begins to illustrate the recurrent dichotomoy in Veblen's social analysis between industry and business, between production (the technological institutions for making the goods) and finance (the pecuniary institutions for making the profits). Anderson begins to play the stock market, becomes an owner, loses the instinct of workmanship and ceases to be a technician on the workers' side. Developing 'a kind of feel for the big money' (p. 1021), he becomes instead a financier immersed in the pecuniary culture with its invidious distinction, competitiveness, and property values.

In addition, there are two other aspects to Veblen's shaping presence in *The Big Money*. Firstly, he is presented as a figure of lonely integrity, standing out against the pressures of intellectual conformity and subservience to the business class, while others like Dick Savage succumb to 'the big money' or like Woodrow Wilson do the dirty work of the monopolies. Secondly, the Sacco and

Vanzetti case of 1927 was crucially important to Dos Passos as his pamphlet *Facing the Chair* makes plain. It became a central experiential source for his sense of class division and the loss of basic rights in modern America. Veblen, however, was an intellectual source. In *The Vested Interests* , as we have noted, he taught that the population 'falls into two main classes: those who own wealth invested in large holdings, and who thereby control the conditions of life for the rest; and those who do not own wealth in sufficiently large holdings, and whose conditions of life are therefore controlled by these others'.[31] It is this sense of the once egalitarian republic having been polarised into the haves and have-nots, into those who control and those who are the victims of control, which underlies Dos Passos' climactic outburst in 'Camera Eye (50)':

all right we are two nations
America our nation has been beaten by strangers who have bought the laws and fenced off the meadows and cut down the woods for pulp and turned our pleasant cities into slums and sweated the wealth out of our people. (p. 1105)

Veblen, then, once an economics instructor in the sweatshop and entrepôt of late nineteenth-century Chicago, began a project of theorising the economic and social behaviour around him, and over the next thirty years of an unsettled academic life wrote a number of works and developed a series of categories: 'the leisure class', 'the vested interests', 'the instinct of workmanship'; and a series of dichotomies: 'production and finance', 'the vested interests and the working man', which became profoundly influential. His ideas affected not only the people in his field, but also major practitioners of fiction in America. Either directly from his works or via the airing his views gained in journals, like *The Dial* or *The New Republic*, such writers as Sinclair Lewis, Theodore Dreiser, Willa Cather, F. Scott Fitzgerald, and John Dos Passos gained a new sense of the tensions operating in American social life. Veblen, therefore, deserves to be considered alongside Freud and Bergson as a significant extra-literary influence upon American fiction between the wars.

Conclusion

Veblen was the great demystifier.

Warren J. Samuels[1]

This study began with setting Veblen in the social and intellectual context of the late nineteenth century in general. Classical economics as derived from Adam Smith and John Stuart Mill was still the orthodoxy, to which resort was made for explanations of the processes of the American economy. Darwin, however, was having a huge influence, as well as Spencer, and the evolutionary point of view was gaining in ascendancy. Critiques of American capitalism were also providing radical analyses of its operations and failures. Marx, Henry George, and Edward Bellamy were important figures in the shaping of Veblen's anti-conservative stance. Important, too, in informing Veblen's perspective were the emerging fields of ethnology associated with Lewis H. Morgan and of anthropology associated with Franz Boas. The immediate milieu of Chicago, in which Veblen lived and worked for fourteen years, was also a shaping influence, bringing him face to face with an industrial city, rapid social change, and the ostentatious display of the city's multimillionaires. Through the university he also came into contact with such materialist scientists as Jacques Loeb and with Franz Boas himself.

Then, it surveyed Veblen's major works in his early phase from the anthropological essays, *The Theory of the Leisure Class*, the essays on classical economics and its shortcomings, *The Theory of Business Enterprise*, *The Higher Learning in America*, and *The Instinct of Workmanship*. In this phase he signalled his break with economic orthodoxy and established his characterstic iconoclasm, his anthropological perspective, and his major formulations – 'conspicuous consumption,' 'pecuniary culture,' 'status emulation,' 'the instinct of workmanship,' and the effect of the resort to credit by corporations.

In the next chapter the discussion turned to the Great War and the Bolshevik Revolution and their aftermath in America with the 'Red Scare', the national strikes, rapid inflation, the depression of 1920–21, and the election of the Harding pro-business administration. We then set Veblen's later phase of publications against this context, following through the articles and editorials in *The Dial*, *The Vested Interests*, *The Engineers and the Price System* with its revolutionary proposal of a soviet of technicians, and, finally, his project's culmination, *Absentee Ownership* with its comprehensive sweep. In this phase Veblen took on a more critical, *engagé* tone, dissecting American capitalism and its mechanisms for survival and exploitation and tentatively pointing to possibilities for change. He is best known for his early analysis of the leisure class, but he deserves to be equally well known for this latter phase which provides a post-Marxian critique of industrial capitalism and its internal tensions. In this phase, *The Engineers and the Price System* has tended to attract critical commentary (partly because it is clearly written and the 'soviet of technicians' is an easy target), while the more penetrating and far-ranging *Absentee Ownership* has tended to be relatively neglected.

Altogether his *oeuvre* is an extraordinary body of work and this study has tried to set it in the context of modern American economic, social and cultural development and to demonstrate the ways in which it provides a cogent, native critical commentary upon that development. Viewed negatively as a whole it may seem a highly repetitious collection of writings, the same points being made again and again from piece to piece and even within the same piece, and there is no doubt that Veblen is vulnerable to this criticism. Yet, a more positive light is cast on the Veblen corpus if we see it as being loosely symphonic in form with early motifs being picked up later and expanded upon, while major earlier themes are faded into the supporting background. So, the instinct of workmanship, first discussed in his article of 1898, is mentioned in *The Theory of the Leisure Class* and then later given book-length treatment in *The Instinct of Workmanship*; the leisure class and its canon of conspicuous consumption is faintly echoed in *The Vested Interests* in a reference to the 'kept classes' and their 'indefinitely expansible consumption of superfluities'; the last chapter of *The Theory of the Leisure Class* refers to the impact of leisure-class values on higher education and this becomes the subject of *The Higher Learning in America*; the role of the engineers in running industry is mentioned in *The Vested Interests* and then gains extended attention in *The Engineers and the Price System*; the growing use of credit by business and the inception of the holding company leading to overcapitalisation are subjects first raised in *The Theory of Business Enterprise* and then returned to in greater depth in *Absentee Ownership*; the 'new order' and 'absentee

ownership' are categories introduced into the essays that made up
The Vested Interests and then given more expansive delineation and
analysis again in *Absentee Ownership*.

We have also surveyed his influence on other writers both within
the social sciences and in fiction, as exemplified in the inter-war
novels of Sinclair Lewis, F. Scott Fitzgerald, Willa Cather, and John
Dos Passos. We have also taken account of the highs and lows which
his reputation has been through over the decades. In addition, we
have looked at the emergence of consumerism in the United States
and the usefulness of Veblen for understanding that phenomenon.

A consideration of the long-running debate that has centred on
Veblen leads us inevitably to the question of his status within
American cultural history. How central or marginal a figure is he?
This is not easy to answer in any definitive way, for any assessment
is inevitably coloured by one's own partisan predilections, and
because there never was and still is no broad agreement on Veblen's
significance. In 1973 Joseph Dorfman could write: 'As to the merits
of his work, opinions differ more widely and more fervently than on
any other writer of equal prominence.'[2] In 1992 Rick Tilman would
reiterate the point: 'no consensus now exists on the value or even
the meaning of Veblen's work.'[3] For some readers, particularly in
orthodox economics, his approach is so wrong-headed and his
analyses so marred by deficiencies as to be worthless. For others, he
is 'arguably the most original and penetrating economist and social
critic that the United States has produced'.[4] For even those
favourable to his work, however, there are aspects which are regret-
table. Common criticisms of his work have been:

- his convoluted language;
- his ambiguous use of 'instinct';
- a lack of detailed empirical evidence;
- a failure to influence any policy or practical measure, in the
  way, say, that Berle and Means brought about the setting up
  of the Securities and Exchange Commission;[5]
- a Rousseauistic view of primitive humankind in the peaceable
  phase of savagery;
- a failure, from a Marxist point of view, to recognise the class
  structure of modern America and the political potential of the
  American working class;
- dichotomies that are too simplistic and rigid;

- an overestimation of the impact of factory production in changing the mindset of industrial workers and bringing about the erosion of archaic habits of thought, such as religion and a respect for property rights;
- a misplaced faith in the revolutionary potential of engineers and technocrats;
- a seeming reduction of such cultural aspects as architecture and fine art to little more than ostentatious display on the part of the leisure class;
- and finally, a utopian cast to his thought.

Many of these criticisms are justified, though the last one is not, as already pointed out earlier. In addition, there are aspects of America to which he pays little or no attention: the growth of bureaucracy, the role of the Federal Government in the economy, the changed role of women in the twentieth century, to name only three.

Yet, despite these shortcomings, his contribution was huge and can be summed up as follows:

- he demonstrated that economic activities must be treated holistically as part of a complete social system from which they derive their aims and values;
- he led the attack on neo-classical economics, whose obsolescence was acknowledged by Berle and Means in 1932, and inspired a new school of heterodox economics, institutionalism;
- he pointed to the business corporation as a key development in finance capitalism, a perception again echoed and expanded upon in 1932 by Berle and Means who concluded that the corporation had become 'the dominant institution of the modern world';
- he was the first to point to the separation of ownership and control, the implications of which were developed later by Berle and Means, and the consequent rise of a new class of salaried managers and technicians;[6]
- he provided early insight into business cycles;
- he paid attention to monopolistic or imperfect competition before other economists;
- his notions of 'cultural lag' and 'the penalty of taking the lead' helped explain Germany's rapid industrialisation and overtaking of Great Britain;

- his dichotomy between business and production enabled an understanding of why factories rarely worked at full capacity;
- although he was not the first to elaborate on the role of conspicuous consumption, for John Rae writing before 1834 had treated this, his focus on it and status emulation enjoyed widespread influence and provided an explanation of the continuing hegemony of the leisure class and of the basis of high mass consumerism;[7]
- he identified the persistent presence of archaic residues in modern American life;
- and, finally, his work provided literary intellectuals with a conceptual framework by which to understand what had gone wrong with the once revolutionary and democratic republic.

One must draw the conclusion after such a survey of his work and its impact that his place in cultural history is assured, that anybody who cares to understand modern America must become acquainted with its foremost analyst and critic – Thorstein Veblen.

Of course, since he died, and in particular since 1945 the shape of the United States economy, as well as of social institutions, has changed a great deal. Veblen could not have foreseen, any more than neo-classical economists, the huge role played in the economy by the American state as a purchaser of armaments during the Cold War. Nor could he have anticipated the extent of the expansion by American corporations into developing countries with the consequent export of a great deal of manufacturing. In addition, there is the huge expansion of the white-collar middle class and the service industries. The mass media, too, film, television, magazines, the Internet, have become significant shapers of 'habits of thought,' and have become constituents of postmodernity. Yet, despite all these contrasts with his America of the first two decades of the twentieth century, I hope, too, that this study has helped ensure that his relevance as a social commentator lives on into the twenty-first century.

John P. Diggins writing in 1998 was able to remark: 'The economic situation that America faces today is right out of Veblen. The making of money has overtaken the making of goods, and the price of goods is more valuable than the goods themselves.'[8] Major corporations have given up manufacturing and conceive themselves entirely as marketing operations. As a Nike CEO has put it: 'For years we thought of ourselves as a product-oriented company, meaning we put all our emphasis on designing and manufacturing the product. We've come around to saying that Nike is a marketing-oriented company, and the product is our most important marketing tool.'[9] Hence, the multimillion sponsorship deals with such sports luminaries as Michael Jordan and Tiger Woods, as well as the sponsoring and branding of major sports events. Their brand-name, their logo, has become their major commodity, a sign, an identification that has great value in itself. In 1988 Philip Morris bought Kraft for $12.5 billion – six times what it was worth on paper. The price difference was the worth of the name 'Kraft'.[10] In Veblen's terms the brand-name is an intangible asset, which provides a marked advantage over competitors in the market-place, where, as today, it is not so much price competition which wages but status competition. As Naomi Klein points out, for today's youth market only certain names – Nike, Reebok, Gap, Benetton, Levis, McDonalds – carry status and there is intense status competition, or 'invidious emulation' within the youth culture.[11]

According to Robert H. Frank, the spirit of conspicuous consumption among the rich is still alive and well. He instances such excesses of consumption as $5,000 patio grills, Patek Phillippe watches for $44,500, $250,000 Lamborghinis, and $10 million mansions.[12] Nieman Marcus, the famous Dallas department store, offered in its 1996 Christmas catalogue: a dog house which was a model of St Peter's Basilica for $9,400; a children's Japanese-style playhouse, $10,000; and a customised house trailer, $195,000. *Robbs Reports*, also a catalogue for the upper class, for 1996 offered a Bentley, $324,000, a wooden bathtub, $34,000, and a walking stick for $795.[13] Frank proposes that a 'luxury fever' has overtaken America, citing an increase in luxury spending in the United States of 21 per cent between 1995 and 1996, while overall spending increased only 5 per cent in the same period.[14] As a further example of leisure-class consumption he cites that in mid-1997 Gulfstream Corporation reported back orders for 98 of its luxury jets, the main model costing more than $37 million. This conspicuous consumption has been fuelled by the huge increases, both relative and absolute, in the wealth of the élite. In 1997 *Forbes 400*, the list of the 400 richest people in America, included 170 billionaires, up from only 13 in 1982. Almost 5 million Americans had a net worth of $1 million in 1996, more than doubling the number just four years earlier. The CEOs of America's largest companies used to earn 35 times as much as the average worker in 1973; today they earn 200 times as much.[15]

However, the effect of such spending is not confined to the top 1 per cent or so but is felt throughout society, for, to recall Veblen, the leisure class's 'example and precept carries the force of prescription for all the classes below it', and so today, according to Frank: 'When the people at the top spend more, others just below them will inevitably spend more also, and so on all the way down the economic ladder.'[16] This spending is encouraged by a massive increase in advertising, reaching $196.5 billion in 1998 in the United States.[17] Thus, a wave of emulatory consumption is set in motion which has three main deleterious effects: greater indebtedness on the part of the lower classes; the neglect of inconspicuous consumption, such as spending more time exercising or being with family and friends; and a starving of funds for projects, such as better roads or hospitals, or cleaner air and water, directed to the benefit of the general public.[18]

There is a further disturbing implication of the effect of the leisure class. To reiterate some points from Chapter Two, it conditions the general notions of happiness and freedom, for under its regime happiness becomes defined as happiness *away from* production and freedom as freedom *from* work, not freedom *in* work. The huge popularity today of such opportunies for amassing wealth instantly and effortlessly as the National Lottery, the football pools, and 'Who Wants To Be A Millionaire?' testifies to the continuing prevalence of this leisure-class-induced life ideal. On both the personal and social levels there seems to be a widespread abandonment of any project to secure some degree of happiness and freedom in work, and the acceptance that the only hope is escape and a life dedicated to hedonistic consumption. Finally, the recruitment into the leisure class of people who have made their fortunes in business, film, popular music, or information technology lends a spurious meritocratic gloss to the institution, when in fact it is overwhelmingly based not on ability but on inherited wealth and privilege and the studious avoidance of even mild tax regimes.

In addition, the recent public disquiet at the significant discrepancies betweeen the prices of new cars in Britain and on the Continent demonstrates that the motor manufacturers still charge what the traffic will bear and through the franchised dealer network seek to limit competition in pursuit of the highest net gain. It is also evident that both in the United Kingdom and the United States we have political systems that are either reluctant or impotent to erect redistributive tax regimes which would channel money from the excessive private consumption noted by Frank into public works which would benefit all. We are still stuck, in Galbraith's memorable phrase, with 'private opulence and public squalor'.[19] These political systems are also impotent to curb corporate power, and in their failure to limit the environmental damage caused by the fossil-fuel burning industries, including transport, they continue to acquiesce in the subordination of human welfare to corporate profits. With a Republican President in the White House America once again has a very pro-business administration which will tailor policies (as we have seen in the reneging on the Kyoto Agreement and the opening up of the Alaska wildlife preserve to oil exploration) to protect corporate profitability. Veblen's view of the US Executive as little more than the civic arm of the corporations thus still, sadly, carries a great deal of validity. In addition, the alarming pervasiveness of Christian fundamentalism in the United States (with its naive belief in the literal truth of the account of Creation given in the Book of Genesis as instanced by the fact that six states – Illinois, Florida, Mississippi, Ohio, Oklahoma, and Tennessee – still make no reference to Darwinian evolution on their science syllabuses) suggests that Veblen's strictures on religion as an archaic legacy of primitive animistic beliefs still carry validity.

The pecuniary culture, the bureaucratisation of universities and influence of business there, status emulation, mass consumerism, salesmanship and advertising, organised religion, the division between the vested interests and the underlying population, absentee ownership are, of course, all still very much with us, and it is educative, as well as liberatory, to go back to the mordant comments of their first observer and analyst. Time and again on reading him and thinking of our contemporary situation, I have inwardly mumured *plus ça change* ... . Paulette Olson writes: 'As with the work of any great scholar Thorstein Veblen's nineteenth-century classic, *The Theory of the Leisure Class* continues to provide many valuable insights as we enter the twenty-first century.' William M. Dugger argues for the continuing relevance of Veblen's analysis to the globalisation of the planetary economy in the new century, as the pecuniary canons of conspicuous consumption and conspicuous leisure are universally propagated through American films and television shows which 'increasingly spread the consumption standards of the American upper class into the villages of the world'.[20]

Accordingly, this so-called 'marginal man' continues to be relevant and he will go on stimulating debate and comment for a long time to come. It is cheering to see that there is now an International Veblen Association, and that his family home has been restored.[21] His most famous volume continues to be in print in cheap paperback editions; the text of some of his articles and other books is freely available on the Internet, allowing a new generation of students world-wide access to his ideas in an unprecedented fashion; and there are dozens of websites pertaining to Veblen that can be visited. Finally, one, minor, index of Veblen's continued survival is that there is a Web domain called 'veblen.com'. What a wry smile the clear-eyed realist, the shrewd exposer of 'intangible assets', the revolutionary iconoclast would have had on his face at learning that!

References

Introduction

1. Albert Einstein, 'Remarks on Bertrand Russell's Theory of Knowledge' in P. A. Schupp (ed.), *The Philosophy of Bertrand Russell* (Evanston, 1944), quoted in Joseph Dorfman, 'New Light on Veblen' in Thorstein Veblen, *Essays, Reviews and Reports,* edited by Joseph Dorfman, p. 310; see W. T. Ganley, 'A Note on the Intellectual Connection between Albert Einstein and Thorstein Veblen,' *Journal of Economic Issues,* **31**, 1(1997)
2. Joseph Dorfman, *Thorstein Veblen and His America,* p. 492
3. Malcolm Cowley, *Books that Changed Our Mind* (New York, 1938), noted by John P. Diggins, *Thorstein Veblen: Theorist of the Leisure Class,* p. 213
4. Quoted by Dorfman, 'New Light on Veblen,' *Essays,* p. 309
5. 'Revolutionary iconoclast',*The International Socialist Review,* (1904), quoted by Dorfman, *Thorstein Veblen and his America,* p. 236; 'the founder of technocracy', quoted by Dorfman, *Thorstein Veblen and his America,* p. 510; 'the American Gramsci', Dorothy Ross, *The Origins of American Social Science,* p. 207; 'the most interesting social scientist the United States has produced', John Kenneth Galbraith, *A Life in Our Times,* p. 29; 'the best critic of America that America has produced', C.Wright Mills, 'Introduction', to Thorstein Veblen, *The Theory of the Leisure Class* (New York,1953) ; John P. Diggins, *Thorstein Veblen: Theorist of the Leisure Class,* p. xv

Chapter One

1. Charles H. Hession and Hyman Sardy, *Ascent to Affluence: A History of American Economic Development* (Boston, 1969), pp. 420, 424
2. Hession and Sardy, *Ascent to Affluence,* pp. 420, 424.
3. United States Department of Commerce, *Historical Statistics of the United States – Colonial Times to 1957* (Washington, 1960), pp. 74, 140
4. Simon Kuznets, 'The Proportion of Capital Formation to National Product', *American Economic Review,* **42** (1952), 507–26, Table I; Simon Kuznets, *Capital in the American Economy: Its Formation and Financing* (Princeton, 1961) pp. 408, 401
5. Hession and Sardy, p. 416; Kuznets, *Capital in the American Economy,* p. 64
6. *Historical Statistics,* p. 139
7. Stuart H. Holbrook, *The Age of the Moguls,* pp. 7, 301, 360
8. Hession and Sardy, p. 469
9. Edward and Eleanor Marx Aveling, *The Working-Class Movement in America* (2nd edition, London, 1891) pp. 64, 77

10. James Bryce, *The American Commonwealth*, II, (1888, revised edition, New York, 1911) pp. 81–2; commentator quoted in Gabriel Kolko, *Wealth and Power in America* (New York, 1962), p. 99

11. Robert H. Frank, *Luxury Fever: Why Money Fails to Satisfy in an Era of Success*, p. 14

12. Rick Tilman, *The Intellectual Legacy of Thorstein Veblen: Unresolved Issues*, p. 120

13. Adam Smith, *The Wealth of Nations* (London, 1910) p. 13

14. Hector St. John de Crevecoeur, *Letters from an American Farmer* (1782, London, 1912) p. 44

15. Smith, p. 398–400

16. John Stuart Mill, *Essays on Some Unsettled Questions of Political Economy* (1844, reprinted London, 1948), pp. 133, 139; Mill quoted in Dorfman, *Thorstein Veblen*, p. 73

17. Joseph Dorfman, 'Background of Veblen's Thought', in Carleton C. Qualey (ed.), *Thorstein Veblen: The Carleton College Veblen Seminar Essays* (New York, 1968), p. 116

18. Thorstein Veblen, 'Some Neglected Points in the Theory of Socialism', *Annals of American Academy of Political and Social Science*, II (1892), reprinted in *The Place of Science in Modern Civilisation* (New York, 1919) 387–408; see Arthur K. Davis's exaggeration of the similarities between Marxism and Veblen in such pieces as 'Thorstein Veblen Reconsidered', *Science and Society*, **26** (Winter 1957) 52–85, reprinted in Arthur K. Davis, *Farewell to Earth: The Collected Writings of Arthur K. Davis*, 2 vols (Adamant, Vermont, 1991) 190–219

19. Richard Hofstadter, *Social Darwinism in American Thought* (London and Oxford, 1945), pp. 91–2, 94

20. Edward Bellamy, *Looking Backwards: 2000–1887*, pp. 36, 131, 133

21. Bellamy, *Looking Backwards*, p. 37

22. Dorfman, *Thorstein Veblen and his America*, p. 70

23. Dorfman in Qualey, p. 123

24. Rick Tilman, 'The Utopian Vision of Edward Bellamy and Thorstein Veblen', *Journal of Economic Issues*, **XIX** (4), December 1985, 879–98, reprinted in Mark Blaug (ed.) *Thorstein Veblen (1857–1929)* (Aldershot, 1992) 241–60

25. Daniel Bell, 'Thorstein Veblen and the New Class,' *American Scholar*, **32**, Autumn 1963, 616–38

26. See Michael Spindler, 'The Origin of Species as Rhetoric', *Nineteenth-Century Prose*, **XIX,** 1 (Winter 1991/92) 26–34

27. Gertrude Himmelfarb, *Darwin and the Darwinian Revolution* (London, 1959) p. 219

28. Hofstadter, p. 6; Ronald N. Numbers, *Darwinism Comes to America* (London, 1998) pp. 30, 44

29. Charles Darwin, *The Descent of Man* (1871, Princeton, 1981) pp. 385–6, 355–6, 365; quoted by Hofstadter, p. 10

30. Quoted by Hofstadter, pp. 24, 27

31. William Graham Sumner, quoted by Hofstadter, p. 37, no source given

32. Quoted by Hofstadter, p. 31

33. Andrew Carnegie, from *The Gospel of Wealth* (1900) in Charles Darwin, *Darwin*, edited by Philip Appleman (second edition, New York, 1979), p. 399

34. Hofstadter, p. 175

35. Rick Tilman, *The Intellectual Legacy of Thorstein Veblen*, p. 29

36. Charles Darwin, *The Origin of Species* in *Darwin*, p.130

37. Tilman, p. 91

38. See Stephen Edgell, 'Rescuing Veblen from Valhalla: deconstruction and reconstruction of a sociological legend', *British Journal of Sociology*, **47**, 4 (December, 1996) 627–42

39. Robert Griffin, 'What Veblen Owed to Peirce – The Social Theory of Logic', *Journal of Economic Issues*, **32**, 3 (September, 1998) 733–57

40. Joseph Dorfman, *Thorstein Veblen and His America* (London, 1935), p. 57

41. Emmet Dedmon, *Fabulous Chicago* (London, 1953), p.183

42. Dedmon, *Fabulous Chicago*, p. 303

43. Andrew Carnegie, from *The Gospel of Wealth* (1900) in *Darwin*, p. 403

44. Bessie Louise Pierce, *A History of Chicago Vol 3: The Rise of the Modern City 1871–1893* (New York, 1957), p. 400

45. Pierce, *A History of Chicago*, p. 390

46. Dorfman, *Thorstein Veblen and His America* p. 92

47. Henry Adams, *The Education of Henry Adams* (London, 1919) p. 339

48. John E. Findling, *Chicago's Great World Fairs* (Manchester, 1994) pp. 26–7

49. Quoted by Dorfman, *Thorstein Veblen and His America*, p. 115

50. Dorfman, *Thorstein Veblen and His America*, p. 107

51. Dedmon, p. 194

52. Veblen, 'Why Is Economics Not An Evolutionary Science?', *Quarterly Journal of Economics*, **12** (1898), reprinted in *The Place of Science in Modern Civilisation*

Chapter Two

1. Wesley C. Mitchell, 'Human Behavior and Economics: A Survey of Recent Literature', *Quarterly Journal of Economics*, **29** (1914–15) 1–47

2. 'The Economic Theory of Women's Dress', *Popular Science Monthly* (1894), reprinted in M. Casson (ed.), *International Library of Critical Writings in Economics*, **83**, 1 (1997), 279–91
   'The Barbarian Status of Women', *American Journal of Sociology*, **IV** (1898–9)
   'The Instinct of Workmanship and the Irksomeness of Labor', *American Journal of Sociology*, **V**(September 1899), 78–96
   'The Beginnings of Ownership', *American Journal of Sociology*, **IV** (November 1898), 32–49

3. Lewis H. Morgan, *Ancient Society* (1877, reprinted Cambridge, Mass. 1964), p. 457

4. Roland Barthes, *Mythologies*, selected and translated by Annette Lavers (Frogmore, 1973), pp. 129, 142

5. Dorfman, *Thorstein Veblen and His America*, p. 174

6. Thorstein Veblen, *The Theory of the Leisure Class* (1899, London, 1970), p. 29. All subsequent page references are to this edition and are included in the text.

7. 'A third moment is that in which one becomes aware that one's own corporate interests, in their present and future development, transcend the corporate limits of the purely economic class, and can and must become the interests of subordinate groups too. This is the most purely political phase, and marks the decisive passage from the structure to the sphere of the complex superstructures; it is the phase in which previously germinated ideologies become "party", come into confrontation and conflict, until only one of them, or at least a single combination of them, tends to prevail, to gain the upper hand, to propagate itself throughout society – bringing about not only a unison of economic and political aims, but also intellectual and moral unity, posing all the questions around which the struggle rages not on a corporate but on a "universal" plane, and thus creating the hegemony of a fundamental social group over a series of subordinate groups', Antonio Gramsci, *Selections from the Prison Notebooks*, edited and translated by Quintin Hoare and Geoffrey Nowell Smith (London, 1971) pp. 181–2; Noam Chomsky, *Necessary Illusions: Thought Control in Democratic Societies* (London, 1989), pp. 46–7; Dorothy Ross even calls Veblen 'the American Gramsci, drawn by the problem of false consciousness and training in idealist philosophy into a revision of Marx's theory of history', *The Origins of American Social Science* (Cambridge, 1991), p. 207

8. I have borrowed the phrase, of course, from Daniel Bell's *The Cultural Contradictions of Capitalism* (London, 1976)

9. Max Weber, *The Protestant Ethic and the Spirit of Capitalism,* translated by Talcott Parsons(1930, reprinted London, 1971)

10. Thorstein Veblen, 'Why is Economics Not An Evolutionary Science?'
—— 'The Preconceptions of Economic Science', *Quarterly Journal of Economics* (January 1899, July 1899, February 1900), reprinted in *The Place of Science in Modern Civilisation*

11. 'Firstly, that labour is exterior to the worker, that is, it does not belong to his essence. Therefore he does not confirm himself in his work, he denies himself ... . Finally, the external character of labour for the worker shows itself in the fact that it is not his own but someone else's, that it does not belong to him, that he does not belong to himself in his labour but to someone else', Karl Marx, 'Alienated Labour', in *Early Texts*, edited and translated by David McLennan (Oxford, 1972) p. 137

12. Henry R. Seager and Charles R. Gulick Jr, *Trust and Corporation Problems* (New York, 1929) 216–42; Donald R. McCoy, *Coming of Age: The United States during the 1920s and 1930s*, p. 76

13. Louis Brandeis, *Other People's Money and How Bankers Use It* (New York, 1914), 32–3

14. Adolf A. Berle and Gardiner C. Means, *The Modern Corporation and Private Property* (1932, reprinted 1967) p. 205

15. Thorstein Veblen, 'Industrial and Pecuniary Employments', *Publications of the American Economic Association*, Series 3, Vol. VII, reprinted in *The Place of Science in Modern Civilisation*, 279–323

16. William Graham Sumner, 'The Concentration of Wealth: Its Economc Justification', in William Graham Sumner, *Social Darwinism: Selected Essays of William Graham Sumner*, edited by Stow Spaulding Persons (Yale, 1963), p. 157; Andrew Carnegie, *The Empire of Business* (1902), quoted in Alun Munslow, *Discourse and Culture: The Creation of America 1870–1920* (London, 1992) p. 25

17. Thorstein Veblen, *The Theory of Business Enterprise* (1904, reprinted New York, 1932) p. 39. All further page references are to this edition and are included in the text

18. Berle and Means, *The Modern Corporation and Private Property* , p. 114

19. Thomas Carlyle, *Selected Writings*, edited by Alan Shelston (Harmondsworth, 1971), pp. 65–7

20. Frederick Winslow Taylor, 'No. 1003 – Shop Management', *Transactions of the American Society of Mechanical Engineers*, **24** (1903) 1337–480; see Martha Banta, *Taylored Lives: Narrative Productions in the Age of Taylor, Veblen, and Ford* (Chicago, 1993) for a discussion of Taylorism and its cultural impact

21. Dorfman, *Thorstein Veblen, Essays*, pp. 141, 396; I have used the text of *The Higher Learning in America* available online at http://www.realuofc.org/libed/veblen/veblen.html which numbers each chapter individually and so I am unable to provide page numbers

22. See Hugh J. Dawson, 'Veblen's Social Satire and Amos Alonso Stagg: Football and the American Way of Life', *Prospects*, **14**, (1989) 273–89

23. John P. Diggins, *The Bard of Savagery: Thorstein Veblen and Modern Social Theory*, p. 174; John Kenneth Galbraith, *A Life in Our Times* (London, 1981), p. 287

24. Thorstein Veblen, 'The Place of Science in Modern Civilisation', *American Journal of Sociology*, **XI**, (March 1906), reprinted in *The Place of Science in Modern Civilisation*, 1–31

25. Thorstein Veblen, 'The Socialist Economics of Karl Marx and His Followers', *The Quarterly Journal of Economics*, XX & XXI, (August, 1906 & February 1907), reprinted in *The Place of Science in Modern Civilisation*, 409–56

26. Dorfman, *Thorstein Veblen and His America*, p. 295

27. Dorfman, *Thorstein Veblen and His America*, p. 324; Diggins, p. 63; for an extended, subtle analysis of *Instinct of Workmanship* see Christopher Shannon, *Conspicuous Criticism: Tradition, the Individual, and Culture in American Social Thought from Veblen to Mills* (Baltimore, 1996) pp. 1–26

28. Thorstein Veblen, *The Instinct of Workmanship* (New York, 1914) p. 1. All other page references are to this edition and are included in the text

29. Diggins, p. 68

Chapter Three

1. Rick Tilman, *The Intellectual Legacy of Thorstein Veblen: Unresolved Issues* (London, 1996), p. 120

2. Dorfman, *Thorstein Veblen and His America*, p. 330

3. Dorfman, *Thorstein Veblen and His America*, p. 344

4. 'Using the IWW to Harvest Grain', memorandum for the Statistical Division of the Food Administration, reprinted in *Essays in Our Changing Order*

5. Dorfman, *Thorstein Veblen and His America*, p. 411; for an extended discussion of Veblen's involvement with *The Dial* see Hartwig Isernhagen, 'A Constitutional Inability to Say Yes: Thorstein Veblen, the Reconstruction Program of *The Dial*, and the Development of American Modernism after World War I', *Sonderdruck aus Real: The Yearbook of Research in English and American Literature* , edited by Herbert Grabes, *et al.*, **1**(1982), 153–90

6. Thorstein Veblen, *The Vested Interests and the Common Man* (London, 1924), p. 39. All subsequent page references are to this edition and are included in the text

7. See John Cummings, 'The Theory of the Leisure Class', *Journal of Political Economy*, **7** (September, 1899), 425–55; and Richard Teggart, *Thorstein Veblen: A Chapter in American Economic Thought* (Berkeley, 1932)

8. 'Suggestions Touching the Working Program of an Inquiry into the Prospective Terms of Peace', Memorandum submitted to the House Inquiry through Walter Lippmann, reprinted in *Essays in Our Changing Order*

9. Quoted by Daniel Bell in his 'Introduction' to Thorstein Veblen, *The Engineers and the Price System* (New York, 1968), p. 20. I am drawing on his account here.

10. Bell, 'Introduction', pp. 21–25

11. Thorstein Veblen, *The Engineers and the Price System* (1921, New York, 1968), p. 43. All subsequent page references are to this edition and are included in the text.

12. Theodor Adorno, 'Veblen's Attack on Culture', *Studies in Philosophy and Social Science*, **9**, 3 (1941), 389–413

13. Bell, 'Introduction,' p. 31

14. Thorstein Veblen, 'Between Bolshevism and War', *The Freeman*, May 25 1921, 248–51, and 'Dementia Praecox' *The Freeman*, June 21 1922, 344–7, both reprinted in *Essays in Our Changing Order*

15. Donald R. McCoy, *Coming of Age*, p. 21

16. Curiously, Dorfman claims that 'Dementia Praecox' is Veblen's expression of the effect to be expected from the loss of the great steel strike, of the Bolshevik scare, and of the policy of the Federal Reserve system in attempting to prevent a complete liquidation in the depression of 1920/21, and that it is prophetic of the great inflation and resulting depression in 1929, *Thorstein Veblen and His America*, p. 464. He must have confused it with another article because this one simply does not deal with these issues.

17. McCoy, p. 24

18. McCoy, p. 75

19. Thorstein Veblen, *Absentee Ownership and Business Enterprise in Recent Times: the Case of America* (1922, New York, 1923), p. 425. All subsequent page references are to this edition and are included in the text.

20. Adolf A. Berle and Gardiner C. Means, *The Modern Corporation and Private Property* (1932, revised edition New York, 1967), p. 308

21. Berle and Means, *The Modern Corporation*, p. 14

22. Berle and Means, p. 14

Chapter Four

1. Joseph Dorfman, *Thorstein Veblen and His America*, p. 372

2. Rick Tilman, *Thorstein Veblen and His Critics, 1891–1963: Conservative, Liberal and Political Perspectives* (Princeton, 1992), pp. 18–25

3. Dorfman, *Thorstein Veblen and His America*, pp. 252, 507

4. Dorfman, *Thorstein Veblen and His America*, p. 194

5. William Dean Howells, 'An Opportunity for American Fiction', *Literature* (28 April and 5 May, 1899), reprinted in Edwin H. Cady (ed.), *W. D. Howells as Critic* (London, 1973), 286–91

6. Dorfman, *Thorstein Veblen and His America*, p. 196; Dorfman, *Essays, Reviews and Reports*, p. 19

7. Dorfman, *Thorstein Veblen and His America*, p. 236; Dorfman, *Essays*, p. 61

8. For Beard see Morton White, *Social Thought in America: The Revolt Against Formalism* (1949, Boston, 1957), p. 35; W. C. Mitchell, 'Human Behavior and Economics: A Survey of Recent Literature', *Quarterly Journal of Economics*, **29** (1914–15), 1–47, p. 30

9. For Sinclair and Hackett, see Dorfman, *Thorstein Veblen*, pp. 273, 344; for Eastman and Dell, see Daniel Aaron, *Writers on the Left* (Oxford, 1977), pp. 34, 51, Patrick Geddes, *Cities in Evolution* (London, 1915), quoted in Jerry L. Simich and Rick Tilman, *Thorstein Veblen: A Reference Guide* (Boston, 1985), p. 8

10. Dorfman, *Thorstein Veblen and His America*, p. 349

11. Daniel Bell, 'Introduction' to *The Engineers and the Price System*, p. 9

12. Dorfman, *Thorstein Veblen and His America*, pp. 370–2; for Dell, Simich and Tilman, *Thorstein Veblen: A Reference Guide*, p. 10–11

13. Dorfman, *Thorstein Veblen and His America*, p. 408

14. Reprinted in H. L. Mencken, *Prejudices: First Series* (New York, 1921), p. 64

15. Dorfman, *Thorstein Veblen and His America*, p. 421

16. Dorfman, *Thorstein Veblen and His America*, pp. 433, 447

17. Quoted by Dorfman, *Thorstein Veblen and His America*, p. 460

18. Dorfman, *Thorstein Veblen, Essays*, p. 187; quoted by Dorfman, *Thorstein Veblen and His America*, p. 484

19. Dorfman, *Thorstein Veblen and His America*, pp. 492–6

20. Thorstein Veblen, 'Economic Theory in the Calculable Future', *American Economic Review – Supplement* (March, 1925), 48–55, reprinted in *Essays in Our Changing Order*

21. Maurice Dobb, 'An American Critic of Capitalist Society',*The Plebs*, **17,** 3 (March, 1925) 119–21

22. John Maurice Clark, 'Recent Developments in Economics,' in *Recent Developments in the Social Sciences*, edited by Edward C. Hayes (Philadelphia, 1927), noted in Simich and Tilman, p. 22

23. Howard W. Odum (ed.), *American Masters of Social Science* (New York, 1927) 231–70; Paul Homan, *Contemporary Economic Thought* (New York, 1928), noted in Simich and Tilman, p. 23

24. John Hobson, 'Thorstein Veblen,' *Sociological Review*, **21** (October, 1930) 342–5

25. Henry Hazlitt, 'Thorstein Veblen', *Century*, **119** (Fall, 1930) 8–10, noted in Simich and Tilman, p. 24; Lewis Mumford, 'Thorstein Veblen', *New Republic*, **67** (5 August 1931) 314–16, quoted by Rick Tilman, *Thorstein Veblen and His Critics*, p. 258

26. Abram L. Harris, 'Types of Institutionalism,' *Journal of Political Economy*, **40** (December, 1932) 721–49, and 'Economic Evolution: Dialectical and Darwinian', *Journal of Political Economy*, **42** (February, 1934) 34–79, noted in Simich and Tilman, pp. 29, 35

27. Rick Tilman, *Thorstein Veblen and His Critics*, pp. 38–46

28. Adolf A. Berle and Gardiner C. Means, *The Modern Corporation and Private Property* (1932, revised edition New York, 1967), pp. 4, 313, 3, 14, 33, 112–18, 303–8

29. Dorfman, *Thorstein Veblen and His America*, pp. 510, 517

30. Dorfman, *Essays, Reviews and Reports*, p. 291

31. Talcott Parsons, 'Sociological Elements in Economic Thought, 1', *Quarterly Journal of Economics*, **49** (May, 1935), 414–53; Simich and Tilman, pp. 38, 41; J. A. Hobson, *Veblen* (London, 1936), p. 224

32. John Patrick Diggins, *Thorstein Veblen: Theorist of the Leisure Class* (Princeton, 1999), p. 215

33. Quoted in Tilman, *Veblen and His Critics*, p. 199

34. Dorfman, *Essays, Reviews and Reports*, p. 306

35. Tilman, pp. 201, 212

36. Tilman, p. 208

37. Henry A. Wallace, 'Veblen's Imperial Germany and the Industrial Revolution', *Political Science Quarterly*, **55** (1940) 435–45

38. Charles Hunt Page, *Class and American Sociology: From Ward to Ross* (New York, 1940), quoted by Simich and Tilman, p. 50; Eric Roll, *A History of Economic Thought* (1942) noted in Simich and Tilman, pp. 49–53

39. Diggins, *The Bard of Savagery*, p. 224

40. Herbert Marcuse, 'Some Sociological Implications of Modern Technology', *Studies in Phliosophy and Social Science*, **9**, 3 (1941) 414–39

41. For a more extended discussion see Michael Spindler, 'Adorno's Critique of Veblen', in Holger Briel and Andreas Kramer (eds), *In Practice: Theodor Adorno and Cultural Theory* (Berne, 2001)

42. Arthur K. Davis, 'Veblen on the Decline of the Protestant Ethic', *Social Forces*, **22** (March, 1944), 282–6; 'Veblen's Study of Modern Germany', *American Sociological Review*, **9** (December, 1944), 603–9; 'Sociological Elements in Veblen's Economic Theory', *Journal of Political Economy*, **53** (1945), 132–49; Tilman, pp. 219–32

43. Alfred Kazin, *On Native Grounds: An Interpretation of Modern American Prose*, pp. 130–42, 'Veblen was an alien to the end', p. 141, 133; Simich and Tilman, *Thorstein Veblen: A Reference Guide*, p. 64

44. Tilman, pp. 177–84

45. Morton White, *Social Thought in America: The Revolt Against Formalism* (1949, Boston 1957), p. 236

46. Stanley Matthew Daugert, *The Philosophy of Thorstein Veblen* (New York, 1950) quoted by Simich and Tilman, p. 70

47. David Riesman, *Thorstein Veblen: A Critical Interpretation* (1953, reissued 1975), p. 6

48. H. W. Coals, 'The Influence of Veblen's Methodology', *Journal of Political Economy*, **62** (December, 1953), 529–37; Lev Dobriansky, *Veblenism: A New Critique* (Washington, 1957); Don M. Wolfe, *The Image of Man in America* (Dallas, 1957, 2nd edn, New York, 1970)

49. Christopher Lasch, 'The Cultural Cold War: A Short History of The Congress for Cultural Freedom', in Barton J. Bernstein(ed.), *Towards a New Past: Dissenting Essays in American History* (New York, 1968) pp. 322–59; Philip Rahv, 'American Intellectuals in the Postwar Situation', *Partisan Review* (May–June,1952), reprinted in *Image and Idea: Twenty Essays on Literary Themes* (London, 1957) 222–30

50. Robert Heilbroner, *The Worldly Philosophers* (New York, 1953); Bernard Rosenberg, *The Values of Veblen: A Critical Appraisal* (Washington, 1956)

51. Paul M. Sweezy, 'The Influence of Marxism on Thorstein Veblen', in *Socialism and American Life*, edited by Donald Drew Egbert and Stow Persons (Princeton, 1952) 473–77, noted in Simich and Tilman, pp. 76, 89, 94

52. Arthur K. Davis, 'Veblen: The Postwar Essays', *Monthly Review*, **9** (1957) 220–7, 'Thorstein Veblen Reconsidered', *Science and Society* , **26** (1957) 52–85, and he contributed 'Thorstein Veblen and the Culture of Capitalism', to Harvey Goldberg (ed.), *American Radicals: Some Problems and Personalities* (New York, 1957), all three pieces reprinted in Arthur K. Davis, *Farewell to Earth: The Collected Writings of Arthur K. Davis*, 2 vols (Adamant, Vermont, 1991)

53. Douglas Dowd (ed.), *Thorstein Veblen: A Critical Reappraisal* (Ithaca, 1958); Forrest G. Hill, 'Veblen and Marx', in Dowd, *Thorstein Veblen*, p. 142; John Kenneth Galbraith, *The Affluent Society*, pp. 42–7, 76, 129; Joseph Dorfman, *The Economic Mind in American Civilization 1918–33* (New York, 1959); Vance Packard, *The Hidden Persuaders* (1957), *The Status Seekers* (1959), pp. 26, 70

54. David Riesman with Staughton Lynd, 'The Relevance of Thorstein Veblen', *American Scholar*, **29** (1961) 543–51, collected in David Riesman, *Abundance for What and Other Essays* (London, 1964) pp. 382–95

55. Daniel Bell, 'Introduction' to Thorstein Veblen, *The Engineers and the Price System* (New York, 1968), p. 28; 'Veblen and the New Class,' *American Scholar*, **32** (1963), 616–32; Tilman,*Veblen and His Critics*, p. 186

56. Clarence Ayres, *Institutional Economics : Veblen, Commons, and Mitchell Reconsidered* (Berkeley,1964); Bernard Rosenberg (ed.), *Thorstein Veblen: Selections from his Work* (New York, 1963); Douglas Dowd, *Thorstein Veblen* (New York, 1964); Carlton C. Qualey (ed.), *Thorstein Veblen : The Carleton College Veblen Seminar Essays* (New York, 1968)

57. See Simich and Tilman, pp. 124, 128, 123; Charles G. Leathers and John S. Evans, 'Thorstein Veblen and the New Industrial State', *History of Political Economy*, **5**, 2 (Fall, 1973) 420–37, reprinted in Mark Blaug (ed.), *Thorstein Veblen (1857–1929)*, pp. 1–18; Stephen S. Conroy, 'Veblen's Progeny', *Colorado Quarterly*, **16** (1968), 413–22

58. Christopher Lasch, *The New Radicalism in America 1889–1963* (New York,1965)

59. Daniel Bell, *The Coming of Post-Industrial Society* (London,1973); *Daedalus*, as noted by Simich and Tilman, p. 149; David Seckler, *Thorstein Veblen and the Institutionalists* (Boulder, 1975)

60. William Akin, *Technocracy and the American Dream : The Technocrat Movement 1900–1941* (Berkeley, 1977); John Kenneth Galbraith, *The Age of Uncertainty* (Boston, 1977), *A Life in Our Times* (London, 1981), pp. 25, 29–30

61. Leonard A. Dente, *Veblen's Theory of Social Change* (New York, 1977), p. 211; John P. Diggins, *The Bard of Savagery: Thorstein Veblen and Modern Social Theory* (1978), p. xv

62. Arthur K. Davis, *Thorstein Veblen's Social Theory* (New York,1980), no pagination given, but 'Veblen Once More: A View From 1979' also reprinted in Arthur K. Davis, *Farewell to Earth: The Collected Writings of Arthur K. Davis*, 2 vols. (Adamant, Vermont, 1991) pp. 150–9

63. Jean Baudrillard, *For a Critique of a Political Economy of the Sign*, translated by Charles Levin, (place of publication not given, 1981), pp. 31–2, 35–7, 115

64. Mark Blaug (ed.), *Thorstein Veblen* (Aldershot, 1992); Jerry L. Simich and Rick Tilman, *Thorstein Veblen: A Reference Guide* (Boston, 1985); John Brooks, *Showing Off in America: From Conspicuous Consumption to Parody Display* (New York, 1981); Roger S. Mason, *Conspicuous Consumption: A Study of Exceptional Behavior* (New York, 1981)

65. Jackson Lears, 'Beyond Veblen: Rethinking Consumer Culture in America', in Simon J. Bronner (ed.), *Consuming Visions: Accumulation and Display of goods in America 1880–1920* (1989)

66. Rick Tilman, *Thorstein Veblen and His Critics* (1992)

67. Dorothy Ross, *The Origins of American Social Science* (Cambridge, 1991); Douglas Tallack, *Twentieth-Century America: The Intellectual and Cultural Context* (London, 1991); Alun Munslow, *Discourse and Culture: The Creation of America 1870–1920* (London, 1992)

68. See the *Zetoc* database for a full listing of articles; Rick Tilman, *The Intellectual Legacy of Thorstein Veblen* (London, 1996); Christopher Shannon, *Conspicuous Criticism: Tradition, the Individual, and Culture in American Social Thought from Veblen to Mills* (Baltimore, 1996); Doug Brown (ed.), *Thorstein Veblen in the Twenty-First Century* (Cheltenham, 1998); Clare Virginia Eby, *Dreiser and Veblen: Saboteurs of the Status Quo* (Columbia and London,1998); John P. Diggins, *Thorstein Veblen: Theorist of the Leisure Class* (Princeton,1999); Elizabeth Watkin and Henry Irving Jorgensten, *Thorstein Veblen: Victorian Firebrand* (New York, 1999)

69. Herbert Marcuse, *One Dimensional Man* (London, 1964)

Chapter Five

1. F. Scott Fitzgerald, *The Crack Up* (Harmondsworth, 1965), p. 59; Arthur Miller, *The Price* (Harmondsworth, 1968), p. 38

2. Louis J. Paradiso, 'Retail Sales and Consumer Incomes', Department of Commerce 1945, quoted in 'Consumption Economics: A Symposium', *American Economic Review*, **35** (May 1945) 52–4; H. T. Oshima, 'Consumer Asset Formation and the Future of Capitalism', *Economic Journal*, **71** (1961), 20–35; Walter Rostow, *The Stages of Economic Growth: A Non-Communist Manifesto* (Cambridge, 1961), pp. 10–11

3. Quoted by Stewart H. Holbrook, *The Age of the Moguls* (New York, 1953), p. 206

4. United States Department of Commerce, *Historical Statistics of the United States: Colonial Times to 1957* (Washington, 1960), p. 462

5. Charles H. Hession and Hyman Sardy, *Ascent to Affluence: A History of American Economic Development* (Boston, 1969), p. 619; Rostow, p. 76; Peter d'A. Jones, *The Consumer Society: A History of American Capitalism* (Harmondsworth, 1965), p. 282; Jim Potter, *The American Economy Between the Wars* (London, 1974), p. 64, also points to consumer durable production as one of the marked features of the 1920s

6. *Historical Statistics*, pp. 139, 601

7. Quoted in Hession and Sardy, p. 617

8. Brookings Institute, *America's Capacity to Produce and America's Capacity to Consume: A Digest* (Pittsburgh, 1934), p. 31

9. Holbrook, p. 209

10. See Vance Packard, *The Hidden Persuaders* (Harmondsworth, 1960), p. 23 and passim for the use by manufacturers of 'psychological obsolescence' to avert the crisis of overproduction

11. J. M. Gillman, *The Falling Rate of Profit: Marx's Law and Its Significance to Twentieth-Century Capitalism* (London, 1957), p. 131

12. Hession and Sardy, p. 624; W. E. Leuchtenberg, *The Perils of Prosperity 1914–1932* (Chicago, 1958), p. 192

13. Hession and Sardy, p. 672; *Historical Statistics*, p. 526

14. T. C. Cochran, *A Basic History of American Business* (Princeton, 1968), p. 68

15. Leuchtenberg, p. 200

16. Cochran, p. 83

17. David M. Potter, *People of Plenty: Economic Abundance and the American Character* (Chicago, 1954), p. 46

18. See 'Consumption Economics: A Symposium,' *American Economic Review*, 35 (May, 1945) pp. 44, 55

19. Rostow, p. 79

20. Oshima, 'Consumer Asset Formation'

21. Dexter M. Keezer, *et al.*, *New Forces in American Business* (New York,1959), p. 75; Harry Magdoff, 'Problems of US Capitalism', *The Socialist Register 1965*, edited by Ralph Miliband and John Saville (New York, 1965), p. 68

22. Keezer, *New Forces*, p. 91

23. *Historical Statistics*, p. 526; see again Packard, *Hidden Persuaders*, for the use of depth psychology in advertising

24. Keezer, pp. 97, 118

25. Norman O. Brown, *Life Against Death: the Psychoanalytical Meaning of History* (London, 1959), p. 224; Dorothy Ross, *The Origins of American Social Science*, p. 206

26. David Riesman, Nathan Glazer, and Reuel Denney, *The Lonely Crowd* (1950, abridged edition, New Haven, 1961), p. 6; William H. Whyte, *The Organisation Man* (London, 1957), pp. 4–6; Potter, p. 173; Daniel Bell, *The Cultural Contradictions of Capitalism* (London, 1976), pp. 21, 61, 64–5

27. Fitzgerald, 'Echoes of the Jazz Age', *The Crack-Up*, p. 11

28. Raymond Williams, *Marxism and Literature* (Oxford, 1977), pp. 121–4

29. Robert S. and Helen M. Lynd, *Middletown in Transition: A Study in Cultural Conflicts* (New York, 1937), pp. 242–3

30. Quoted in Hession and Sardy, p. 669

31. Malcolm Cowley, *Exile's Return: A Narrative of Ideas* (New York, 1934), pp. 69–72

32. Cowley, *Exile's Return*, p. 72

33. Thorstein Veblen, 'The Economic Theory of Women's Dress', *Popular Science Monthly* (1894), reprinted in M. Casson (ed.), *International Library of Critical Writings in Economics*, **83**, 1 (1997) 279–92

34. Theodore Dreiser, *Sister Carrie* (1900, New York, 1961), p. 3

35. Thorstein Veblen, *The Theory of the Leisure Class* (1899, London, 1970), p. 110

36. Harvey Leibenstein, 'Bandwagon, Snob and Veblen Effects in the Theory of Consumers' Demand', *Quarterly Journal of Economics*, **64** (May, 1950) 183–207, reprinted in *Beyond Economic Man: A New Foundation for Micro-economics* (Cambridge, Mass., 1976), p. 52

37. Veblen, *Leisure Class*, p. 85

38. Gary Cross, *Time and Money: The Making of Consumer Culture* (London, 1993), p. 5

39. Veblen, *Leisure Class*, pp. 70, 81

40. Andrew Carnegie, 'Wealth', *North American Review* (June, 1889), reprinted in Gail Kennedy (ed.), *Democracy and the Gospel of Wealth* (Boston, 1949), p. 1

41. Veblen, *Leisure Class*, pp. 37, 42–3, 218

42. James Bryce, *The American Commonwealth* (1888, revised edition, New York, 1911) II, pp. 21, 624–5; Lynd and Lynd, *Middletown*, pp. 247, 455

43. See Paula S. Fass, *The Damned and the Beautiful: American Youth in the 1920s* (New York, 1977)

44. F. Scott Fitzgerald, 'Echoes of the Jazz Age', in *The Crack-Up* (Harmondsworth, 1965) p. 11

45. Frederick Townsend Martin, *The Passing of the Idle Rich* (New York, 1911), p. 220

46. Herbert L. Stewart, 'The Ethics of Luxury and Leisure', *American Journal of Sociology*, **24**, 3 (1918) 241–59; James Russell Lowell, *Democracy and Other Addresses* (Boston and New York, 1887), p. 28; C. D. Burns, *Leisure and the Modern World* (London, 1932), p. 148

47. Jean Baudrillard, *Selected Writings*, edited by Mark Poster (Cambridge, 1988), pp. 44, 46, 35

48. George Katona, *The Mass Consumption Society* (New York, 1964) p. 61

49. Vance Packard, *The Status Seekers* (London: 1960), p. 7

50. Robert H. Frank, *Luxury Fever: Why Money Fails to Satisfy in an Era of Excess*, p. 174

51. Jackson Lears, 'Beyond Veblen: Rethinking Consumer Culture in America,' in Simon J. Bronner (ed.), *Consuming Visions: Accumulation and the Display of Goods in America 1880 and 1920* (New York, 1989) pp. 73–97

52. Andrew B. Trigg, 'Veblen, Bourdieu, and Conspicuous Consumption', *Journal of Economic Issues*, **35**, 1 (March, 2001) 99–115; Yngve Ramstad, 'Veblen's Propensity for Emulation: Is It Passé?' in Doug Brown (ed.), *Thorstein Veblen in the Twenty-First Century* (Cheltenham, 1998) pp. 3–27

Chapter Six

1. William Dean Howells, 'An Opportunity for American Fiction', Literature, 28 April and 5 May, 1899, reprinted in Edwin H. Cady, *W. D. Howells as Critic* (London, 1973)

2. Stuart Chase, 'Foreword,' to Thorstein Veblen, *The Theory of the Leisure Class* (New York: 1934), p. xiii

3. Walter B. Rideout, *The Radical Novel in the United States 1900–1954* (Cambridge, Mass., 1956) mentions Veblen in connection with Dos Passos; Joseph Blotner, *The Modern American Political Novel 1900–1960* (Austin and London, 1966) mentions him once; Nelson Memfred Blake, *Novelists' America: Fiction as History 1910–1940* (Syracuse, 1969) fails to mention him at all; and Eric Homberger, *American Writers and Radical Politics, 1900–39* (London, 1986) mentions him in passing just three times

4. Alfred Kazin, *On Native Grounds: An Interpretation of Modern American Prose Literature* (London, 1943), pp. 130–42, 344–5; John P. Diggins in 'Dos Passos and Veblen's Villains', *Antioch Review*, **23** (Winter, 1963) 485–500, points out the Veblenian themes present in Dos Passos, and in *Thorstein Veblen: Theorist of the Leisure Class* mentions that Veblen's ideas 'echoed through the Chicago-based novels of Robert Herrick and Ben Hecht', p. 211; Thomas Reed West, *Flesh of Steel: Literature and the Machine in American Culture* (Vanderbilt, 1967), pp. 71–94, links Carl Sandburg and Veblen; D. W. Noble brings together Veblen and Dreiser, contrasting their social perspectives in two articles, 'Dreiser and Veblen in the Literature of Cultural change,' in Joseph J. Kwiat and Mary Christine Turpie (eds), *Studies in American Culture* (Minneapolis, 1960) 139–52, and 'Progress versus Tragedy: Veblen and Dreiser' in Cushing Strout (ed.), *Intellectual History in America*, 2 vols (New York, 1968) 60–72; recently Clare Virginia Eby has brought together Dreiser and Veblen in a very fruitful manner in *Dreiser and Veblen: Saboteurs of the Status Quo* (Columbia and London,1998) in which she treats both as radical cultural critics and emphasises 'the striking parallels between their works'

5. Daniel Aaron, *Writers on the Left* (Oxford, 1977)

6. Sinclair Lewis, *Main Street* (1920, New York, 1961), pp. 255, 116, 117, 59

7. Robert S. and Helen M. Lynd, *Middletown: a Study in contemporary American Culture* (New York, 1929), pp. 278, 309

8. Mark Schorer, *Sinclair Lewis: An American Life* (London, 1961), p. 72

9. Sinclair Lewis, *Babbitt* (1922, London, 1924), p. 99

10. For representative readings see Philip L. Gerber, *Willa Cather* (Boston, 1975), pp. 112–7, and James Woodress, *Willa Cather: A Literary Life* (London, 1987), pp. 371–5, e.g. 'The public theme of the novel is a strong indictment of materialism,' p. 372

11. Thorstein Veblen, *The Theory of the Leisure Class*, pp. 215, 220–1, 237

12. Willa Cather, *The Professor's House* (London, 1981), p. 154

13. Cather, *The Professor's House*, p. 223

14. Theodore Dreiser, *An American Tragedy* (New York, 1964), pp. 29, 48

15. Dreiser, *An American Tragedy*, p. 149; Veblen, *Leisure Class*, pp. 334, 105; see Eby, *Dreiser and Veblen*, pp. 135–47, for a similar Veblenian reading of *An American Tragedy*

16. See Paula S. Fass, *The Damned and the Beautiful: American Youth in the 1920s* (New York, 1977) for a discussion of the significance of the youth culture and its hedonism and consumerism

17. William Dean Howells, 'An Opportunity for American Fiction', *Literature* (28 April and 5 May, 1899), reprinted in Edwin H. Cady (ed.) *W. D. Howells as Critic* (London, 1973)

18. F. Scott Fitzgerald, *Collected Short Stories* (Harmondsworth, 1986), p. 100

19. F. Scott Fitzgerald, *This Side of Paradise*, pp. 30, 230, 243

20. F. Scott Fitzgerald, *The Beautiful and the Damned*, pp. 9–10, 364

21. Letter to Maxwell Perkins (January, 1925), *Letters*, p. 195

22. F. Scott Fitzgerald, *The Great Gatsby*, p. 119

23. Fitzgerald, *Gatsby*, p. 99; See E. R. Canterbery, 'Thorstein Veblen and *The Great Gatsby*,' *Journal of Economic Issues*, **33**, 2 (1999) 297–304

24. Quoted by Malcolm Cowley in his 'Introduction' to F. Scott Fitzgerald, *Tender is the Night*, (Harmondsworth, 1955), p. 13

25. *Tender is the Night*, p. 122–3

26. From his memorandum to himself, quoted by Cowley, 'Introduction', p. 13

27. Veblen, *Theory of the Leisure Class*, p. 21

28. Quoted by Townsend Ludington (ed.) in *The Fourteenth chronicle: Letters and Diaries of John Dos Passos* (Boston, 1973), p. 443; Donald Pizer, *Dos Passos' USA: a Critical Study* (Charlottesville, 1988), p. 163, also points to the relevance of Veblen to the Charley Anderson narrative.

29. John Dos Passos, *U.S.A.* (Harmondsworth, 1966) pp. 554–5, 830. Subsequent page references are to this edition and are included in the text.

30. John Dos Passos, 'Introduction', *U. S. A.* (New York, 1937)

31. Thorstein Veblen, *The Vested Interests and the Common Man* (London, 1924), p. 160

Conclusion

1. Warren J. Samuels, 'Reflections on the Intellectual Context and Significance of Thorstein Veblen', *Journal of Economic Issues*, **29**, 3 (1995), 916–22

2. Joseph Dorfman, 'New Light on Veblen,' in Thorstein Veblen, *Essays, Reviews and Reports*, edited by Joseph Dorfman, p. 596

3. Rick Tilman, *Thorstein Veblen and His Critics*, p. 13

4. Warren J. Samuels, 'Foreword' to Tilman, *Thorstein Veblen and His Critics*, p. ix
5. Adolf A. Berle and Gardiner C. Means, *The Modern Corporation and Private Property* (1932, revised edition New York, 1967), p. vii
6. Berle and Means, pp. 303, 313, Chapter 6 'The Divergence of Interest between Ownership and Control', 112–18
7. Harvey Leibenstein makes this point in *Beyond Economic Man; A New Foundation for Microeconomics* (Cambridge, Mass., 1976) p. 48–9
8. John P. Diggins, *Thorstein Veblen: Theorist of the Leisure Class*, p. xxviii
9. Quoted in Naomi Klein, *No Logo* (New York, 2000), p. 22
10. Klein, *No Logo*, p. 7
11. Klein, *No Logo*, pp. 7–10
12. Robert H. Frank, *Luxury Fever: Why Money Fails to Satisfy in an Era of Excess* (New York, 1999) p. 18
13. William Hildred, 'Executive Consumption: Not Conspicuous, but still Invidious', in Doug Brown (ed.), *Thorstein Veblen in the Twenty-First Century* (Cheltenham, 1998) pp. 85–103
14. Frank, p. 33
15. Frank, p. 11
16. Klein, p. 8
17. Frank, pp. 46, 177, 53
19. John Kenneth Galbraith, *The Affluent Society*, p. 195
20. Paulette Olson, 'My Dam is Bigger than Yours: Emulation in Global Capitalism', in Doug Brown (ed.), *Thorstein Veblen*, pp. 189–207; William M. Dugger, 'Thorstein Veblen and the Upper Class', Brown, *Thorstein Veblen*, 73–84
21. See Jonathan Larson, 'A Restoration of Significance', *Journal of Economic Issues*, **29**, 3 (1995), 910–15

Bibliography

Works by Thorstein Veblen

'The Economic Theory of Women's Dress', *Popular Science Monthly* (1894), reprinted M. Casson (ed.), *International Library of Critical Writings in Economics*, **83**, 1 (1997) 279–91

The Theory of the Leisure Class (1899, London, 1970)

The Theory of Business Enterprise (1904, reprinted 1932)

The Instinct of Workmanship and the State of the Industrial Arts (1914, reprinted New York, 1964)

Imperial Germany and the Industrial Revolution (1916, reissued 1939, and 1990)

An Inquiry into the Nature of Peace (1917)

The Higher Learning in America: A Memorandum on the Conduct of Universities by Business Men (1918), available at http://www.realuofc.org/libed/veblen/veblen.html

The Place of Science in Modern Civilisation, ed. Leon Ardzrooni, Wesley C. Mitchell, and Walter W. Stewart (New York, 1919)

The Vested Interests and the Common Man (1919, London,1924)

The Engineers and the Price System (1921, New York,1968)

Absentee Ownership and Business Enterprise in Recent times: the Case of America (1922, New York, 1923)

Essays in Our Changing Order, ed. Leon Ardzrooni and Wesley C. Mitchell (New York,1934)

What Veblen Taught, ed. Leon Ardzrooni and Wesley C. Mitchell (New York,1936)

Essays, Reviews and Reports: Previously Uncollected Writings edited with an introduction, 'New Light On Veblen', by Joseph Dorfman (Clifton, New Jersey, 1973)

Secondary Sources

Aaron, Daniel *Men of Good Hope: A Story of American Progressives* (1951)
—— *Writers on the Left* (Oxford, 1977)
Adams, Henry *The Education of Henry Adams* (New York,1918)
Adorno, Theodor 'Veblen's Attack on Culture', *Studies in Philosophy and Social Science*, **9**, 3 (1941), 389–413
Akin, William *Technocracy and the American Dream: The Technocrat Movement 1900–1941* (Berkeley, 1977)
Aveling, Edward and Eleanor Marx *The Working-Class Movement in America* (London, 1891)
Ayres, Clarence *Institutional Economics: Veblen, Commons, and Mitchell Reconsidered* (Berkeley, 1964)
Banta, Martha *Taylored Lives: Narrative Productions in the Age of Taylor, Veblen, and Ford* (Chicago, 1993)

Barthes, Roland *Mythologies*, selected and translated by Annette Lavers (Frogmore, 1973)

Baudrillard, Jean *For a Critique of the Political Economy of the Sign*, transl. Charles Levin (place of pub. not given, 1981)

Bell, Daniel 'Thorstein Veblen and the New Class', *American Scholar*, **32** (Autumn 1963), 616–38

—— 'Introduction,' to Thorstein Veblen, *The Engineers and the Price System* (New York, 1968)

—— *The Cultural Contradictions of Capitalism* (London, 1976)

Bellamy, Edward *Looking Backward: 2000–1887* (1888, London, 1942)

Berle, Adolf A. and Gardiner C. Means *The Modern Corporation and Private Property* (New York, 1932, revised edition 1967)

Blaug Mark (ed.) *Thorstein Veblen (1857–1929)* (Aldershot, 1992)

Blotner, Joseph *The Modern American Political Novel 1900–1960* (Austin and London, 1966)

Brandeis, Louis *Other People's Money and How Bankers Use It* (New York, 1914)

Bronner, Simon J. (ed.) *Consuming Visions: Accumulation and Display of Goods in America 1880–1920* (New York, 1989)

Brookings Institute, *America's Capacity to Produce and America's Capacity to Consume: A Digest* (Pittsburgh, 1934), p. 31

Brown, Doug (ed.) *Thorstein Veblen in the Twenty-first Century* (Cheltenham, 1998)

Brown, Norman O. *Life Against Death: The Psychoanalytical Meaning of History* (London, 1959)

Bryce, James *The American Commonwealth*, 2 vols (1888, rev. edn New York, 1911)

Burns, C. D. *Leisure and the Modern World* (London, 1932), p. 148

Cady, Edwin H. (ed.), *W. D. Howells as Critic* (London, 1973)

Canterbery, E. R. 'Thorstein Veblen and *The Great Gatsby* ', *Journal of Economic Issues*, **33**, 2 (1999), 297–304

Carlyle, Thomas *Selected Writings*, ed. Alan Shelston (Harmondsworth, 1971)

Carnegie, Andrew 'Wealth', *North American Review* (June 1989), repr. in Gail Kennedy (ed.) *Democracy and the Gospel of Wealth* (Boston, 1949), p. 1

Carnegie, Andrew *The Gospel of Wealth and Other Timely Essays* (New York, 1900), selections from, in Philip Appleman (ed.), *Darwin* (2nd edn, New York, 1979)

Cather, Willa *The Professor's House* (1925, London, 1981)

Chase, Stuart 'Foreword', to Thorstein Veblen *The Theory of the Leisure Class* (New York, 1934), p. xiii

Chomsky, Noam *Necessary Illusions : Thought Control in Democratic Societies* (London, 1989)

Coals, H. W. 'The Influence of Veblen's Methodology', *Journal of Political Economy*, **62** (December, 1953), 529–37

Cochran, T. C. *A Basic History of American Business* (Princeton, 1968)

Conroy, Stephen S. 'Veblen's Progeny', *Colorado Quarterly*, **16** (1968), 413–22

Cowley, Malcolm *Exile's Return : A Narrative of Ideas* (New York, 1934)

Cross, Gary *Time and Money: The Making of Consumer Culture* (London,1993)

Cummings, John 'The Theory of the Leisure Class', *Journal of Political Economy*, **7** (September, 1899), 425–55

Darwin, Charles *The Origin of Species* (1859) in Philip Appleman (ed.), *Darwin* (2nd edn, New York, 1979)
—— *The Descent of Man and Selection in Relation to Sex* (1871, Princeton, 1981)
Davis, Arthur K. 'Veblen on the Decline of the Protestant Ethic', *Social Forces*, **22** (March, 1944), 282–6
—— 'Veblen's Study of Modern Germany', *American Sociological Review*, **9** (December, 1944), 603–9
—— 'Sociological Elements in Veblen's Economic Theory', *Journal of Political Economy*, **53** (1945), 132–49
—— *Thorstein Veblen's Social Philosophy* (New York, 1980)
—— *Farewell to Earth: the Collected Writings of Arthur K. Davis*, 2 vols (Adamant, Vermont, 1991)
Dawson, Hugh J. 'Veblen's Social Satire and Amos Alonso Stagg: Football and the American Way of Life', *Prospects*, **14** (1989), 273–89
Dedmon, Emmet *Fabulous Chicago* (London, 1953)
Dente, Leonard A. *Veblen's Theory of Social Change* (New York, 1977)
Diggins, John P. 'Dos Passos and Veblen's Villains', *Antioch Review*, **23**, (Winter, 1963), 484–500
—— *The Bard of Savagery : Thorstein Veblen and Modern Social Theory* (New York, 1978)
—— *Thorstein Veblen: Theorist of the Leisure Class* (Princeton, 1999)
Dobb, Maurice 'An American Critic of Capitalist Society', *The Plebs*, **17**, 3 (March, 1925) 119–21
Dorfman, Joseph *Thorstein Veblen and His America* (London, 1935)
—— *Thorstein Veblen: Essays, Reviews and Reports* (Clifton N.J., 1973)
—— *The Economic Mind in American Civilization 1918–33* (New York, 1959)
Dos Passos, John *U.S.A.* (1937, Harmondsworth, 1966)
Dowd, Douglas (ed.) *Thorstein Veblen: A Critical Reappraisal* (Ithaca, 1958)
Dreiser, Theodore *Sister Carrie* (1900, New York, 1958)
—— *The Financier* (1912, reprinted New York, no date)
—— *The Titan* (1914, reprinted New York, no date)
—— *An American Tragedy* (1925, New York, 1964)
Eby, Clare Virginia *Dreiser and Veblen: Saboteurs of the Status Quo* (Columbia and London, 1998)
Edgell, Stephen 'Rescuing Veblen from Valhalla: deconstruction and reconstruction of a sociological legend', *British Journal of Sociology*, **47**, 4 (December, 1996), 627–42
Fass, Paula S. *The Damned and the Beautiful: American Youth in the 1920s* (New York, 1977)
Findling, John E. *Chicago's Great World Fairs* (Manchester, 1994)
Fitzgerald, F. Scott *This Side of Paradise* (1920, Harmondsworth, 1963)
—— *The Beautiful and Damned* (1922, Harmondsworth, 1966)
—— *The Great Gatsby* (1925, Harmondsworth 1950)
—— *Tender is the Night* (1934, rev. edn ed. Malcolm Cowley, Harmondsworth, 1955)
—— *Collected Short Stories* (Harmondsworth, 1986)
—— *The Crack-up* (Harmondsworth, 1965)
—— *Letters* ed. Andrew Turnbull (Harmondsworth, 1968)

Frank, Robert H. *Luxury Fever: Why Money Fails to Satisfy in an Era of Excess* (New York, 1999)

Galbraith, John Kenneth *The Affluent Society* (3rd edn, Boston, 1976)

—— *The New Industrial State* (London, 1967)

—— *The Age of Uncertainty* (Boston, 1977)

—— *A Life in Our Times* (London, 1981)

Gerber, Philip L. *Willa Cather* (Boston, 1975)

Gillman J. M. *The Falling Rate of Profit: Marx's Law and Its Significance to Twentieth-Century Capitalism* (London, 1957)

Gramsci, Antonio *Selections from the Prison Notebooks* , ed. and transl. Quinton Hoare and Geoffrey Nowell Smith (London, 1971)

Griffin, Robert 'What Veblen Owed to Peirce – The Social Theory of Logic', *Journal of Economic Issues*, **32**, 3 (September, 1998), 733–57

Heilbroner, Robert *The Worldly Philosophers* (New York, 1953)

Hession, Charles H. and Hyman Sardy *Ascent to Affluence: A History of American Economic Development* (Boston, 1969)

Himmelfarb, Gertrude *Darwin and the Darwinian Revolution* (London, 1959)

Hobson, John 'Thorstein Veblen', *Sociological Review*, **21**(October, 1930), 342–5

—— *Veblen* (London, 1936)

Hofstadter, Richard *Social Darwinism in American Thought* (1944, rev. edn Boston, 1955)

Holbrook, Stewart H. *The Age of the Moguls* (New York, 1953)

Homberger, Eric *American Writers and Radical Politics, 1900–39* (London, 1986)

Horkheimer, Max 'Preface', *Studies in Philosophy and Social Science*, **9**, 3 (1941), 365

Howells, William Dean 'An Opportunity For American Fiction', *Literature*, 28 April and 5 May, 1899, collected in Edwin H. Cady (ed.) *W. D. Howells as Critic* (London, 1973)

Isernhagen, Hartwig 'A Constitutional Inability to Say Yes: Thorstein Veblen, the Reconstruction Program of *The Dial*, and the Development of American Modernism After World War I', in Herbert Grabes *et al.* (eds) *Sonderdruck aus Real: The Yearbook of Research in English and American Literature*, **1** (1982), 153–90

Jorgensen, Elizabeth Watkins and Henry Irving Jorgensen *Thorstein Veblen: Victorian Firebrand* (New York, 1999)

Katona, George *The Mass Consumption Society* (New York, 1964)

Kazin, Alfred *On Native Grounds: An Interpretation of Modern American Prose Literature* (London, 1943)

Klein, Naomi *No Logo* (London, 2000)

Kolko, Gabriel *Wealth and Power in America* (New York, 1962)

Kuznets, Simon 'The Proportion of Capital Formation to National Product', *American Economic Review*, **42** (1952), 507–26

—— *Capital in the American Economy: Its Formation and Financing* (Princeton, 1961)

Kwiat, Joseph J. and Mary Christine Turpie (eds) *Studies in American Culture* (Minneapolis, 1960)

—— 'Progress versus Tragedy: Veblen and Dreiser' in Cushing Strout (ed.) *Intellectual History in America*, 2 vols (New York, 1968), 60–72

Larson, Jonathan 'A Restoration of Significance', *Journal of Economic Issues*, **29**, 3 (1995), 910–15

Lasch, Christopher 'The Cultural Cold War: A Short History of The Congress for Cultural Freedom', in Barton J. Bernstein (ed.), *Towards a New Past: Dissenting Essays in American History* (New York, 1968), pp. 322–59

—— *The New Radicalism in America 1889–1963: The Intellectual as Social Type* (New York, 1965)

Lears, Jackson 'Beyond Veblen: Rethinking Consumer Culture in America', in Simon J. Bronner (ed.) *Consuming Visions: Accumulation and Display of Goods in America 1880–1920* (New York, 1989)

Leibenstein, Harvey 'Bandwagon, Snob and Veblen Effects in the theory of Consumer Demand', *Quarterly Journal of Economics*, **64** (May 1950) 183–207, reprinted in *Beyond Economic Man: A New Foundation for Microeconomics* (Cambridge, Mass., 1976)

Lewis, Sinclair *Main Street* (1920, New York, 1961)

—— *Babbitt* (1922, London, 1924)

Lowell, James Russell *Democracy and Other Addresses* (Boston and New York, 1887)

Ludington, Townsend (ed.) *The Fourteenth Chronicle: Letters and Diaries of John Dos Passos* (Boston, 1973)

Lynd, Robert S. and Helen M. *Middletown: A Study in Contemporary American Culture* (New York, 1929)

Magdoff, Harry 'Problems of US Capitalism', *The Socialist Register 1965*, ed. Ralph Milibrand and John Saville (New York, 1965)

Marcuse, Herbert 'Some Social Implications of Modern Technology', *Studies in Philosophy and Social Science*, **9**, 3 (1941), 414–39

—— *One Dimensional Man* (London, 1964)

Martin, Frederick Townsend *The Passing of the Idle Rich* (New York, 1911)

Marx, Karl *Capital*, Volume 1, (1867, London 1968)

—— *Early Texts*, ed. and transl. David McLennan (Oxford, 1972)

Mason, Roger S. *Conspicuous Consumption: A Study of Exceptional Behavior* (New York, 1981)

McCoy, Donald R. *Coming of Age: The United States during the 1920's and 1930's* (Harmondsworth, 1973)

Mencken, H. L. *Prejudices : First Series* (New York, 1921)

Miller, Arthur *The Price* (Harmondsworth, 1968)

Mitchell, Wesley C. 'Human Behavior and Economics: A Survey of Recent Literature,' *Quarterly Journal of Economics*, **29**, 1914–15

Morgan, Lewis H. *Ancient Society* (1877, reprinted Cambridge, Mass., 1964)

Morris, William *News From Nowhere* (1891, Harmondsworth, 1985)

Munslow, Alun *Discourse and Culture: The Creation of America 1870–1920* (London, 1992)

Norris, Frank *The Pit* (1903)

Numbers, Ronald N. *Darwinism Comes to America* (London, 1998)

Odum, Howard W. *American Masters of Social Science* (New York, 1927)

Oshima, H.T. 'Consumer Asset Formation and the Future of Capitalism', *Economic Journal*, **71** (1961), 20–35

Packard, Vance *The Hidden Persuaders* (Harmondsworth, 1957)
—— *The Status Seekers* (London, 1960)
Paradiso, Louis J. 'Retail Sales and Consumer Incomes', Department of Commerce 1945.
Parsons, Talcott 'Sociological Elements in Economic Thought,1', *Quarterly Journal of Economics*, **49** (May, 1935), 414–53
Pierce, Bessie Louise *A History of Chicago Vol. 3: The Rise of the Modern City* (New York, 1957)
Pizer, Donald *Dos Passos' U.S.A. : A Critical Study* (Charlottesville, 1988)
Potter, David M. *People of Plenty: Economic Abundance and the American Character* (Chicago, 1954)
Potter, Jim *The American Economy Between the Wars* (London, 1974)
Qualey, Carlton C. (ed.) *Thorstein Veblen* (New York, 1968)
Rahv, Philip 'American Intellectuals and the Postwar Situation', *Partisan Review* (1952) reprinted in *Image and Idea* (London, 1957)
Riesman, David *Thorstein Veblen: A Critical Interpretation* (1953, reissued 1975)
Riesman, David, Nathan Glazer and Reuel Denney *The Lonely Crowd* (1950, abr. edn, New Haven, 1961)
Rosek, Carl *Lewis Henry Morgan: American Scholar* (Chicago, 1960)
Rosenberg, Bernard *The Values of Veblen: A Critical Appraisal* (Washington, 1956)
—— (ed.) *Thorstein Veblen: Selections from his Work* (New York, 1963)
Ross, Dorothy *The Origins of American Social Science* (Cambridge, 1991)
Rostow, Walter *The Stages of Economic Growth: A Non-Communist Manifesto* (Cambridge, 1961)
Samuels, Warren J. 'Reflections on the Intellectual Context and Significance of Thorstein Veblen', *Journal of Economic Issues*, **29**, 3 (1995), 916–22
Schneider, Louis *The Freudian Psychology and Veblen's Social Theory* (1948)
Schorer, Mark *Sinclair Lewis: An American Life* (London, 1961)
Seager, Henry R. and Charles R. Gulick Jr, *Trust and Corporation Problems* (New York, 1929)
Shannon, Christopher *Conspicuous Criticism: Tradition, the Individual, and Culture in American Social Thought from Veblen to Mills* (Baltimore,1996)
Simich, Jerry L. and Rick Tilman, *Thorstein Veblen: A Reference Guide* (Boston,1985)
Smith, Adam *The Wealth of Nations* (1776, London, 1910)
Spencer, Herbert *Structure, Function and Evolution*, ed. Stanislav Andreski (London, 1971)
Spindler, Michael 'The Origin of Species as Rhetoric', *Nineteenth-Century Prose*, **XIX**,1 (Winter 1991–92), 26–34
—— 'Adorno's Critique of Veblen', in Holger Briel and Andreas Kramer (eds) *In Practice: Theodor Adorno and Cultural Theory* (Berne, 2001)
Stewart, Herbert L. 'The Ethics of Luxury and Leisure', *American Journal of Sociology*, **24**, 3 (1918), 241–59
Sumner, William Graham *Social Darwinism: Selected Essays of William Graham Sumner*, ed. Stow Persons (Boston, 1963)
Tallack, Douglas *Twentieth-Century America: The Intellectual and Cultural Context* (London, 1991)

Teggart, Richard *Thorstein Veblen: A Chapter in American Economic Thought* (Berkeley, 1932)

Tilman, Rick *Thorstein Veblen and His Critics, 1891–1963: Conservative, Liberal, and Radical Perspectives* (Princeton: 1992)

—— *The Intellectual Legacy of Thorstein Veblen : Unresolved Issues* (London, 1996)

Trigg, Andrew B. 'Veblen, Bourdieu, and Conspicuous Consumption', *Journal of Economic Issues*, **35**, 1 (March, 2001), 99–115

United States Department of Commerce, *Historical Statistics of the United States – Colonial Times to 1957* (Washington, 1960)

Wallace, Henry A. 'Veblen's "Imperial Germany and the Industrial Revolution"' *Political Science Quarterly*, **55** (1940), 435–45

Weber, Max *The Protestant Ethic and the Spirit of Capitalism* (1905), transl. Talcott Parsons (1930, reprinted London, 1971)

West, Thomas Reed *Flesh of Steel: Literature and Machine in American Culture* (Vanderbilt, 1967)

White, Morton *Social Thought in America: The Revolt Against Formalism* (1949, Boston, 1957)

Whyte, William H. *The Organisation Man* (London, 1957)

Williams, Raymond *Marxism and Literature* (Oxford, 1977)

Wolfe, Don M. *The Image of Man in America* (New York, 1957, 2nd edn, 1970)

Woodress, James *Willa Cather: A Literary Life* (London, 1987)

Index

Absentee Ownership 1, 46, 76–85, 90–1, 93, 107, 108, 128, 142, 144
Adams, Henry 22, 61
Addams, Jane 20
Adorno, Theodor 74, 97, 98
advertising 3, 67, 82, 94, 98, 112, 113, 115, 122, 125, 148
Agassiz, Louis 14
American Economic Association 2, 91
Ardzrooni, Leon 69, 94
Armour, Philip D. 20, 24

'Barbarian Status of Women' 1, 26, 27, 30, 32
Barthes, Roland 32
Baudrillard, Jean 107, 124
Beard, Charles 88, 94, 99
'Beginnings of Ownership' 26, 27, 29, 30, 60
Bell, Daniel 13, 74, 89, 104, 106, 117
Bellamy, Edward 11, 12, 13, 29, 35, 87, 142
    Looking Backward 11, 29, 66, 73, 120
Berle, Adolf A. 48, 79, 85, 93, 108, 144, 145
'Between Bolshevism and War' 74
Boas, Franz 23, 142
Bolshevik Revolution 63, 68, 142
Bolshevism 75
'Bolshevism is a Menace – To Whom?' 64
Brookings Institute 112
Brown, Norman O. 116
Bryce, James 7, 122

Carleton College 1, 12, 18, 105
Carlyle, Thomas 49, 50, 51
Carnegie, Andrew 6, 16, 20, 41, 47, 121

Cather, Willa 3, 127, 129–32, 141, 144
Chicago 18–24, 142
Chicago, University of 1, 21, 54, 55
Chomsky, Noam 38
Columbian Exposition 21, 22–3
Communist Manifesto, The 10, 49, 67
conspicuous consumption 3, 26, 34, 35, 38, 66, 87, 108, 120, 123, 125, 131, 137, 142, 147, 149
Cooke, Morris L. 69, 71
Coolidge, Calvin 61, 77, 78
Cornell 1, 12
Cowley, Malcolm 94, 118
Coxey, Jacob 23
Crèvecooeur, Hector St. John de 9
Cross, Gary 35, 120

Darwin, Charles 14, 16, 17, 25, 27, 30, 37, 43, 142
    The Origin of Species 13, 17
    The Descent of Man 14, 15, 30
Davenport, William 56
Davis, Arthur K. 98, 103, 107
Debs, Eugene 24, 69
'Debs Rebellion' 23
'Dementia Praecox' 74, 75
Depression 2, 85, 92, 93, 95, 97, 114, 127
Dewey, John 2, 87, 89, 94, 99
Dial, The 1, 21, 63, 64, 68, 74, 89, 90, 141, 143
Diggins, John P. ix, 56, 60, 97, 106–7, 109, 146
Dobb, Maurice 91
Dorfman, Joseph ix, 10, 87, 94, 95, 96, 104, 138, 144
Dos Passos, John 3, 61, 126, 127, 138–41, 144
Dreiser, Theodore 3, 21, 24, 109, 119, 127, 132–4, 141
Durkheim, Emile 2, 101, 107

Eastman, Max 88, 90
'Economic Theory of Women's
    Dress' 1, 26, 27, 60
Einstein, Albert 1
Engels, Frederick 10, 29, 49
Engineers and the Price System, The 1,
    2, 68–74, 86, 90, 93, 97, 104,
    142
Essays in Our Changing Order 94

Field, Marshall 20, 21
Fitzgerald, Francis Scott 3, 110, 117,
    123, 127, 134–8, 141, 144
Ford, Henry 41, 42, 98, 111, 113,
    139
Freud, Sigmund 2, 56, 94, 99, 141
    Civilization and Its Discontents 56

Galbraith, John Kenneth 54, 103,
    105, 106, 149
Gantt, Henry L. 69, 71
Geddes, Patrick 88
George, Henry 8, 11, 12, 142
Gramsci, Antonio 2, 38, 98, 108
Gray, Asa 14
Great War 51, 61, 64, 78, 142

Harding, Warren 77–8
Harvard 55
Haymarket Riot 20
Higher Learning in America, The 1,
    51–4, 60, 89, 106, 142, 143
Hobson, John ix, 92, 94
Horkheimer, Max 97
Howells, William Dean 12, 87, 126,
    134
Huxley, Thomas Henry 13, 14

Imperial Germany ix, 62, 88, 96, 128
*Inquiry into the Nature of the Peace,
    An* ix, 63, 89, 138
instinct of workmanship 2, 26, 28,
    33, 34, 41, 52, 56, 59, 60, 63,
    141, 152, 143
'Instinct of Workmanship' 26, 27,
    28, 32, 58
Instinct of Workmanship 1, 17,
    56–60, 88, 97, 140, 142
Institutionalism 88

International Thorstein Veblen
    Association 109, 150
IWW (International Workers of the
    World) 13, 63, 68, 69, 72, 84,
    90

James, William 17, 29, 56
Johns Hopkins 1, 18, 54

Keynes, John Maynard 44, 86, 97,
    103, 108

Laughlin, J. Laurence 1, 10, 12, 18
Lasch, Christopher 102, 105
Lewis, Sinclair 3, 127–9, 141, 144
Locke, John 64, 78
Loeb, Jacques 17, 142
Lynd, Helen M. and Robert S. 117,
    128
    Middletown 128

Marcuse, Herbert 97, 109
marriage 14, 27, 30, 31, 32, 33
Marx, Karl 2, 10, 11, 12, 13, 26, 29,
    40, 41, 44, 46, 49, 50, 51, 55,
    79, 85, 88, 98, 103, 107, 126,
    142
    Capital 10, 12, 46, 84
Marxism 11, 12
McCarthy, Senator Joe 102
McCormick, Cyrus 20
McDougall, William 17
Means, Gardner 48, 79, 85, 93, 108,
    144, 145
Mencken, H. L. 89
Mill, John Stuart 9, 10, 42, 142
Mills, C. Wright 99, 105
Miller, Arthur 110
Missouri, University of 1, 56, 89
Mitchell, Wesley C. 28, 88, 94, 95,
    108
Morgan, C. Lloyd 17, 28
Morgan, J. P. 6, 45, 46, 47, 71, 76
Morgan, Lewis H. 23, 29, 30, 57,
    132, 142
Morris, William 11, 36, 41, 49, 50
Mumford, Lewis 92, 94

New Deal 2, 86, 95, 96

New Republic, The 2, 63, 88, 89, 92, 94, 105, 138, 141
New School for Social Research 1, 74, 91
Norris, Frank 21, 24

Packard, Vance 104, 125
Parsons, Talcott 94, 96, 101
pecuniary emulation 2, 34, 35, 39, 40, 119, 122, 125
Peirce, Charles S. 18
People's Party 8, 20
'Place of Science in Modern Civilisation, The' 55, 57
Place of Science in Modern Civilisation, The 90
Populism 8
'Preconceptions of Economic Science, The' 42, 44
Protestant ethic 117, 121, 122, 124

'Red Scare' 68, 72, 76, 77, 78, 142
Riesman, David 100, 104, 105, 116
Rockefeller, John D. 6, 16, 21, 45, 54
Rolfe, Ellen 12, 18
Roosevelt, Franklin D. 2, 95
Russian Revolution 61, 64, 68, 74

sabotage 2, 70
Sandburg, Carl 22
Sinclair, Upton 24, 88, 94, 127
Smith, Adam 9, 24, 42, 44, 64, 93, 142
Social Darwinism 15, 16, 24, 127
'Socialist Economics of Karl Marx and His Followers, The' 55
Sombart, Werner 46
'Some Neglected Points in the Theory of Socialism' 55
Spencer, Herbert 15, 17, 44, 87, 98, 142

Stanford 1, 54, 55, 91
status symbols 122
Sumner, William Graham 10, 12, 15, 47

Taylor, Frederick Winslow 50, 69, 139
Technicians, Soviet of 73, 90, 143
Technocracy 2, 93
Theory of Business Enterprise, The 1, 46–51, 58, 59, 60, 64, 65, 81, 88, 93, 138, 140, 142, 143
Theory of the Leisure Class, The ix, 1, 22, 33–42, 51, 58, 60, 86–7, 89, 90, 91, 94, 97–8, 103, 109, 120, 130, 138, 139, 142, 143, 149
Tilman, Rick ix, 13, 87, 95, 104, 108, 109, 144

Vanderbilt, Cornelius 6, 8
'Veblen Effect' 120
Veblen, Thomas 18
Vested Interests, The 1, 64, 68, 90, 91, 138, 140, 141, 142, 144

Wall Street Crash 2, 42
Wallace, Henry 96
Ward, Lester Frank 87
Webb, Sidney and Beatrice 90
Weber, Max 2, 20, 40, 101, 103, 107, 124
    Protestant Ethic and the Spirit of Capitalism, The 20
What Veblen Taught 94
'Why is Economics Not An Evolutionary Science?' 25, 42–4
Williams, Raymond 117
Wilson, Woodrow 61, 69, 75, 90, 140

Yale 1, 12, 15
Yerkes, Charles T. 21, 24

Robert Anton Wilson Klausité

Joyce's Metamorphosis